Strike Hard! Anti-Crime Campaigns
and Chinese Criminal Justice, 1979-1985

Strike Hard!

Anti-Crime Campaigns
and Chinese Criminal Justice
1979-1985

Harold M. Tanner

 East Asia Program
Cornell University
Ithaca, New York 14853

The Cornell East Asia Series is published by the Cornell University East Asia Program and has no formal affiliation with Cornell University Press. We are a small, non-profit press, publishing reasonably-priced books on a wide variety of scholarly topics relating to East Asia as a service to the academic community and the general public. We accept standing orders which provide for automatic billing and shipping of each title in the series upon publication.

If after review by internal and external readers a manuscript is accepted for publication, it is published on the basis of camera-ready copy provided by the volume author. Each author is thus responsible for any necessary copy-editing and for manuscript formatting. Submission inquiries should be addressed to Editorial Board, East Asia Program, Cornell University, Ithaca, New York 14853-7601.

An earlier version of chapter 6 was published in *China Information: A Quarterly Journal on Contemporary China Studies,* Leiden, Vol. IX, Nos. 2/3, Winter 1994-95, pp. 40-71.

Cover design by Karen K. Smith.

Number 104 in the Cornell East Asia Series.
© 1999 Harold M. Tanner. All rights reserved
ISSN 1050-2955
ISBN 1-885445-64-4 hc
ISBN 1-885445-04-0 pb

13 12 11 10 09 08 07 06 05 04 03 02 01   10 9 8 7 6 5 4 3 2 1

CAUTION: Except for brief quotations in a review, no part of this book may be reproduced or utilized in any form, without permission in writing from the author. Please address inquiries to Harold M. Tanner in care of East Asia Program, Cornell University, 140 Uris Hall, Ithaca, NY 14853-7601.

To the memory of my father
Earl C. Tanner
Historian and physicist.
1919-1985

CONTENTS

LIST OF TABLES

ACKNOWLEDGMENTS

Throughout years of research, I have been asked whether it was not difficult or impossible to find materials relevant to my subject. While there is a lack of certain types of information such as statistics, a great deal of material on the theory and the practice of Chinese criminal justice is available for those who are willing to look. In locating and digesting a variety of sources, I was assisted by numerous individuals and institutions. For their assistance in locating a variety of primary and secondary sources, I would like to express my gratitude to the librarians of the School of Oriental and African Studies, Columbia University's Starr East Asian Library, Princeton University's Gest Library, and the Willis Library of the University of North Texas. In my research at Beijing University I was aided by Professor Yang Dunxian of the Department of Law and by the helpful staff of the Beijing University Library. Professor Fang Liufang of People's University offered valuable advice and assistance in locating materials, as did a number of law students, legal workers, and several hooligans and former criminal offenders who shared with me their insights into the Chinese legal system. Research in Beijing was followed by a year of research at the Universities Service Centre at the Chinese University of Hong Kong. I owe great thanks to Professor Kwan, the director of the Universities Service Centre and especially to managing director Jean Hung.

Research at Beijing University was funded by The Committee on Scholarly Relations with the People's Republic of China, while research in Hong Kong was supported by the Fulbright Foundation. A Developing Faculty Research grant from the College of Arts and Sciences of the University of North Texas made it possible for me to work on the manuscript during the summer session of 1998.

A number of friends and colleagues have read parts of or, in some cases, all of the manuscript and offered valuable suggestions. In this regard, I would like to thank Don Chipman, Catherine Keyser, Shawn Hsieh, Andrew J. Nathan, Robert Hymes, Stuart Schram, and Michael Tsin. Special thanks must go to my adviser at Columbia University, Madeleine Zelin, who guided this work through the dissertation stage, and to James Seymour and Mark Seldin for reading and offering valuable suggestions on later stages of the manuscript. I would also like to express my gratitude to Karen K. Smith, managing editor at the Cornell East Asia Series, for helping me to cope with the process of transforming a manuscript into a book. Needless to say, I remain solely responsible for any weaknesses or errors that remain.

Last, but not least, I would like to thank my family. My parents, Mary Tanner and the late Earl Tanner took my passion for aimless world travel and channeled it into the more respectable path of an academic career. My wife, Yiyun Jiang, has remained strong and cheerful through years of sacrificed weekends and unpredictable moves from one hemisphere to another while reminding me periodically that there is life beyond research. Our children, William and Sophia, have offered many welcome moments of joy and distraction while giving up more playtime than they realize to the all-consuming research project. Finally I am deeply indebted to my father-in-law, Professor Jiang Youyi, and especially to my mother-in-law, Professor Huang Kefan who gave generously of their time and energy in extended visits to the United States when they helped to care for their grandchildren with tremendous patience and dedication.

INTRODUCTION

Under the leadership of the Central Committee and the State Council, let us advance courageously to change the backward state of our country and turn it into a modern and powerful socialist state.

Deng Xiaoping, "Emancipate the Mind, Seek Truth From Facts and Unite as One in Looking to the Future." In *Selected Works of Deng Xiaoping (1975-1982)*, 165.

In the late 1970s the Chinese Communist leadership called upon the Chinese people to unite in the struggle to modernize their poor and backward country. It was a task that the Party leadership understood in terms of two areas or spheres: the material and the spiritual. As explained in a Party document of 1982:

The material achievements of the people in reshaping the natural world are what is meant by 'material' civilization, which is manifest in the progress of the people's material production and in the improvement of their material lives. At the same time as they reshape their objective world, the people also reshape their subjective world. Society, spiritual production, and spiritual life are further developed. Accomplishments in this area are what is referred to as 'spiritual civilization.' They are manifest in the development of education, science, and cultural knowledge and in the raising of the people's ideological, political and moral levels.[1]

---

1. *Zhongguo gongchandang di shier ci quanguo daibiao dahui wenjian huibian* (Documents of the Twelfth National Congress of the Chinese Communist Party), 33-34, quoted in Jia Chunfeng, *Lun shehui zhuyi jingshen wenming*, 4-5. Note that the definition of "spiritual civilization" is so shaped as to leave the political system of the dictatorship of the proletariat, the leadership of the Chinese Communist party, and Communist Party ideology outside the scope of things to be reshaped, so that the Party, along with "the people," stands as the subject, rather than the object, of the reshaping.

A modern China would possess all the material accouterments of modern life as seen in the developed world. The people would have a high standard of living as measured in terms of food, housing, automobiles, television sets, computers, refrigerators, air conditioners, rice-cookers, micro-wave ovens, video cassette recorders, in-home kara-OK sets, and name-brand clothing. China would have factories employing the latest technology, ready access to large quantities of fossil and nuclear energy, extensive road, rail, and air transport systems, a blue-water navy, and a world-class arsenal of inter-continental ballistic missiles. But in addition to all this, the ideal modern China would be a country of cultured, educated, polite, politically astute, responsible, disciplined and moral people. Only by constructing both material and spiritual civilization would China truly achieve modernity—not the modernity of the morally bankrupt west, but a modernity in which the heights of material production and the heights of moral perfection would be achieved simultaneously.

The goal of material modernization is relatively easy to comprehend and easy to measure. After a decade or more of economic reform and opening to the outside world, it could be observed that, while they had not yet attained parity with the West, the Chinese, both as individuals and as a nation, were militarily stronger, wealthier, more technologically advanced, and consumed significantly more goods and services than they had in 1978. It is much more difficult to define "spiritual civilization" and to measure the level of its attainment. In its most fundamental respect, "spiritual civilization" represents the moral tenor of society, and is described in the criminal law. It is through the definition of crime in the criminal law that the outer limits of acceptable behavior are established, and it is in the enforcement of the criminal law and in the punishment and the reform of criminal offenders that we see the attempts of the state to bring social practice into conformity with the vision of spiritual civilization that finds its expression in the criminal law.[2]

To recognize the role of the criminal law and the criminal justice system in the attempt to lay forth and to bring into reality a particular vision of modern Chinese spiritual civilization we must look seriously at both the laws themselves and their application in practice. It is easy to dismiss the Chinese criminal justice system of the 1980s as having been backward, dictatorial, an instrument of political repression, or as a mere travesty. But in doing so, we learn more about ourselves, our ideals, and China's failure to have lived up to them than we do about the goals,

---

2. I would not suggest that the criminal law and the criminal procedure are the only areas in which the vision of spiritual civilization is expressed and put into action. Mass campaigns for social morality, such as the long-standing "Five Emphasizes and Four Beauties" and the educational system are also areas in which the attempt to define the ideal "spiritual civilization" and to bring it into being can be found. For an extended discussion of the Communist Party's efforts to recreate China in moral terms, see Bakken, *The Exemplary Society*.

the techniques, the philosophical bases, the practice, and the results of Chinese criminal justice. As we look at Chinese criminal justice in the era of Deng Xiaoping, we may see the influence of the Chinese past, but also the hopes and dreams of the future; we may see the rejection of Maoist class-struggle politics along with the continued use of some of the institutions, the techniques, and the rhetoric of the Maoist years; we may observe the attempts of the Communist Party Center to impose a higher degree of standardization and central control over the use of the state's coercive power against the individual along with the continued undermining of legality by local authorities, by infrastructural weakness, and by a lack of material and human resources; we may see a vision of a stable society in which crime should be decreasing and eventually eliminated while at the same time, we observe rising crime rates, the appearance of new, un-imagined forms of crime, and pervasive corruption. When we look at these phenomena in comparative perspective, we may see that developments in China in the 1980s parallel in some ways the phenomenon of rising crime rates observed in the context of capitalist industrial modernization in the West; but at the same time, we may see the development of a system of law and government that, at least as of the 1990s, did not appear to converge with the pattern of modernization experienced by the West and which Western governments hoped would be replicated by a modernizing, economically vibrant China.

The following chapters deal with the reform and the practice of Chinese criminal justice in the 1980s. In doing so, I have tried to focus on the reconstruction of the Chinese criminal justice system in 1979-1980 and at the development of criminal justice in the context of the anti-crime campaigns of the early to mid-1980s. In doing so, I have purposely concentrated on the functioning of the criminal justice system as seen in the struggle against common crime, rather than political offenses. I have done so, not because the issue of political dissidents and their treatment is unimportant, but because it has been well documented by human rights organizations including Amnesty International, Human Rights Watch, and Human Rights in China and discussed in a number of excellent books. Furthermore, I believe that a study of the definition, the prosecution, and the punishment of common crime can tell us much about the development of Chinese law and Chinese society.

The first three chapters of this book describe the reform of the criminal justice system and the practice of criminal justice from 1979 through 1982. Where I have felt it necessary to do so, I have included background information concerning the development of the criminal justice system in the 1950s through the 1970s as well as discussion of the influence of the Soviet model. Chapter Four deals with a crucial turning-point in the development of criminal justice under Deng—the first "Strike Hard" anti-crime campaign of the 1980s. This campaign saw some substantial revisions of the criminal justice code and set the stage for future campaigns against crime in the 1980s and 1990s. Chapter Five addresses the issue of crime itself, while Chapter Six deals with the two major forms of punishment used in China: execution and labor reform. The seventh chapter is devoted to a discussion of the broader historical issue of the relationship of modernization both to changes in the rate and structure of crime and to the development of the criminal justice system. The Afterward discusses the significance of the revisions made to the criminal law and the criminal procedure law in 1996 and 1997.

1

THE LAWS

To ensure people's democracy, we must strengthen our legal system. Democracy has to be institutionalized and written into law, so as to make sure that institutions and laws do not change whenever the leadership change their views or shift their focus of attention.

> Deng Xiaoping, "Emancipate the Mind, Seek Truth From Facts and Unite As One In Looking to the Future." In *Selected Works of Deng Xiaoping (1975-1982)*, 158.

'The affairs under heaven are inexhaustible, yet what is written in the books of punishment is limited; with finite laws it is difficult to comprehend an infinity of affairs.' And so it is necessary that we have recourse to the power of legal interpretation in order to supplement the weaknesses inherent in the laws.

> *Zhonghua renmin gongheguo falu guifanxing jieshi jicheng*, (Collected normative legal interpretations of the People's Republic of China), 1.

Two basic laws guided the administration of criminal justice during the period of Deng Xiaoping's leadership: the Criminal Law and the Criminal Procedure Law of the People's Republic of China. These laws, promulgated in 1979 and effective as of 1 January 1980, were the first laws of their type in the history of the PRC. The promulgation of these laws marked a decisive step toward the greater institutionalization and central regulation of the state's power to establish fundamental behavioral norms and to enforce those norms by coercive means. In comparison to the more secretive and *ad hoc* nature of criminal justice under Mao and the chaos of the Cultural Revolution, the new laws displayed a greater concern for the protection of the rights of the individual from the abuse of state power by

5

individuals within the police, the procuratorates and the courts.[1] At the same time, however, the way in which behavioral norms were set forth in the criminal law and the provisions for the enforcement of those norms established in the criminal and in the criminal procedure laws displayed a substantial degree of continuity with the ideals and the practices of the period of Mao Zedong's leadership.

Some of the causes of this continuity may be located in the history of the development of the laws themselves. The text of both laws harkens back to the 1950s, when China began the construction of its socialist legal system on the basis of the Soviet model. In their underlying faith in the malleability of the individual, in their assumption of an instrumentalist view of law, and in their assumption that a direct relationship exists between the moral and spiritual uplift of the nation and the economic tasks of development, the laws bring to mind Chairman Mao's voluntarist reading of Marxism, although not his methods of spiritual regeneration. In their moralistic tone and their inherent flexibility (provided for through the use of unspecific language, broadly drawn categories, wide sentencing guidelines and the principle of analogy), and in the use of an ever-changing body of "legal interpretation" as a mediating agent between law and its practical application too, the new laws bore a striking resemblance to the legal practice of the Maoist era.

THE CRIMINAL LAW

The first Criminal Law of the People's Republic of China was promulgated on 6 August 1979.[2] This law, which had been twenty-five years in the making, drew on the Soviet criminal code, Marxism-Leninism, Mao Zedong Thought, and on the lessons of the Cultural Revolution. The result was a code of law that was clearly based on German law as filtered through the Soviet Union, yet revealing, upon closer examination, certain characteristics drawn from China's historical experience.

The Criminal Law of 1979 was short and simple, consisting of 192 articles in two sections: General Provisions and Special Provisions. The General Provisions were divided into four chapters in which were set forth the guiding ideology, tasks, and scope of application of the law (Chapter 1), definitions of basic concepts such as crime and criminal responsibility (Chapter 2) and in which

---

1. For a description and documentation of the practice of criminal justice in the People's Republic prior to the reform era, see Cohen, *The Criminal Process in the People's Republic of China, 1949-1963.*

2. The Chinese and English texts of the Criminal Law of the PRC as promulgated in 1979 (hereafter cited as "Criminal Law, 1979") can be found in *The Criminal Law and the Criminal Procedure Law of China.* All future references to the Criminal Law of 1979 are to the English translation that appears in that volume, as are all direct quotations.

both the types of punishment that might be imposed for criminal offenses and rules for the concrete application of punishments are prescribed (Chapters 3 and 4). The second section, Specific Provisions, described in nine chapters the particular offenses, including Crimes of Counterrevolution, Crimes of Endangering Public Security, Crimes of Undermining the Socialist Economic Order, Crimes of Infringing Upon the Rights of the Person and the Democratic Rights of Citizens, Crimes of Property Violation, Crimes of Disrupting the Order of Social Administration, Crimes of Disrupting Marriage and the family, and Crimes of Dereliction of Duty. This structure and the basic concepts defined within it (the person who is responsible for his/her intentional acts, the distinction between consummated and attempted crimes, the concepts of negligence, mental illness and self-defense, for example) have led one Western scholar to describe the Criminal Law as "simply a Western penal code drafted on the German model," one that "an American lawyer might curse at . . . but [with which] he could work . . . without developing any radically different techniques"[3] While not denying the familiarity of the basic structure and concepts of the Criminal Law, a closer examination of the code, its historical context, and the process by which it was drafted will reveal characteristics peculiar to the socialist economic system and to the Chinese historical experience.

Plans for a criminal code began in 1950 when the Legal System Committee of the Central People's Government began preparatory work for the drafting of such a law. Over the next four years, two documents were produced: "Draft Outline for a Criminal Law of the PRC" and "Draft Guiding Principles for a Criminal Law of the PRC (first draft)"[4] The circumstances were not deemed right, however, for the drafting and promulgation of the criminal law itself. In the economic sphere, the process of socialist transformation was in full swing. In the legal sphere, the Judicial Reform Movement was being carried out to purge the judicial system of unreliable elements and to subject the methods, assumptions and legal philosophy of the old society to a thorough criticism.[5] In the context of the rapid and fundamental transformation of China's economic, governmental, and judicial systems, it was impossible—perhaps even undesirable—to set forth fixed definitions of right and wrong in the form of a criminal law. To do so would imply that the state sought to preserve the status quo, while in fact, the goal of the Communist Party at this point was revolutionary change. How, for instance, could one legally define the offense of theft when the status and definition of property itself was still in flux?

---

3. Jones, "The Criminal Law of the People's Republic of China," 409, 411.
4. Gao Mingxuan. *Zhonghua renmin gongheguo xingfa de yunyu he dansheng*, 2. The following discussion of the drafting of the Criminal Law is based largely on Gao, 2-7.
5. Gao Mingxuan, ed. *Xin Zhongguo xingfaxue*, 4.

In 1954, with the promulgation of the first Constitution of the PRC, the time was judged to be more favorable. The work of drafting a criminal code was thus formally undertaken by the Legal Section of the General Office of the Standing Committee of the National People's Congress. By June 1957, the twenty-second draft had been sent to the Legal Committee of the Party Center and to the Party Secretariat for revision and then circulated to the members of the NPC. Following this review, the twenty-second draft was about to be issued for experimental use. But it was precisely at this point, in June 1957, that Mao Zedong unleashed the Anti-Rightist Movement, a mass movement that aimed to denounce and purge critics of Communist Party rule. One aspect of the Anti-Rightist Movement was the denigration of law and of lawyers and a parallel strengthening of the position that policy, rather than law, provided the most flexible guide for the application of the coercive power of the state to wrong-doers.[6] The drafting process was consequently suspended for four years.

In late 1961 and early 1962, the situation changed again. In his talk at the enlarged national work conference (the "Seven-thousand Cadres Work Conference") in January, 1962, Chairman Mao Zedong remarked that China needed to promulgate criminal and civil codes. In May, the Legal Affairs Office again took up the criminal law. Revisions of the twenty-second draft were completed with the assistance of the Party Center's Politico-Legal Affairs Group. By October, a thirty-third draft law had been produced and was transmitted to the Politburo and to Mao himself for consideration. Again, the law was on the point of being promulgated when another mass movement, the Socialist Education Movement, was begun. This time, as the Socialist Education Movement was followed by the Cultural Revolution, the task of drafting the criminal law was put aside for fifteen years.

Only in October 1978, with Deng Xiaoping's call for the promulgation of laws as a guarantee of democracy and a defense against chaos was work on the criminal law taken up once again. Following Deng's remarks, the Central Politico-Legal Affairs Group met to discuss the question of constructing the legal system and organized a Draft Criminal Law Revision Team. The thirty-third draft was taken up again as the basis for the next three drafts. The second of these was passed in principle by the Politburo of the Central Committee on 20 May 1979, considered by the Legal System Committee and then by the Standing Committee of the NPC, revised, and passed along to the Second Session of the Fifth NPC for consideration. There, further additions and revisions were made. The final draft of the Criminal Law of the PRC, passed unanimously on 1 August 1979, was promulgated on 6 August to go into effect on the first day of January 1980.

---

6. For descriptions of the Anti-Rightist Movement and of the Socialist Education Movement (mentioned below), see Meisner, *Mao's China and After*, 192-200 and 288-306.

The drafting process (excluding the years of preparatory work prior to 1954) had extended over a period of twenty-five years from 1954 to 1979, during which the actual working time (subtracting the time during which work was suspended owing to the political climate) amounted to five years scattered across three decades. The Criminal Law of 1979 was thus an amalgam of the ideas and experiences of the 1950s, the 1960s and the 1970s.

In its form, in its major legal concepts, in the definition of most of the offenses and in its language, the Criminal Law remained largely a product of the 1950s. During the early part of the 1950s, the newly established People's Republic had repudiated the laws and institutions of the Republican period and learned the new arts of socialist government from its "elder brother," the Soviet Union. China drew freely upon Soviet penal law theories while Soviet law and the Soviet legal system were taken as models. In its basic form, then, the Criminal Law, although it is certainly not a mere copy, does bear some resemblance to the Soviet Code of 1928, particularly in the matter of arrangement into sections of General and Special Provisions, the initial statement of the tasks of the law, and the placement of counter-revolution at the head of the list of particular offenses. But it is in the Marxist-Leninist legal philosophy underlying the codes, rather than the formal arrangement of the sections, chapters, and articles, that the shared characteristics of the Chinese code and the Soviet socialist codes may be identified.

The socialist characteristics of the Criminal Law of 1979 are evident in the role of law as an instrument of the dictatorship of the proletariat, in the explicit assumption of a socialist economy, and in the assumption that crime, as a product of class society, will be reduced and eventually eliminated as the dictatorship of the proletariat guides society through the transitional stage of socialism toward the realization of the communist ideal. Thus the criminal code was based on an explicitly articulated instrumentalist philosophy in which law was regarded as a weapon of class struggle, an instrument of social engineering and of the engineering of human souls. The goal of the law was not to maintain control over a static society, but to "safeguard the smooth progress of the cause of socialist revolution and socialist construction."[7] Punishments were explicitly designed, not to satisfy the desire for retribution or revenge, but to reform the offender and to instruct the general public.[8] Counter-revolution, as the most serious of all possible crimes, took first place in the list of individual offenses. As concerns the protection of property, the code clearly placed the greatest emphasis on the protection of socialist property, with an entire chapter of the law devoted to "Crimes Undermining the Socialist Economic Order." The protection of personal property was

---

7. Criminal Law, 1979, Article 2.
8. Gao Mingxuan, *Zhonghua renmin gongheguo xingfa de yunyu he dansheng,* 15.

addressed later in Chapter Five, "Crimes of Property Violation," that dealt with violations of both public and private property.

While sharing certain characteristics with the Soviet code, the Chinese criminal law of 1979 also reflects elements of China's historical experience. Materials consulted for the earlier drafts in the 1950s included the laws of the Communist base areas of the 1930s and 1940s and a compilation, based on research carried out by the Supreme People's Court, of the names and types of offense and the ranges of punishment then in use in the adjudication of criminal cases in courts around the country in the early 1950s.[9] In 1957, as the preparation of the twenty-second draft was underway, a uniquely Chinese element was added to the theoretical bases of the Chinese criminal law. This was the concept of the "two types of contradiction" expounded by Party Chairman Mao Zedong in his speech "On the Correct Handling of Contradictions Among the People."

In this speech, delivered on 27 February 1957 to the Supreme State Conference and published (with editorial changes) in *People's Daily* on 19 June, Mao suggested that in the further development of socialism, the Chinese Party/state and the Chinese people were confronted with "two types of social contradictions—those between ourselves and the enemy and those among the people themselves."[10] Contradictions between the people and the enemy (referred to as "antagonistic contradictions") were to be resolved through the exercise of proletarian dictatorship. Thus ". . . to arrest, try and sentence certain counter-revolutionaries, and to deprive landlords and bureaucrat-capitalists of their right to vote and their freedom of speech for a specified period of time . . ." and to "exercise dictatorship over embezzlers, swindlers, arsonists, murderers, criminal gangs and others who severely disrupt public order . . . " were all examples of the use of dictatorship to "resolve the external contradiction between ourselves and the enemy."[11] The resolution of contradictions among the people, said Mao, should rely on "the democratic method, the method of discussion, of criticism, of persuasion and education, and not . . . the method of coercion or repression." Mao did envisage the possibility that elements of "the people" might break the law, but denied that the people could exercise dictatorship over themselves: "Law-breaking elements among the people will be punished according to law, but this is different in principle from the exercise of dictatorship to suppress the enemies of the people."[12]

Mao's comments quoted above inspired decades of debate concerning the standards by which criminal offenders should be judged. Should his remarks be

---

9. *Ibid.*, 18; Gao Mingxuan, ed. *Xin Zhongguo xingfaxue*, 7.

10. Mao, "On the Correct Handling of Contradictions Among the People," 433.

11. *Ibid.*, 435-36.

12. *Ibid.*, 436, 438.

taken to mean that serious criminal offenses ought to be understood as "antagonistic contradictions" and thus subject to heavier punishment, while lesser crimes might be considered contradictions among the people and the offenders thus treated with greater leniency and correspondingly larger doses of "education?" Did he mean that crimes committed by persons of "enemy class" background (capitalist, landlord, and counter-revolutionary) should be considered manifestations of the contradiction between the enemy and the people and thus subject to heavier penalties than the same acts would be if committed by a person of "good class" background? Or was it the case that all persons who committed acts that brought them into the purview of the organs of dictatorship (police, procuratorates and courts) were automatically to be regarded as enemies of the people?

Further confusion was caused by the fact that Mao saw contradictions, not as permanent, but as developing in an ever-changing historical context. What was a contradiction between the enemy and the people in one context might well become a contradiction among the people in another, and vice versa, all depending on the state of class struggle at any given historical moment.

The need of the criminal law to provide a basis for the correct identification and handling of the two different types of contradiction, as understood in the context of a constantly-changing situation of class struggle formed a part of the theoretical basis of the criminal law as it was drafted in 1957, in 1962, and in 1978. The concrete understanding of these concepts and their manifestation in the text of the criminal law, however, changed substantially over time.

In the 1950s and 1960s, it was assumed that class struggle was an important, and often intense, part of China's on-going socialist revolution and construction. Most offenders, it was assumed, were enemies of the people, most crime a manifestation of class struggle Thus most, though not all, criminals were considered to be "objects of dictatorship."[13] Although there were differences of opinion, most agreed in the late 1950s that the class status of the criminal should play a key role in determining whether or not his/her offense should be considered a contradiction between the people and the enemy or a contradiction among the people. Crimes committed by persons of enemy class background were manifestations of class struggle and thus antagonistic contradictions, while those committed by inexperienced or misled persons of working-class origin were clearly not a manifestation of class struggle.[14]

The need to distinguish between these two types of contradiction in the context of the class struggle was manifest in the wide array of punishments prescribed in the law and in the wide range of possible punishments assigned to each individual offense. The wide choice of punishment thus incorporated into the

---

13. Gao Mingxuan, ed. *Xin Zhongguo xingfaxue*, 29.
14. *Ibid.*, 26.

law was intended to give judges the discretionary power to fit the punishment to each individual crime as it appeared in the changing historical context of the class struggle in China.

Drawing on the legal experience of the pre-1949 Communist base areas and on the early years of the People's Republic, the twenty-second (1957) draft of the criminal law provided nine punishments. Control, criminal detention, fixed-term imprisonment, life imprisonment, and death (including death with two years' reprieve) served as principle punishments. Supplementary punishments including fines, deprivation of political rights, and confiscation of property could be added to the principle punishments. In addition, deportation was provided as a principle or a supplementary punishment for foreign criminal offenders.

This structure of punishment was designed not merely to serve retributive purposes, but also to distinguish between the treatment of criminal offenders, offering the possibility of education and reform as well as the threat of life imprisonment or death. Control and criminal detention, for example, were forms of punishment particularly suited to the resolution of "contradictions among the people." Those sentenced to criminal detention were to be confined in a local detention house and allowed to return to their homes and families on a regular basis. Those sentenced to control were to continue to live at home and to work in their regular places of employment while under the supervision, not only (or even primarily) of the police, but also of the masses.

In control and in criminal detention, the law assumed the existence of an active, concerned populace whose interests were essentially identical to those of the state. Indeed, this assumption extended beyond the relatively mild punishments of detention and control to include imprisonment and even, in the form of death with two years' reprieve, the death penalty.[15] In all cases, punishment was expressly combined with programs of reform through participation in collective labor and through an "education" exercised not only through an appeal to the intellect via ideological indoctrination, but also through an appeal to the emotions via care for the individual's physical and emotional needs.[16]

The combination of the assessment of the current state of class struggle, the need to distinguish between the two types of contradiction, and the desire to produce in the offender an attitude of regret and reform was underlined in the thirty-third (1962) draft, which stated that punishment should be assessed "on the basis of the facts of the crime, the nature and circumstances of the crime, and the degree of harm to society" while also "taking into consideration the individual

---

15. Death with two years' reprieve is an innovation of the Chinese criminal law. Persons so sentenced serve two years in prison. If they have expressed true regret for their crimes and shown progress toward reform, their sentence may be converted to life or fixed-term imprisonment. If they have not, they may be executed. See Criminal Law, 1979, Art. 43, 46.

16. The theory and the practice of reform through labor is discussed below in chapter six.

situation of the criminal offender, the degree of sincerity with which he/she confesses his/her crime, and his/her penitential attitude."[17]

The need to distinguish between the two different types of contradiction as manifest under the changing conditions of class struggle also found expression in the range of punishment that could be meted out for any given criminal offense. This too was given particular attention in the thirty-third (1963) draft criminal law. In addition to allowing the courts to mete out sentences below the minimum, this draft also contained a provision that would allow the courts (subject to the approval of the Supreme People's Court) to mete out sentences *above* the maximum allowed by law in particularly severe cases or in cases with "odious circumstances." The rationale for this was that while the ordinary range of punishment might be suitable to ordinary times, there might be special situations in which the class struggle manifest itself in sharper form than usual. Such extraordinary circumstances would clearly require that the dictatorship of the proletariat respond with especially severe punishment.[18]

The final draft of the criminal law, written in 1978-79 on the basis of the thirty-third draft, shared the basic theoretical assumptions, framework, and much of the language of the previous drafts. Law was still considered to be an instrument of class dictatorship, and the socialist criminal law in particular to be a weapon in the hands of the dictatorship of the proletariat. Crime was assumed to be the product of the system of private ownership, a characteristic of the bourgeois stage of historical development and thus amenable, under socialism, to a process of reduction and eventual elimination. In legal theory and in jurisprudential practice, it was still considered essential to distinguish between the two different types of contradiction as manifest in the context of the class struggle.

But these basic concepts, introduced during the 1950s, were now filtered through the experience of the Cultural Revolution. During the years 1966-1976, Chinese intellectuals and Party leaders had witnessed the utter breakdown of law and order. Class struggle had been elevated to a position of supremacy. Law had been criticized, denounced, and freely violated. The organs of the legal system—the public security, the procuratorates and the courts—had been rhetorically and literally attacked as the state lost its monopoly on coercive power. Torture under interrogation and framed-up, often utterly absurd cases of "counter-revolution" were common during those years, and many intellectuals and Party leaders fell victim to a "dictatorship of the proletariat" that seemed to have run amuck.

The experience of the Cultural Revolution led the Communist Party to reassess the role of class struggle in China's ongoing socialist transformation in

---

17. Quoted in Gao Mingxuan, *Zhonghua renmin gongheguo xingfa de yunyu he dansheng*, 88.
18. *Ibid.* 94.

1978. According to the new party line of the post-Mao era, class struggle would continue within a limited scope, but was no longer the major task facing the Communist Party and the Chinese people. This reassessment led to (or justified) a reassessment of the nature of law and of crime. Law, while still regarded as an expression of the interests of the ruling class (in the case of China, of the proletariat), was also admitted to have a certain universal regulatory character. Crime, previously considered to be primarily a manifestation of contradictions between the people and the enemy, was now thought to be primarily a matter of contradictions among the people. In the final drafts of the Criminal Law, these changes in the theoretical understanding of law and of the role of the legal system were manifest in greater degree of attention to the protection of the property rights and the personal rights of the individual than had been evident in previous drafts.

Increased concern for the protection of individual rights is evident in a number of revisions and additions made in the final draft versions of the criminal law in 1978-79. In respect to the concrete application of punishments, for example, the thirty-third draft's stipulation that the offender's "individual situation, degree of sincerity of confession and attitude of regret" be considered in sentencing was eliminated from the law. The excessive stress on attitude was seen to conflict with the defendant's right of defense, while consideration of "individual situation" might easily lead to the assessment of punishment on the basis of the defendant's class background rather than on the facts of the crime. The thirty-third draft's provision that punishment above the maximum prescribed by law might be meted out under special circumstances was likewise eliminated as it appeared to make a mockery of sentencing guidelines, conflicted with the principle that the punishment should fit the crime, and also because no such provision could be found in the criminal law of any other country.

Although it may seem strange to discuss the protection of rights in the law on counter-revolution, Gao Mingxuan describes how, in the final drafting process, the various articles on counter-revolutionary offenses were revised in a conscious effort to limit the scope of the offense and to reduce the level of punishment.[19] Counterrevolution was defined as behavior endangering the state and committed with the conscious intent of "overthrowing the political power of the dictatorship of the proletariat and the socialist system."[20] While this definition may seem unremarkable to us, the legal requirement that both behavior dangerous to the state *and* counter-revolutionary intent be present was a significant step in light of the experience of the Cultural Revolution, when the merest appearance of counter-revolutionary behavior was enough to gain a conviction.

---

19. *Ibid.*, 137-139.
20. Criminal Law, 1979, Art. 90.

15

In addition to this more precise legal definition of "counter-revolution," the final draft of the criminal law, as compared to previous drafts, made lighter punishments possible for numerous counter-revolutionary offenses by expanding the range of punishment on the lower end.[21] Definitions of "aiding the enemy" and of "counter-revolutionary incitement" (Articles 97 and 102) were tightened in order to prevent the overly broad construction of "counter-revolution" characteristic of the Cultural Revolution. The phrase "have illicit relations with another country," originally included in the thirty-third (1962) draft was eliminated. The offense of distributing counter-revolutionary propaganda, described in the thirty-third draft as to "write, post, [or] distribute counter-revolutionary slogans [or] leaflets, to produce [and] disseminate rumors, or by other means carry out counter-revolutionary propaganda [or] threats" was revised to read: "Through counter-revolutionary slogans, leaflets or other means, propagandizing for and inciting the overthrow of the dictatorship of the proletariat and the socialist system."[22]

Greater interest in protecting individual rights was also evident in certain changes and additions made to Chapter IV (Crimes of Infringing Upon the Rights of the Person and the Democratic Rights of Citizens). In previous drafts, this chapter had been entitled "Crimes Infringing Upon the Rights of the Person of Citizens." It included crimes that seriously infringe upon the integrity of the person, such as homicide, injury, rape and other sexual offenses.[23] It also included a number of what William Jones called "Cultural-Revolution crimes," that is, provisions that criminalized behavior typically associated with the Cultural Revolution and the Red Guards.[24] Prohibition of the use violence, public posters, or other means to insult or trump up charges against another person (Art. 145) and of the provision of criminal sanctions for state personnel who unlawfully deprive citizens of their freedom of religious belief or infringe upon the customs of national minorities (Art. 147) were new, the latter being added in June 1979 at the suggestion of religious and national minority figures in the National People's Congress (NPC). Provisions relating to other offenses, such as the use of torture to coerce confessions (Art. 136), unlawful detention (Art. 143) and the illegal subjection of another person to control (Art. 144), while present in previous drafts,

21. Articles on the offenses of colluding with foreign states to harm the motherland (Article 91), plotting to subvert the government or dismember the state (Article 92), defecting to the enemy and turning traitor (Article 94), leading a mass rebellion (article 95), and leading a mass prison raid or organizing a jailbreak (Article 96) expanded the range of sentence at the lower end as compared to previous drafts, making lighter sentences theoretically possible. In Article 97 (espionage and aiding the enemy), the range of punishment was reduced on the upper end by making life imprisonment, rather than death, the maximum penalty. See Gao Mingxuan, *Zhonghua renmin gongheguo xingfa de yunyu he dansheng*, 137-143.
22. *Ibid.* 147-48; Criminal Law, 1979, Art. 102.
23. Meijer, "The New Criminal Law of the People's Republic of China," 135.
24. Jones, "The Criminal Law of the People's Republic of China," 410.

were revised in order to provide greater protection of the individual not only from citizens and from judicial personnel, but from all state personnel.[25]

While we acknowledge the extent to which the new Criminal Law reflected a thoughtful response to the violence and lawlessness of the Cultural Revolution, we must not exaggerate the scope or significance of the changes. The concepts of proletarian dictatorship and class struggle had been revised, but they were not rejected. The many additional protections against civilian and even official infringement of the "democratic rights" of the citizen and the protection of private as well as socialist property were still watered down by a continued emphasis on the importance of confession and by an underlying commitment to the need to protect the social order from political dissidents who, it was feared, would use their ideas to instigate riots and unrest. Expansion at the lower end of the range of punishment for many counter-revolutionary offenses and the reduction in the total number of offenses punishable by the death meant that lighter sentences and a minimal use of the death penalty were a theoretical possibility, but these changes in the law could not guarantee that lighter punishments would actually be assessed. Most significantly, any protection of individual rights was compromised by the continued assumption that the law functioned as an instrument of social transformation in the hands of the Communist Party. Nonetheless, it is notable that the lessons of the Cultural Revolution did inspire changes in the draft criminal laws, and we should understand that after the traumatic experience of the 1960s and 1970s, making such changes must have appeared as something like a moral imperative.

While looking back toward the experience of the Cultural Revolution, the final draft of the criminal law looked forward as well toward the task of administering criminal justice in a large country during a period in which significant social and economic changes were expected. In order that the law should be applicable over the tremendous breadth of territory of the PRC, and in order to be able to address the multifarious possibilities inherent in a complex and constantly changing society, the criminal law attempted, in the words of Gao Mingxuan, (quoting Mao Zedong) to "combine principle with flexibility."[26] Flexibility was incorporated into the letter of the Criminal Law through the use of vague language, wide sentencing guidelines, and the inclusion of the principle of analogy.

Vague terms such as "serious circumstances," "very serious circumstances," "odious circumstances," "especially odious circumstances," "relatively large amounts," and "heavier punishment" were used throughout the articles on particular offenses. Inasmuch as these terms were employed in combination with

---

25. Gao Mingxuan, *Zhonghua renmin gongheguo xingfa de yunyu he dansheng*, 182, 190-92, 196-97.

26. *Ibid.*, 17. Gao refers to Mao's statement, in "Qingniantuan de gongzuo yao zhaogu qingnian de tedian," 87 that "There must be flexibility in applying principles."

broad ranges of punishment, their precise meaning in any particular case would be of the utmost importance in the determination of an offender's sentence. These vague terms were purposely used in order to allow local judicial officials the flexibility to adjust the principles of the law to the concrete circumstances of their own particular time and place.[27]

The principle of analogy was set forth in Article 79 of the Criminal Law: "A crime that is not expressly stipulated in the Special Provisions of this Law may be determined and punished according to the most analogous article of the Special Provisions, but the matter shall be submitted to the Supreme Court for approval." This use of analogy in Chinese Communist law can be traced to the 1951 law on the punishment of counter-revolutionary crimes and, before that, to the base area laws of the 1930s.[28]

The stated purpose for including provision for the punishment of undesirable behavior by analogy was to allow room for the principles of the Criminal Law to adapt to the changing social situation of a rapidly developing country. In practice, as Dana Gianovetti has argued, the provision that cases decided by analogy must be approved by the Supreme People's Court (SPC) demonstrates that the Party sought both to incorporate a degree of flexibility into the law and to exercise a greater degree of supervision over base-level discretion than had been thought necessary in the past. The greater concern with central supervision over the application of analogy is reflected in the provision that cases be approved by the SPC; in previous drafts of the criminal law, it was felt sufficient that cases be approved by the higher level people's courts. In practice, the trouble of referring cases to the SPC for approval made judges disinclined to make use of Article 79. According to one source, only fifty-one cases decided by analogy were approved by the SPC between 1979 and 1991.[29]

THE CRIMINAL PROCEDURE LAW

The Criminal Procedure Law was drafted in a process similar to that of the Criminal Law. The earliest drafts were prepared in the 1950s on the basis of Soviet law and with reference to summaries of the various procedures actually followed by courts throughout China.[30] As with the Criminal Law, work on the

---

27. Gao Mingxuan, *Zhonghua renmin gongheguo xingfa de yunyu he dansheng*, 134.

28. Zhang Xipo, ed. *Geming genjudi fazhishi*, 275.

29. Gianovetti. "The Principle of Analogy," 382-401; Gao Mingxuan, *Zhonghua renmin gongheguo xingfa de yunyu he dansheng*, 127; Interview file 11.

30. Ma Xiwu, "Zai sifa zuotanhui shang dui liangge shenli chengxu chubu zongjie de jidian shuoming," 615-620; "Geji renmin fayuan xingshi anjian shenpan chengxu zongjie," 627-637; Chen Guangzhong, "Zhongguo xingshi susongfaxu," 6.

Criminal Procedure was suspended in 1957 and resumed in 1962. In 1963 a "Preliminary Draft of the Criminal Procedure Law of the PRC" was completed.[31] This draft was taken up again in 1978. After several rounds of revision, including review by the Central Committee of the CCP, the final draft passed and was promulgated as the first Criminal Procedure Law of the PRC in 1979. The new Criminal Procedure Law took effect on 1 January 1980.[32]

Like the Criminal Law, the Criminal Procedure Law of 1979 shows a greater concern for the protection of individual rights when compared to its earlier draft versions. The changes can clearly be seen of we compare the 1963 draft criminal procedure to the 1979 law. But as in the case of the Criminal Law, these tentative moves toward the greater protection of the individual from the power of the state were seriously compromised not only by the instrumentalist theory of law that underlay all the Chinese codes and thus made the law susceptible to *ad hoc* manipulation by both central and local Communist Party leadership, but also by passages within the code that placed narrow limits upon defendant's rights and provided incentives for the defendant to confess all and submit him/herself utterly to the mercy of the dictatorship of the proletariat.

The Criminal Procedure Law of 1979 consisted of four parts: Part One, General Provisions; Part Two, Filing a Case, Investigation and Initiation of Public Prosecution; Part Three, Adjudication: and Part Four, Execution of Sentences. Part One defined the tasks of the Criminal Procedure as "to guarantee the accurate and timely clarification of the facts of crimes, to apply the law correctly, to punish criminal elements, to safeguard innocent people from criminal prosecution, to educate citizens to struggle against criminal conduct actively, in order to uphold the socialist legal system, to protect the rights of the person and the democratic rights of citizens, and to safeguard the smooth progress of the cause of socialist revolution and socialist construction."[33] To accomplish these ends, the law laid forth the outlines of a three-stage procedure: "The public security organs are responsible for investigation, detention and preparatory examination of criminal cases. The People's Procuratorates are responsible for approving arrest, conducting procuratorial work (including investigation) and initiating public prosecution. The people's courts are responsible for adjudication."[34] The three

---

31. "Zhonghua renmin gongheguo xingshi susongfa caoan (chugao)." Hereafter cited as "Preliminary Draft Criminal Procedure Law (1963)."

32. Zhongyang zhengfa ganxiao, ed. *Zhonghua renmin gongheguo xingshi susongfa jiangyi*, 96-97.

33. "The Criminal Procedure Law of the People's Republic of China," Art. 2. The Chinese text and an English translation of "The Criminal Procedure Law of the People's Republic of China" as promulgated in 1979 appear in *The Criminal Law and the Criminal Procedure Law of China*, Beijing: Foreign Languages Press, 1984. Hereafter this law will be cited as "The Criminal Procedure Law, 1979." All quotations will be taken from the English translation appearing in the volume cited above.

34. Criminal Procedure Law, 1979, Art. 3.

organs of justice were to carry out their tasks independently of each other, yet coordinating and restraining each other (Art. 5). All citizens were to be treated equally before the law (Art. 4). Accused persons had the right of defense and were (in most cases) to be tried in open courts (Art. 8). Both the defendant (Art. 129) and the procuratorate (Art. 130) had the right to a single appeal; the second instance was the final instance (Art. 7).

The structure of the criminal process and the language in which it was laid forth followed the 1963 Preliminary Draft of the Criminal Procedure. As with the Criminal Law, however, the lessons of the Cultural Revolution are evident in certain differences between the 1963 draft and the law as promulgated in 1979. These differences concern the issue of confessions coerced under torture and the role of lawyers in the criminal procedure.

The practice of obtaining confessions by coercive means is addressed in both the Preliminary Draft and in the 1979 law. But while the Preliminary Draft deals with the issue in a bland admonition prohibiting the use of threats, enticement or other illegal means to obtain evidence, the Criminal Procedure Law states unequivocally in Article 32: "The use of torture to coerce statements and the gathering of evidence by threat, enticement, deceit or other unlawful methods are strictly prohibited."[35] Related to the express prohibition of torture introduced into the 1979 law is the placement of "material evidence and documentary evidence" at the top of the list of six types of evidence, above "testimony of witnesses" (a reversal of the order in the 1963 draft). Also significant is the addition of Article 35, which states that material evidence should take precedence over oral statements, that a defendant cannot be found guilty and punished if there is no evidence other than his/her statement, and that, conversely, a defendant may be convicted on the basis of "complete and reliable" evidence even if he/she has not confessed.

The right to defense and the role of lawyers, while recognized in the 1963 draft, were expanded in 1979. As seen in Article 2 (quoted above), the 1979 Criminal Procedure Law stated specifically (as the 1963 draft did not) that one of the tasks of the law is to "safeguard innocent people from prosecution." To that end, the Criminal Procedure Law strengthened the role of defense lawyers beyond what had been envisioned in 1963. For instance, where the Preliminary Draft states that the defense lawyer may, with the permission of the court, "acquaint himself" the materials relevant to the case, the Criminal Procedure Law drops the phrase "with the permission of the court" and uses the word "consult," which, unlike "acquaint himself" implies direct perusal of the case materials.[36] According

---

35. Compare Preliminary Draft Criminal Procedure (1963) Art. 31 with Criminal Procedure, 1979, Art. 32.
36. Compare Preliminary Draft Criminal Procedure (1963) Art. 28 with Criminal Procedure Law, 1979, Art. 29.

to Art. 110, the defendant must be notified of the trial date and be told that he/she may appoint a defender no later than seven days in advance of the trial. The 1979 law also adds an explicit statement to the effect that "In adjudicating a case appealed by a defendant or his legal representative . . . a people's court of the second instance may not increase a defendant's criminal punishment."[37] In the Preliminary Draft there was no such guarantee, and in practice it had been the rule that sentences would be increased on appeal, as an appeal was regarded as a clear demonstration that the defendant had failed to confess, to repent, and to accept the justice of the punishment meted out to him, and thus would require a relatively longer period of labor reform.[38]

Despite these changes, the Criminal Procedure Law still contained numerous provisions that placed severe limits on defendants' rights and on the protection of those rights. The provision that defense lawyers could only be retained seven days before trial meant that in practice, defense lawyers could do very little for their clients. By the time a defense lawyer was retained, the defendant may have been under investigation, including intensive interrogation, for weeks or months. During interrogation, the defendant was legally obligated to answer truthfully all questions regarding the case (Art. 64). The law provided no right to remain silent. Once retained, the defense lawyer was required "on the basis of the facts and the law, to present material and opinions proving that the defendant is innocent, that his crime is minor, or that he should receive a mitigated punishment be exempted from criminal responsibility . . ."[39] Even if she or he were retained precisely seven days prior to trial, the defense lawyer would have relatively little time to consult the materials of the case. Furthermore, while the courts, the procuratorates and the public security were expressly given the power to "gather and obtain evidence from the relevant state organs, enterprises, institutions, people's communes, people's organizations and citizens" (Art. 34), the defense was not granted similar rights. Once the trial was begun, the defendant did not benefit from the presumption of innocence—a legal concept rejected on the grounds that it was unscientific; if a person were to be presumed innocent, then why should he/she have been brought to trial for a criminal action? In general, the defense lawyer was, then, limited to arguing that there were mitigating circumstances, that his/her client had confessed and regretted, and that a relatively lighter sentence might thus be justified.

---

37. Criminal Procedure Law, 1979, Art. 137.
38. Cohen, *The Criminal Process in the People's Republic of China*, 38-40.
39. Criminal Procedure Law, 1979, Art. 28.

REGULATIONS AND LEGAL INTERPRETATION

In his study of the Chinese legal system of the 1950s and 1960s, Jerome Alan Cohen observed that the practice of criminal justice was based not on published codes of law, but on "a vast body of unpublished regulations, rules, orders, instructions, policies, reports, interpretations, and syntheses of judicial decisions . . . subject to continuing revision in light of experience and China's evolving needs . . . [which] may be applied both analogically and retroactively in order to ensure that legal standards do not lag behind the policy demands of the day, and to prevent previously un-prescribed but socially dangerous acts from going unpunished."[40] Despite the promulgation of the Criminal and Criminal Procedure Laws in 1979, Cohen's description continues to be relevant to our understanding of the practice of criminal justice in the 1980s.

Both the Criminal and the Criminal Procedure laws were highly programmatic in nature. They laid forth basic principles intended to guide the practice of criminal justice, but did so in purposely vague language that would allow the authorities sufficient flexibility to adapt those principles to the complex and constantly changing reality of each individual case as considered in the context of its circumstances (be they "mitigating," "serious," "odious," or "extremely odious") and in the context of the constant process of social change. For example, Peng Zhen, who had supervised the drafting of the new laws and their passage through the NPC, explained that the Criminal Procedure Law was intended simply to prescribe the relations between the public security, the procuratorates and the courts and to lay down the basic principles to be followed in the criminal procedure; the concrete procedure to be followed in the handling of criminal cases by each organ of the criminal justice system would be laid forth separately in individually established regulations.[41] Thus, while the laws set forth the basic principles or structural guidelines of the criminal justice system, the concrete handling of cases would continue to be determined in large part by additional rules, regulations, legal interpretations and policies.

To take the public security organs as an example, the preparation of internal criminal procedural regulations took nearly six years. Work begun in 1981-82 was quickly overtaken by the events of 1983—the Strike Hard anti-crime campaign of that year and the revisions of the Criminal Procedure Law that accompanied the campaign as well as the transfer, in the same year, of responsibility for the administration of the labor reform and re-education camps from the Ministry of Public Security to the Ministry of Justice. Work on the regulations was resumed

---

40. Cohen. *The Criminal Process in the People's Republic of China*, 23.
41. For a summary of Peng's remarks, see "Yu Lei fubuzhang zai guanche shishi 'gongan jiguan banli xingshi anjian de chengxu guiding' dianhua shang de jianghua," 42.

in 1987.[42] Before the Procedural Regulations for the Public Security Organs' handling of Criminal Cases were completed and took effect, the procedure, responsibilities and powers for the handling of criminal cases within the public security organs were simply not clearly delineated.[43]

Even with the promulgation of the regulations in 1987, there remained unresolved questions. The relationship between the Ministry of Public Security and the Ministry of National Security remained, in the words of one official, subject to "the regulations of the relevant documents."[44] Other issues remained not only unclear, but contradictory. For example, the 1987 regulations of the Ministry of Public Security stipulated that cases of theft, swindling or forcible seizure had to involve a minimum of forty yuan in rural areas or eighty yuan in urban areas before criminal responsibility would be pursued. At the same time, the threshold of criminal responsibility in such cases was set by the internal regulations of the people's courts at two hundred yuan and four hundred yuan, respectively.[45]

While regulations established concrete rules and procedures on the basis of the principles contained in the law, legal interpretations provided a mechanism by which the law was explained, adapted and up-dated to conform with the complex and ever-changing needs of the practice of criminal justice across time and space. In its "Decision Regarding Strengthening Legal Interpretation Work" (June 1981), the Standing Committee of the NPC defined three types of legal interpretation. First, legislative interpretations (*lifa jieshi*), which may be issued only by the Standing Committee of the NPC, were those that further defined or supplemented an existing law. Up to the end of 1992, the Standing Committee of the NPC had not issued any legislative interpretations directly relevant to criminal justice. Second, judicial interpretations (*sifa jieshi*), issued individually or jointly by the Supreme People's Court and/or the Supreme People's Procuratorate (SPP) were concerned with the concrete application of law in judicial or procuratorial work. If the SPC and the SPP should differ in their interpretation of law, the issue was to be resolved by the Standing Committee of the NPC. In practice, this did not occur during the 1980s because the SPP and the SPC made a practice of consulting with each other during the drafting of legal interpretations.[46] Third, there were administrative interpretations (*xingzheng jieshi*) issued by organs of state other than the SPP and the SPC regarding the application of laws not relevant

---

42. "Gonganbu faguiju fujuzhang Liu Enqi 'guanyu gongan jiguan banli xingshi anjian chengxu guiding de shuoming,'" 38.
43. "Yu Lei fubuzhang zai guanche shishi 'gongan jiguan banli xingshi anjian de chengxu guiding' dianhua shang de jianghua," 42.
44. "Gonganbu faguiju fujuzhang Liu Enqi 'guanyu gongan jiguan banli xingshi anjian chengxu guiding de shuoming," 38.
45. Ibid.
46. Interview file 12.

to judicial or procuratorial work. For example, the Ministry of Public Security could issue administrative interpretations concerning the enforcement of the Security Administration Punishment Act.

Neither the distinctions between legislative, administrative and judicial interpretation, the issue of which organs were empowered to issue interpretations, nor the forms that interpretation might take and the format for the publication of legal interpretation were entirely clear. Prior to the 1981 decision of the Standing Committee of the NPC referred to above, there was no legal definition of "legal interpretation." In practice, the line between administrative and judicial interpretation appears to have been quite vague. This is particularly true for the period up to 1984, when it was common for the SPC and the SPP to issue legal interpretations jointly with the Ministry of Public Security and often with other state organs as well.[47] Before 1985, legal interpretations were not openly published, but only circulated internally within the relevant bureaucracies. After 1985, legal interpretations were published in a bewildering variety of forms. The SPC and the SPP each circulated its judicial interpretations both as internal documents and in openly published communiques. In addition, the judicial interpretations of the SPC and the SPP, as well as a variety of administrative interpretations, policy documents, regulations, and even talks by high-ranking legal officials were compiled and issued in a number of collections and handbooks published by work units, educational institutions, and state-run publishing houses. According to Zhou Daoluan, Director of the Policy Research Bureau of the Supreme People's Court in 1992, there was no central control over the publication of such collections.[48]

Within the court system, judicial interpretations could be issued in response to a request from a lower level court or administrative bureau for clarification of some point of law, or they could be issued by the SPC on its own initiative in response to a question that it had taken note of, either in its own adjudication work or in its review of work done by lower level courts. Once an issue was brought up for interpretation, it would be referred to the SPC Policy Research Office for discussion. If the Policy Research Office concluded that a judicial interpretation was called for, then it would compose a draft interpretation with the help of the

---

47. In many instances, such as the definition of the offense of writing "counter-revolutionary contact letters" (*fangeming guagouxin*), it was essential that the public security organs, the procuratorates and the courts agree on such concrete details as the name of the offense and the type of evidence to be transferred from one organ to the next in the case files. Inasmuch as base level units outside the SPP and SPC might not acknowledge SPC and/or SPP documents as legally binding, it was essential that all units involved in the identification and handling of any particular type of case jointly issue the relevant interpretative documents to the units within their respective bureaucracies.

48. Interview file 12. One of the reasons for the publication of such volumes was simply the desire to make a profit in the growing market for legal publications. Another reason is that units such as provincial cadre schools compile collections for instructional purposes, thus saving the work unit or the students from having to purchase expensive, formally published collections.

relevant division of the SPC. The draft would then be passed along to the leaders of the SPC, who would consider it and circulate it to the lower levels of the court system and to legal scholars in order to solicit opinions. On the basis of opinions and suggestions thus gathered, the draft interpretation would be revised and sent to the SPC Adjudication Committee (a leadership body within the SPC). Following approval by the SPC, the interpretation would be promulgated.

Judicial interpretations were issued in a number of different forms. Different forms of judicial interpretation were designed to fulfill different purposes, but the proliferation of overlapping categories and the absence of clear definitions could be confusing. In the case of the Supreme People's Court, "letters" were used to reply to specific questions from a higher people's court. They did not have to be approved by the adjudication committee of the SPC, nor did they have general normative authority. "Replies with instructions" were issued to the entire court system in response to a single concrete question raised by several different courts. They were legally binding on all courts. "Circulars" and "regulations" dealt with broader questions, and were also sent to and binding on all courts. As a whole, however, the various forms of interpretation were not standardized throughout the 1980s. Even in 1992, more than ten years after China began reforming its legal system, the judicial interpretations and their various forms were still, in the words of a high-ranking SPC official, "a big mess."[49]

It was not only the variety of forms that judicial interpretation might take and the numerous formats in which they were published that were messy. Legal questions concerning the power to issue judicial interpretation and the question of retroactivity were also obscure. Some judicial interpretations contained explicit statements of retroactive force. For example, the SPP's 9 January 1984 "Answers to Certain Questions Regarding the Concrete Application of Law in the Struggle to Deal Strong Blows to Serious Criminal Offenders" stated that in cases of offenders who had been punished previous to the introduction, in August 1983, of the new sentencing standards for serious criminal offenses, the original sentence should be revoked and the offender re-arrested and re-tried on the basis of the new legal standards if there had been great public outrage at their offense or if the original sentence had been "abnormally light."[50] Zhou Guanghan, writing in *Adjudication* in 1985 argued that after a judicial interpretation was issued, all cases previously decided in ways that conflicted with the new interpretation should be regarded as having been incorrectly handled and thus were open to revision.[51]

As regards the legal basis of the power of judicial interpretation, Kong Xiaohong argues that although the 1981 decision of the Standing Committee of the

---

49. Interview file 12. See also Ren Yiqiu. "Zhiding xingshi sifa jieshi de jige yuanze"

50. "Zuigao renmin jianchayuan guanyu zai yanli daji xingshi fanzui douzheng zhong juti yingyong falu de ruogan wenti de dafu," 36-39.

51. Zhou Guanghan. "Sifa jieshi qianxi," 14.

NPC granted the power of legal interpretation to the SPC, the SPP and organs under the State Council, there was still no constitutional basis for the institution of legal interpretation. Also, while Article 33 of the Organic Law of the People's Courts granted the power of judicial interpretation to the SPC, the Organic Law of the People's Procuratorate did not grant such power to the SPP. One cannot help but agree with Kong's conclusion that "Chinese legislators do not intend to treat the exercise of the interpretative power as a very sensitive issue."[52] But regardless of its legal basis or the many forms in which it was manifest, legal interpretation, and particularly judicial interpretation, played an essential role in the practice of criminal justice and the development of the criminal justice system during the Deng era. Inasmuch as legal interpretation functioned as law, public security, procuratorate and court personnel could not do their work without reference to legal interpretations.[53] Likewise, we cannot hope to understand the practical workings, the development, the strengths and the weaknesses of the Chinese criminal justice system unless we consider legal interpretations as well as the laws themselves.

THE SIGNIFICANCE OF THE CRIMINAL
AND CRIMINAL PROCEDURE LAWS

Did the promulgation of criminal and criminal procedure laws in 1979 indicate a significant change in the Chinese Communist regime's attitude toward law and its usefulness in establishing norms for behavior and for the guidance of the use of the coercive power of the state? Or were the laws no more than a screen barely concealing the continued reality of a leadership committed to the arbitrary use of state power as an instrument of social engineering and of political repression?

Shao-chuan Leng and Hung-dah Chiu have suggested that the legal history of the PRC can be understood in terms of the dialectical movement between two co-existing and competing models of law: the jural (formal) model and the societal (informal) model. The jural model "stands for formal, elaborate, and codified rules enforced by a regular judicial hierarchy . . . " The societal model "focuses on socially approved norms and values, inculcated by political socialization and enforced by extrajudicial apparatuses consisting of administrative agencies and social organizations."[54] Seen in terms of these two models of law, the Chinese

---

52. Kong Xiaohong, "Legal Interpretation in China," 498.

53. *Ibid.*, 491-506; Ren Yiqiu, "Zhiding xingshi sifa jieshi de jige yuanze," 31-32.

54. Leng and Chiu, *Criminal Justice in Post-Mao China*, 7. Conceptually, the societal model is linked to Chairman Mao's dislike for bureaucracies, the ideas of the mass line and of the need for constant revolution, and to the traditional Chinese tendency to assign greater value to rule by moral virtue,

approach to criminal justice may be described as having gone through six stages.[55] In the first stage, from 1949-1953, although the formal organs of criminal justice were established, in practice the societal model held sway as revolutionary justice was dispensed by administrative agencies or by the people themselves under Party leadership. From 1954 through 1957, the PRC moved decisively in the direction of the jural model, as a constitution was adopted (1954), some laws were written, and class struggle de-emphasized. From 1957 through 1960, law was attacked as bourgeois; the societal model had returned to favor. The years 1961 through 1963 are characterized by a turn in the direction of the jural model, while the period from 1964 through 1977 represent the nearly complete domination of the societal model. In the period from 1978 through the present, the jural model has returned to an ascendancy even more marked than that of the mid-1950s.

According to this developmental scheme, the laws of 1979 appear as the re-assertion of the jural model, and thus as a reassertion of the Soviet-style socialist legality that served as a model for the construction of the Chinese legal system of the 1950s.[56] Inasmuch as the laws of 1979 were based on research and drafting work begun in the 1950s (and carried out under substantially the same leadership and involving many of the same personnel), this interpretation does have some merit. However, it does tend to obscure the complex nature of socialist legality.

As Richard Baum has pointed out, more than one model of socialist legality can be derived from the Soviet experience.[57] The policy of the War Communism years (1918-1921) was revolutionary justice untrammeled by legal restraints, a socialist legal nihilism in which law itself was considered to be a bourgeois institution to would be eliminated as socialism was established. With the New Economic Plan (1921-1927), the need for codification and legal system-building

---

persuasion, internalization of norms, and resolution of disputes by conciliation than to the regulation of behavior by punishment and the resolution of disputes in court. In terms of institutions, the societal model is manifest in street committees, propaganda organs, "mass organizations" (Youth League, Women's Federation, unions and so on) and, above all, in the Party and its policies. The jural model, by contrast, is linked to Marxist-Leninist ideology and to the ancient Chinese school of Legalism (whose philosophers believed that draconian laws firmly and swiftly enforced would lead to social stability) and concretely manifest in the laws and legal organs adapted from the Soviet Union—which were also, of course, under Party leadership.

55. Leng and Chiu present the development of Chinese criminal justice in terms of four stages, 1949-53 (societal), 1954-57 (jural), 1957-65 (societal), and 1966-76 (societal). My periodization is based on that presented in Baum, "Modernization and Legal Reform in Post-Mao China," 95.

56. Chiu, "China's Legal Reform," 268-271.

57. The following analysis of the development of Soviet criminal justice and the derivation from that development of three models of socialist legality is inspired by Baum, "Modernization and Legal Reform in Post-Mao China." My analysis, however, differs from that of Baum in its emphasis. Baum discusses both civil and criminal law under the rubric of "socialist legality" but in fact, as is indirectly indicated by some of his own comments (73, 100), the models of socialist legality that he has constructed fit the case of civil law better than that of criminal justice. In what follows, I am concerned with socialist legality only as it concerns the criminal justice system.

was admitted, but "only as a temporary bow to the necessities of a social order part socialist but also . . . part capitalist."[58] Socialist legality was thus born in reluctance, but soon led to the development of a system of laws and legal institutions. Class reconciliation, rather than class struggle, was the order of the day; punishments were mild, and the death penalty was eliminated.

Following Stalin's consolidation of power and under the theoretical as well as practical leadership of chief procurator Vyshinsky, socialist legality took on new characteristics. Rather than looking forward to the imminent withering away of the state under socialism, Stalin argued that in order to accomplish the goals of the revolution and to safeguard the socialist order, the state must become more powerful and more efficient than it had ever been. Under the conditions of "socialism in one country," the causes of crime were said to be located entirely outside the USSR in either left-over feudal and capitalist ideology or in the machinations of world capitalism. All crime, then, took on class attributes, and criminal law was thus an aspect of class struggle, a means by which to eliminate obstacles to socialist construction.[59] Punishment was swift and harsh, and included the death penalty. Under the influence of Vyshinsky, confession came to be regarded as the "queen of evidence." The number of laws increased, as did the number of bureaucrats, police, procurators and judges charged with enforcing them. In cases of undesirable behavior not expressly prohibited by law, punishment could be assessed by analogy.

In the years following Stalin's death, the Soviet approach to criminal justice went through an initial phase of liberalization and popularization and then entered an era which, although characterized by a greater respect for legality and less emphasis on class struggle than the Stalinist system, saw nevertheless an attempt to deal with social problems through the creation of new offenses and the use of harsher punishments and campaign tactics. In the initial phase of liberalization and popularization, Nikita Kruschev repealed draconian Stalinist laws, reduced punishments, and decriminalized some less dangerous offenses. The authority of the legal organs (procuratorates and courts) was restored, and that of the Ministry of Internal Affairs (the police) reduced; in the process, L.P. Beria, the notorious chief of the Ministry of Internal Affairs, was executed. The trend toward liberalization was given concrete expression in the drafting and promulgation of the new Soviet criminal code of 1958 and of a criminal procedure law.

Accompanying the liberalization of criminal justice was a trend toward popularization. Criminologists and political leaders argued that in the fight against crime, preventive and educational measures were more important than punish-

---

58. Juviler. *Revolutionary Law and Order*, 28. The description of the development of Soviet justice that follows is based on Juviler.
59. *Ibid.*, 48.

ment. There appeared then a tendency to substitute non-judicial, preventive measures for judicial punishment. Particularly after 1959, such non-judicial institutions as comrades courts, people's detachments, collective reeducation, street committees, parents' committees, legal propaganda, and campaigns against drunkenness and immorality proliferated. But in 1961, the Soviet approach to criminal justice turned again toward greater emphasis on the punitive than the preventive, on the legal apparatus rather than on popular organizations. Revisions of the criminal law in 1961 and 1962 added new crimes and new penalties, including harsher penalties for recidivism and increased use of the death penalty. This trend continued beyond Kruschev's death into the Brezhnev era, which saw further increases in the use of criminal punishment, the use of campaign tactics (including a campaign against hooliganism in 1966), and a tendency to address any and all social problems, including the ever-growing problem of alcohol abuse, through coercive legal means.

Taking the various types of socialist legality represented by the Soviet experience as reference points, we can see more clearly the nature of the Chinese socialist legal system of the 1980s. The system certainly does not fall under the Stalinist model of socialist legality. In fact, the revisions of the draft criminal and criminal procedure codes included specific rejection of such basic characteristics of Stalinist law as the class nature of crime and the value attached to confession. If anything, the promulgation of the new criminal and criminal procedure laws and the propaganda effort with which they were introduced bears a certain resemblance to the de-Stalinization of Soviet law during the early Kruschev years.

In both instances, we see a deliberate down-playing of class struggle, re-emphasis on the authority of the procuratorates and the courts, a reduction in the scope of punishment, more strict construction of counter-revolutionary offenses, and a new emphasis on the importance of prevention as opposed to punishment. Similarities appear also in the implementation of criminal justice. Both the Kruschev and the Deng regimes began with the rhetoric of liberalization, popularization and prevention, but soon turned in frustration to stricter laws and heavier punishments as they attempted to address seemingly intractable social problems. But where Kruschev, and Brezhnev after him, dealt with the problems of an increasingly moribund socialist planned economy, the criminal justice system of the Deng era aimed both to preserve of social order in a lively, growing market economy and to assist in the creation of the spiritual or moral construction that was deemed an essential part of China's modernization.

In conclusion, the laws as promulgated in 1979 were clearly a step toward greater clarity, stability, and accountability in regard to the establishment of behavioral norms and their enforcement by the coercive power of the state. Underlying the new laws, however, were some of the same assumptions that had informed the application of state power during the Maoist years. The dictatorship of the proletariat was still charged with the goal of transforming China into a strong, powerful socialist state. As will be seen below, this task was understood as involving the moral as well as the material transformation of the Chinese people. This was rule by law, but not rule of law. The legal system, including the criminal justice system, remained an instrument with which the Party leadership was to carry out the historical project of socialist transformation.

2

THE ORGANS OF DICTATORSHIP

In conducting criminal proceedings, the people's courts, the people's procuratorates and the public security organs shall have a division of labor with separate responsibilities and coordinate with each other in order to guarantee the accurate and effective enforcement of the law.

Criminal Procedure Law of the PRC (1979), Article 5.

The Criminal Law was administered by the three legal organs, or organs of dictatorship: public security, procuratorates, and courts. All three were centralized bureaucracies which had been established in the 1950s. In 1967, during the Cultural Revolution, all three were the objects of rhetorical and physical attack by Red Guards acting according to the slogan "smash the public security, courts and procuratorates."[1] The public security organs and courts continued to exist, although in a weakened state; the procuratorate was dissolved, and its prosecutorial functions taken over by the public security organs until it was restored in 1977. In 1978-79, the system of public security, procuratorates and courts was reconstructed as a part of the overall reconstruction of socialist legality.

In the criminal procedure, the public security organs, the procuratorates and the courts were to coordinate with each other and to restrain each other in the task of establishing the facts and circumstances of any given criminal case and applying the law as appropriate.[2] In their relationship to each other, the three organs of justice were sometimes compared to three stations on an assembly line, processing the raw material (criminal offenders) and finally passing it along to the next

---

1. Zhou Zhenxiang and Shao Jingchun, ed. *Xin Zhongguo fazhi jianshe sishinian yaolan*, 131.
2. Criminal Procedure Law, 1979, Art. 5.

31

stage—labor reform—in which criminals were to be made into "useful timber" for the construction of socialism.[3] The division of labor in the criminal justice system between public security, procuratorates, and courts thus did not bring about a meaningful institutional autonomy, much less an adversarial relationship between the three organs of criminal justice—nor was it intended to do so. In practice, the working relationship of the three organs, the subordination of all three organs at each level of government to the people's congress and Communist Party committee of that same level, and the inherent conflict of interest in the procuratorate's dual role of prosecutor and supervisor of the legality of the entire criminal procedure meant that in practice, mutual coordination was a more significant factor than mutual restraint. This lack of institutional autonomy, combined with factors including the lack of material and human resources, lack of the presumption of innocence, the overlap between administrative and judicial policies toward crime control and a general unfamiliarity and impatience with law, and particularly with procedural law, led to recurrent violations of defendants' rights. The endemic violations of defendants' rights was regarded by leading cadres and by legal scholars as a serious, problem, not simply because such violations resulted in unnecessary suffering, but also because they indicated a lack of efficiency on the part of the public security, the procuratorates and the courts.

PUBLIC SECURITY

China's public security (police) system consisted of a single, centralized bureaucracy led by the State Council's Ministry of Public Security. The *Encyclopedia of Criminal Sciences* described the Ministry of Public Security thus:

> Its main tasks are to be in charge of national public security work, to lead the public security and the People's Armed Police forces, to protect the political power of the people's democratic dictatorship and the socialist system, to maintain social order, to suppress counter-revolutionary activity, to punish criminal activities that harm public security, undermine the socialist economy and other criminal activities, and to safeguard the personal, democratic and other rights of citizens. Its main duties are: on the basis of the constitution and the laws to draw up the concrete policies and principles for public security work; issue public security regulations and orders in accordance with departmental authority; direct the public security work of public security organs at all levels; organize and lead preventive and punitive work against

---

3. For example, see Wu Lei, ed. *Zhongguo sifa zhidu*, 93. For a discussion of the concept of offenders as "useful timber," see Dutton, *Policing and Punishment*, 253-262.

the wrecking activities of counter-revolutionary elements and other criminal elements; organize and lead the work of guarding the safety of state property, state secrets and key departments; organize and lead the administrative management of public security, household registration management, traffic safety management, and fire prevention work. Within the Ministry of Public Security are established the operational departments of public security management, criminal investigation, frontier inspection, management of foreigners, traffic safety, fire prevention, preliminary examination, and the Chinese central office of the International Criminal Police Organization (Interpol).[4]

As we can see from this description, the Ministry of Public Security was designed not only to investigate criminal acts and arrest and interrogate criminal offenders, but also to maintain social order by exercising a wide range of preventive and administrative powers. Thus in addition to those functions prescribed by the Criminal Procedure Law, the coercive power of the Public Security apparatus extended to include the administrative detention and interrogation of suspected criminals, the enforcement of the Security Administration Punishment Act (an administrative regulation concerning what in American law would be referred to as misdemeanors), and for the sentencing of minor offenders to periods of "re-education through labor."

In practice, these powers were exercised by a unified police bureaucracy. Within the government of each province, autonomous region and centrally administered city was a department of public security (*gonganting*), while each city or county government included a bureau of public security (*gonganju*) and each city district (*qu*) a Public security sub-bureau (*gongan fenju*). At the base level—town, street, busy urban areas —were the public security stations (*gongan paichusuo*). Public security stations were agencies of public security bureaus or sub-bureaus; they exercised the basic organizational, administrative and investigative functions of public security, but did not have the authority to initiate criminal detention or to transfer cases to the procuratorate for prosecution. Each public security organ (i.e. the public security departments, bureaus and sub-bureaus) was a part of the people's government of the same level, but also reported to the public security organ of the next higher level, with all public security work coming under the national leadership of the Ministry of Public Security. Each public security organ, then, was subject to the dual leadership of the people's government and Communist Party committee of the same level and of the public security organ of the next higher level.[5]

---

4. Yang Chunxi, Gao Mingxuan, Ma Kechang and Yu Shutong, ed. *Xingshi faxue da cishu*, 182-83.
5. *Ibid.*, 183-84.

The public security apparatus (and the same could be said of the courts and procuratorates) entered the era of economic reform and opening to the outside world with two distinct, but related problems. First, the bureaucracy had to be purged of the work habits and, to some extent, the organizational structure and personnel of the Cultural Revolution. Second, public security organs and personnel had to adapt to the new and constantly changing context of the 1980s. As with the laws themselves, the public security, courts and procuratorates sought in the present to adapt the assumptions, the methods, the structures and the personnel of the past to meet the imagined needs of a largely unknown future. For the public security apparatus, this meant that the *ad hoc*, policy-driven, and highly politicized public security work of the Cultural Revolution was to be replaced by a more formally structured, law-guided administration of public security, in which the public security bureaus would have to place more emphasis on professionalism and on cooperation with the now strengthened procuratorates and courts than ever before.

The challenges posed by the circumstances of the new era were discussed by Peng Zhen in a talk delivered to chiefs of public security bureaus in September, 1979. Echoing the slogans of the time, Peng urged the public security organs to "seek truth from facts," "take practice as the sole criterion of truth," and make a clean break with the practices that had allegedly characterized the years of the Cultural Revolution.[6] Classes as such had long since ceased to exist, said Peng, their economic basis having been eliminated and their individual members having either reformed or passed away. Now, the public security organs must revive and develop the "excellent traditions" of the past—that is to say, of the seventeen years of Communist government preceding the Cultural Revolution—and exercise the powers of dictatorship in accordance with the law. That the public security organs, in cooperation with the procuratorates and the courts, should carry out the law was the wish of the Party Center—therefore it was incumbent upon all public security personnel to study and understand the law. Public security personnel, both old and new would require training and study. Personnel newly transferred from the PLA (such newly transferred personnel accounted for half the public security force of Beijing, for example) stood in particular need of instruction in the nature of their new duties. Past mistakes—in particular the extraction of testimony under coercion and beatings—should be admitted and apologized for in order to restore the public reputation of the public security organs. In future, those guilty of beating and torturing suspects would be punished.

In this context, Peng Zhen laid particular stress on the need for public security organs to remain close to and submit to the authority of the Party. As a counter-

---

6. "Peng Zhen tongzhi zai quanguo gongan juzhang huiyi shang de jianghua," 114-129. The following two paragraphs draw on this talk.

example, he pointed to the Soviet Union. "Of the Soviet ministers of public security, from Drzhinski through Beria, excepting only Drzhinski, none came to a good end—just about every one was killed. With that vertical leadership that they do, the Party hasn't any means of control, [central authority] extends straight to the bottom, with the result that, if there is a problem, you take responsibility, so what is to be done then? Kill the minister of public security. Before the Zunyi conference, we used this method too. During the Yan'an period, we changed . . . to dual leadership. When the Party committees exercise leadership, there are not many mistakes."[7] All errors, said Peng, should be confessed to the Party organization, and all problems should be taken to the Party organization. If the public security organs believed that the procuratorates or the courts had made incorrect decisions regarding cases transferred to them from the public security, then public security could demand re-consideration.

As reflected in Peng Zhen's comments, the reform of public security brought with it a number of new challenges. Public security men and officers were used to working under the guidance of policy rather than within the narrower and less flexible framework of the Criminal Law and Criminal Procedure Law. They were trained in and accustomed to class struggle rather than struggle against common crime, and they had a reputation for avoiding the hard work of detection and investigation, preferring instead to extract testimony by means of threats, marathon interrogations, beatings and torture. These problems, and particularly the problem of extraction of testimony under coercion, remained commonplace throughout the 1980s and beyond. The reasons for this are complex. They involved infrastructural weakness, poorly trained personnel, ingrained attitudes toward suspected wrong-doers, the structure of the criminal justice system and its subordination to Party leadership, and the administrative as well as legal coercive measures used by the public security organs in their work of maintaining public order and punishing wrong-doers.

There were four administrative sanctions available to the public security organs in the 1980s. They could take suspicious people into custody and return them to their home areas under "shelter and deportation" (*shourong qiansong*) or hold them for "shelter and investigation" (*shourong shencha*). Minor infractions of public security could be punished under the Security Administration Punishment Act, and more serious infractions still not considered to constitute a crime could be punished by re-education through labor.

Shelter and deportation and shelter and investigation were related institutions. Their roots can be traced back to the early 1960s, when the Great Leap Forward had caused a nation-wide famine in which the rural areas suffered disproportionately. Rural people fleeing starvation flocked to the cities searching for food. In

---

7. *Ibid.*, 126.

1961 the Central Committee of the Chinese Communist Party and the State Council jointly instructed large cities and major transportation centers to establish "shelter and deportation centers" (*shourong qiansong zhan*). The purpose of these centers was to detain, investigate and return transients to their places of origin. Two years later, evidently taking "shelter and deportation" as a model, the Ministry of Public Security established the institution of "shelter and investigation" as a means of detaining and investigating criminal suspects who had no known residence and/or whose identity was unclear.[8]

Up until 1975, the practice of shelter and investigation seems to have existed without any formal legal basis. In that year, it was further defined in a State Council document entitled "Major Points of the Meeting on Railway Security." Public security units at the locality (*di*) and city (*shi*) level and above were authorized to establish shelter and investigation centers for the detention and interrogation of persons whose residence or identity was in question and who were suspected of having committed criminal offenses. It is clear that shelter and investigation was not intended for dealing with persons of known identity. In 1978, the Ministry of Public Security issued another document in which it stated again that shelter and investigation centers were to be operated only by public security organs at the locality and city level and above. All facilities established by county level public security offices were to be closed. Rules of procedure, time limits and the rules concerning targets of shelter and investigation were to be strictly observed. Only reliable and incorruptible cadres were to be entrusted with the supervision of shelter and investigation.[9]

In 1980, the State Council ordered that shelter and investigation be combined with another administrative sanction, re-education through labor. Those detained under shelter and investigation were to be integrated into labor re-education facilities rather than being held in separate shelter and investigation centers.[10] But in 1984, the Ministry of Public Security issued 'Provisional Regulations for the Management of Shelter and Investigation Work."[11] These procedural regulations for the management of shelter and investigation Centers still referred to the 1975 "Major Points" report as the basis for shelter and investigation.

According to the "Provisional Regulations," shelter and investigation required the approval of public security organs of the county level or higher. Suspects were to be interrogated within twenty-four hours and their families or work units

---

8. *Dangdai zhongguo de gongan gongzuo* 404-405; Zhou Guojun. "Guanyu shourong shencha cunfei zhi yanjiu," 36.

9. "Gonganbu guanyu zhengdun he jiaqiang dui liucuan fanzuifenzi shourong shencha gongzuo de tongzhi," 248-250.

10. "Guowuyuan guanyu jiang qiangzhi laodong he shourong shencha liangxiang cuoshi tongyiyu laodong jiaoyang de tongzhi," Art. 2.

11. "Shourong shencha guanli gongzuo zanxing guiding," 250-252.

notified of their whereabouts and the reason for their detention—indicating that shelter and investigation was no longer limited to the detention of transients. In general, the facts of a case were to be clarified within one month, although in complex cases, the period of detention could be extended to two or three months. Those who refused to divulge their real names or places of origin could be held indefinitely.[12]

None of these documents constituted a formal legal basis for the institution of shelter and investigation. In June 1986 an internal document issued by the Legal Work Committee of the Standing Committee of the NPC declared: "The State Council's 'Notice of the State Council on the Unification of the Two Measures of Forced labor and Shelter and Investigation Together With Re-education Through Labor' . . . may be regarded as an administrative regulation and, prior to official legislation, it may serve as the legal basis for shelter and investigation."[13] But also in 1986 the Ministry of Public Security cited the lack of a legal basis as a reason for prohibiting the Chinese press from reporting news about people being held in shelter and investigation and forbidding public security units or personnel from writing on or discussing shelter and investigation in the openly published media.[14]

Despite the Ministry's concern about unflattering publicity, routine abuse of the power of shelter and investigation was revealed and criticized both within the public security apparatus and in the Chinese legal press. In the 1985 "Notice Regarding Strict Control of the Use of Shelter and Investigation," the Ministry of Public Security expressed concern with the widespread use of shelter and investigation as a means of detaining suspects without having to follow the procedural rules concerning administrative detention, criminal detention, and arrest. The document also pointed out that suspects were being held beyond the three-month maximum.[15] Some legal scholars and members of the Chinese legal profession suggested that shelter and investigation be abandoned. Defenders of the system argued that abuses could be brought under control if the leaders of the public security organs would just conscientiously follow the relevant regulations.[16]

In addition to the power to detain suspects for shelter and investigation, the public security organs enforced a sort of shadow criminal law known as the Security Prevention Punishment Act (SAPA). The first Security Administration Punishment Act was promulgated on October 22, 1957. A revised version was passed by the Standing Committee of the National People's Congress in September 1986.[17] The SAPA defined various types of behavior considered to be

---

12. *Ibid.*
13. Zhou Guojun, "Guanyu shourong shencha cunfei zhi yanjiu," 35.
14. "Gonganbu guanyu shourong shencha xuanchuan wenti de qingshi' de pifu."
15. "Guanyu yange kongzhi shiyong shourong shencha shouduan de tongzhi," 3-75.
16. Zhou Guojun, "Guanyu shourong shencha cunfei zhi yanjiu," 35-41.
17. Xu Hanmin, ed. *Renmin zhian 40 nian*, 1992, 99.

harmful to public security and prescribed the punishments to be assessed against offenders. The SAPA gave the public security offices formal guidelines for the maintenance of public order through the imposition of warnings, fines of up to 200 yuan and up to fifteen days of detention of persons guilty of SAPA offenses.[18] It also empowered the public security offices to mediate minor conflicts, to order offenders to pay for financial losses or medical expenses incurred by their victims, and to take drunkards into custody. In addition, the police were supposed to convince those who were punished to admit their guilt and to willingly accept the punishment imposed.[19] As SAPA was an administrative law, it was enforced by the public security organs alone, without the cooperation of the procuratorates or the courts.

A very wide range of offenses was made punishable by the SAPA. Some, such as disturbing public order, harassing women, illegal possession of guns and knives, and ticket-scalping were also offenses under the Criminal Law. Serious offenses would thus be criminal matters, while minor violations would be handled as SAPA offenses. Other offenses, most notably prostitution, were not punishable under the Criminal Law but were punishable under the SAPA. Under the SAPA, the public security bureaus also had jurisdiction over a wide range of cultural activities. To take two examples at random, the Ministry of Public Security once issued a document banning the import of foreign postage stamps bearing nude portraits and another prohibiting the import and broadcast of laser discs. The goal in both cases was the maintenance of what the authorities viewed as a "healthy" cultural environment.[20]

Overlap between the Criminal Law and the SAPA meant that public security personnel were responsible for determining whether or not an offender should be pursued for criminal responsibility or should merely be given a warning, a fine, or a short period of detention. In some types of case, a clear line could be drawn. In other cases, public security personnel would have to make a distinction between a crime and a SAPA offense on the basis of their analysis of the facts and circumstances of the case. In the enforcement of the SAPA, public security officers

---

18. According to regulations on SAPA, people being punished by administrative detention were to be organized to perform labor, the income from would go toward defraying the expense of their food, daily necessities, and study materials. "Zhian juliusuo guanli banfa (shixing)," Art. 12.

19. SAPA, Arts. 6, 8, 9, 13; Ma Zhongzhi, ed. *Zhian chufa anli xiangjie*, 9-15; "Zhian juliusuo guanli banfa (shixing)," Art. 12.

20. See "Gonganbu guanyu chuli waiguo luoti renxiang youpiao wenti de pifu," 1178; "Zhonggong zhongyang xuanchuanbu, xinwen chubanshu, guangbo dianying dianshibu, wenhuabu, gonganbu, haiguan zongshu Guanyu tingzhi jinkou he bofang jiguang shipian (gushipian) de tongzhi," 218-220. According to the latter document, laser discs were prohibited because mainland China lacked the technology either to produce its own laser discs or to censor the films on those that were imported, and feared the negative social consequences alleged to be caused by Western, Hong Kong, and Taiwanese movies.

also exercised administrative discretion when they decided whether to punish an offense by fines or detention or to impose the most severe administrative sanction available to them: re-education through labor.

Re-education through labor (*laodong jiaoyang*) had its origins in the 1950s. In two policy documents of 1955 and 1956, the Central Committee of the Chinese Communist Party ordered that counter-revolutionaries and other "bad elements" whose political unreliability made them unfit for retention in their original jobs but whose behavior was not serious enough to deserve a long sentence of labor reform be subject to a shorter period of re-education through labor. This allowed the Party to remove politically unreliable people from their jobs without adding to the already severe unemployment problem which the Party was also working to resolve in the mid-1950s.[21]

As was often the case, an institution originally established by a Party policy document was followed by legislation designed to supply a legal basis. The 1957 "Decision of the State Council of the PRC Regarding the Question of Re-Education Through Labor" served as the legal basis for re-education through labor. According to the 1957 "Decision," the targets of re-education through labor were to be urban residents and rural residents temporarily living in urban areas who had committed offenses not considered serious enough to merit criminal punishment. As defined in the 1957 'Decision," these offenders included:

1) Those who do not engage in proper employment, those who behave like hooligans, and those who, although they steal, swindle, or engage in other such acts, are not pursued for criminal responsibility, who violate security administration and whom repeated education fails to change.

2) Those counter-revolutionaries and anti-socialist reactionaries who, because their crimes are minor, are not pursued for criminal responsibility, who receive the sanction of expulsion from an organ, organization, enterprise, school or other such unit and who are without a way of earning a livelihood.

3) Those persons who have the capacity to labor but who for a long period refuse to labor or who destroy discipline and interfere with public order, and who [thus] receive the sanction of expulsion from an organ, organization, enterprise, school or other such unit and who have no way of earning a livelihood.

4) Those who do not obey work assignments or arrangements for getting them employment, or those who do not accept the admonition to engage in labor

---

21. These documents were the "Directive regarding thorough elimination of hidden counter-revolutionary elements" (August 1955) and the "Directive regarding each province and city immediately establishing labor re-education organs" (January 1956). See Wu Lei, ed. *Zhongguo sifa zhidu*, 288-89.

and production, who ceaselessly and unreasonably make trouble and interfere with public affairs and whom repeated education fails to change."[22]

As this list indicates, re-education through labor had developed from a technique for the incarceration of politically unreliable elements to a tool for the maintenance of social order in a broader sense.

In the 1980s, Re-education Through Labor was further refined in order to meet the needs of the reform era. In 1980, the 1957 "Decision" was re-promulgated. In 1982, the State Council approved and issued the Ministry of Public Security's "Trial Implementation Methods for Re-education Through Labor," which became the documentary basis fort that institution.[23]

According to the 1982 "Trial Implementation Methods," the targets of re-education through labor were now to be:

1) Those counter-revolutionary elements and anti-party, anti-socialist elements whose acts are too minor to be pursued for criminal responsibility;

2) Those who formed criminal gangs to commit crimes such as murder, robbery, rape, arson etc., but [whose acts] are to minor to be pursued for criminal responsibility;

3) Those who behave like hooligans, or engage in prostitution, or stealing, swindling, or other such acts, and who do not change their ways despite repeated education, but [whose acts] are too minor to be pursued for criminal responsibility;

4) Those who fight or beat up people, or provoke quarrels, stir up trouble and other acts which disrupt public order, whose acts are too minor to be pursued for criminal responsibility;

5) Those who have a job but who for a long time refuse to labor or destroy labor discipline, and who ceaselessly and unreasonably make trouble, who disturb the order of production or work, or the order of teaching or research and the order of life, who hinder public affairs, and who do not listen to advice and instructions to stop;

6) Those who instigate others to break the law or commit crimes, but [whose acts] are too minor to be pursued for criminal responsibility."[24]

The list is similar to that contained in the 1957 "Decision." Most of the targeted behavior is not overtly political. It is interesting to note, however, that the political category, relegated to second place in 1957, returned to the top of the list in 1982.

---

22. Translation from Cohen, *The Criminal Process in the People's Republic of China*, 249-250.
23. Wu Lei, *Zhongguo sifa zhidu*, 289.
24. Translation from Amnesty International, *Administrative Detention in China*, 36.

According to the "Trial Implementation Methods," people who stood in need of re-education through labor were to have their cases reviewed by "labor re-education administration committees" that were to be established by provincial-level public security organs. If the offender did not accept the decision of the committee, he or she would be allowed a single appeal to the same committee. No other avenue of appeal was established. In practice, the "Labor Re-education Committees" were no more than the provincial public security bureaus. Thus the 'Trial Implementation Methods" allowed the police to imprison people in labor camps for up to three years without having to go to the trouble of arrest, prosecution and trial.[25]

In theory, re-education through labor was distinguished from the reform through labor (*laodong gaizao*, also referred to as "labor reform") to which convicted criminal offenders were sentenced by the courts. Persons undergoing re-education through labor were officially considered to be among the ranks of "the people," whereas criminals sentenced to labor reform were guilty of such serious offenses that they were considered to have become 'enemies of the people." Accordingly, inmates undergoing re-education through labor were to receive a token wage for their labor, while those undergoing labor reform received no wages.

The distinction between the two forms of forced labor was also manifest in the terms used to refer to the different types of offender. Persons undergoing re-education through labor were "labor re-education personnel." Those in labor reform were "prisoners" or "criminals." Prisoners or criminals were "released on completion of sentence"(*xingman shifang*). Labor re-education personnel were "released on fulfillment of term" (*qiman shifang*). This distinction was made not only for reasons of clarity and to distinguish the different types of offender within China, but also in a conscious effort to convince foreigners that re-education through labor was not a criminal sanction, and thus to improve the negative international image if the Chinese criminal justice system.[26]

When a case of deviant behavior was thought to deserve criminal punishment rather than administrative sanctions, the public security organs were responsible for the detection and investigation of crimes, the arrest of criminal suspects, and the "preliminary hearing" (*yushen*, sometimes translated "preliminary investiga-tion" or "preliminary examination"). Of these responsibilities, the nature and function of the preliminary hearing is most important to our understanding of the criminal procedure.

Preliminary hearing was the responsibility of the preliminary hearing section within the public security organ. Preliminary hearing was to begin within twenty-

---

25. Wu, *Laogai*, 13; Amnesty International, *China: Punishment Without Crime*, 48-49.
26. Yang Guoyue, "'Zonghe zhili' chengji xianzhu," 14.

four hours of a suspect's arrest or criminal detention. The process would continue until it had been decided whether or not to transfer the case to the procuratorate for prosecution. According to public security regulations, the goal of preliminary hearing was to "accurately and in a timely manner clarify the facts of the defendant's crime in their totality, to investigate other people whose criminal responsibility should be pursued, and to protect the innocent from suffering injustice or being falsely accused."[27] Both the Criminal Procedure Law and the public security regulations expressly forbade the use of torture or threats to extract testimony during the preliminary hearing. Investigation (*zhencha*) was regarded as the basis upon which the preliminary hearing was carried out, but the two activities were understood and practiced as feeding into each other, as information obtained during preliminary hearing led to further investigation and as the suspect undergoing preliminary hearing was confronted with evidence obtained through investigation.[28] When the twin processes of investigation and preliminary hearing had established the facts of a crime, the public security organs had completed their task. The case would then be passed on to the procuratorate for prosecution.

THE PEOPLE'S PROCURATORATE

The people's procuratorates, like the public security organs, were organized in a single national bureaucracy. At the top, exercising leadership over all procuratorial organs and activities and issuing judicial interpretations of law relevant to procuratorial affairs, was the Supreme People's Procuratorate (SPP). Beneath the SPP were various levels of local people's procuratorates: provincial (including autonomous region and directly administered city) procuratorates; branch procuratorates of the provincial level procuratorates; autonomous prefecture and provincially administered city procuratorates; county, city, autonomous county and city district procuratorates.[29] In order to understand the procuratorate, its role in the 1980s, and its relations with the local people's congresses and Party committees, it will be helpful to consider briefly the establishment of the procuratorate and its development in the 1950s.

When the Chinese procuratorate was established in 1949, it took the Soviet procuratorate as its model. In the Soviet system, the procuratorate had been designed as an independent organ of government that supervised the legality of the actions of other branches of the government and the correct implementation of laws in society in general. In respect to criminal affairs, the Soviet procuratorate

---

27. "Yushen gongzuo guize," Article 3.

28. Ibid., Art. 5 and 27.

29. Yang Chunxi, *Xingshi faxue da cishu*, 405. There were also military procuratorates and railway procuratorates, which fall outside the scope of this study.

was responsible not only for the work of prosecution, but also for supervising the legality of the entire criminal process, from investigation and preliminary hearing to the judgments, decisions and rulings of the police and the courts to the execution of sentence in the prisons, labor camps and execution grounds. In short, the procuratorate was to see to it that the laws of the state were followed and implemented in a correct and uniform manner throughout the country. Because it was intended to guarantee the uniform implementation of law, the procuratorate itself was organized in a highly centralized fashion in order to prevent local level procuratorial organs from coming under the influence of local interests. It was thus "the only Soviet agency that [was] exempt from the principle of 'dual subordination' to both local and higher levels."[30]

Following the Soviet model, the Chinese procuratorate of the 1950s was given the power to ensure that all citizens, state organs and state personnel properly carried out both the laws and the policies of the state. In the criminal procedure, the procuratorate was responsible both for the prosecution of criminal offenders and for supervising the legality of the entire criminal process. Initially, the Chinese also followed the Soviets in organizing the procuratorates on the vertical leadership pattern. In order to overcome localism, procuratorial organs at each level were to be responsible solely to the procuratorate at the next higher level.[31] But in practice, the vertical leadership model proved to be unworkable in the China of the early 1950s. Lack of personnel meant that local procuratorates and local public security organs were often one and the same.[32]

In 1951, the Chinese procuratorate changed over to a system of dual leadership in which each procuratorial organ was placed under the leadership of the procuratorial organ of the next higher level and of the people's government of the same administrative level.[33] Concern with the drawbacks of localism led to a restoration of vertical leadership in 1954, but with a difference: while coming under the professional leadership of the procuratorate of the next higher level, each local procuratorate remained subject to the leadership of the Communist Party Committee at the same level.[34] Furthermore, each procuratorate established a "procuratorial committee" under the leadership of the chief procurator of that

30. Berman, *Soviet Criminal Law and Procedure*, 111.
31. Ginsburgs and Stahnke, "The Genesis of the People's Procuratorate,'"26-8; "Zhonggong zhongyang guanyu jianli jiancha jigou wenti de zhishi," 21-22; "Zhonggong zhongyang pifa zuigao renmin jianchashu dangzu 'guanyu jiancha gongzuo fangzhen renwu de yijian de baogao' ji zhongyang zhengfa weiyuanhui dangzu de jianyi," 23-6.
32. "Zhonggong zhongyang guanyu zhongyang renmin jianchashu sixiang guiding de tongzhi," 20-21.
33. Dual leadership was established in "Geji difang renmin jianchashu zuzhi tongze"
34. See "Zhonggong zhongyang guanyu 'dierjie quanguo jiancha gongzuo huiyi' ji Gao Kelin tongzhi 'guanyu guoqu jiancha gongzuo de zongjie he jinhou jiancha gongzuo fangzhen renwu de baogao' de pishi," 36, 50 and "Zhonggong zhongyang pizhuan zuigao renmin jianchayuan dangzu guanyu jiancha yewu gongzuo huiyi qingkuang he jinhou gongzuo yijian xiang zhongyang de baogao," 58.

level. The procuratorial committees consisted of a small number of procurators who exercised leadership over procuratorial work, resolved difficult questions and made sure that in its work, the procuratorate followed the current polices of the Communist Party.[35] Since the chief procurator at each level chaired the procuratorial committee, and since he/she had the final say on all questions that the committee could not agree on, the procuratorial system from 1949 through 1979 essentially ran on the principle of one-man leadership.[36]

When it was reconstructed in 1978, the responsibilities of the procuratorate included the investigation of certain types of complicated criminal cases, the approval of arrests and the prosecution of criminal cases. The procuratorate also supervised of the legality of the public security organs' investigation of crimes, criminal trials, the execution of sentences the administration of detention centers and labor reform and re-education facilities, and the legality of the handling of civil cases and of administrative suits.[37] These functions can be summed up as supervisory, investigatory, and prosecutorial. Within the design of the criminal justice system, the procuratorates played a key role. It is the procuratorates that decided whether or not to prosecute a case, and it is they who were charged with ensuring that the law was followed correctly throughout the criminal procedure—a function that put them in a supervisory position vis-a-vis both the public security organs and the courts. The issues of leadership and of staffing of the procuratorate were thus of considerable importance.

In 1979 the new Organic Law of the People's Procuratorates[38] restored the principle of dual leadership that had been in place between 1951 and 1954. According to law, the local people's governments at the provincial and county levels were to appoint the chief procurator of the procuratorate of their level of government. The chief procurators were to be responsible to and make regular reports to the same people's congress that had appointed them. Assistant procurators, members of the procuratorial committee and other procuratorial staff were to be nominated by the chief procurator and approved by the standing committee of the people's congress. But in their day to day work, the procuratorates were to be subject to the leadership and direction of the procuratorate of the next higher level, with all procuratorial organs coming under the leadership of the SPP.[39]

This was the system of dual leadership as defined by the Organic Law of the People's Procuratorates. But the principle of dual leadership was itself ambiguous. In 1989, *Encyclopedia of Criminal Sciences* noted that there were two opinions

---

35. Ginsburgs and Stahnke, "The Genesis of the People's Procuratorate," 9.
36. Zhang Siqing, ed., *Zhonghua renmin gongheguo jiancha yewu quanshu*, 1991, 34.
37. For an overview of procuratorial functions, see Liang Guoqing, ed. *Jiancha yewu gailun*, 51-53.
38. "Zhonghua renmin gongheguo renmin jianchayuan zuzhifa."
39. "Zhonghua renmin gongheguo renmin jianchayuan zuzhifa," articles 21-23.

concerning the meaning of the term "dual leadership of procuratorial organs." Some believed that it meant that procuratorates were subject to the leadership of the procuratorial organ of the next higher level and the people's congress of the same level; others believed that it meant that the procuratorial organs were subject to the leadership of the next higher procuratorate and of the Party organization of the same level.[40] The "Experimental Criminal Procuratorial Work Regulations of the People's Procuratorates," issued in 1980, reflected the latter view when it stated that procuratorates "under the leadership of the Party committee and the next higher procuratorial organ, practice division of responsibilities, mutual cooperation and mutual restriction with the public security organs and the people's courts."[41]

Whether understood in terms of leadership by local level people's government or local level Party committees, dual leadership could, in practice, mean that local interests might be placed above those of the state as local Party cadres would find it easy to interfere in the legal process, substituting their personal orders for law and undermining the procuratorate's role as watch-dog of the legal system. Such was the argument of critics of the dual leadership system who suggested that a restoration of vertical leadership would ensure a more clear division between Party and state and thus guarantee the independent exercise of procuratorial power.[42] In fact, the process in which the people's procuratorate was reconstituted in the late 1970s-early 1980s reveals an intertwining of state and Party organization that makes us doubt that the Party leadership was at all interested in bringing about a real separation between Party and state or to guarantee a meaningful independence of the judiciary.

One aspect of the continued close relationship between the procuratorial organs and the Party committees may be seen in the reconstruction of the procuratorate in the wake of the Cultural Revolution. Since it had been absorbed by the public security apparatus during the Cultural Revolution, the procuratorate had to be reconstructed from the ground up in the late 1970s and early 1980s. Cadres had to be transferred from other work units into the procuracy. Some resisted transfer into the procuracy because procuratorial organs lacked housing and office facilities—a major weakness in a society in which one's material life is almost entirely dependent on the resources of one's work unit.

In a talk delivered in 1980 Jiang Hua, then president of the SPC, described the process of transferring leading cadres into the public security, procuratorate and court organs as follows:

---

40. Yang Chunxi, *Xingshi faxue da cishu*, 246.
41. "Renmin jianchayuan xingshi jiancha gongzuo shixing xize," Article 4, para. 4.
42. Jin Mosheng, "Jiancha jiguan ying huifu chuizhi lingdao tizhi," 3; Gao Xun, "Jianchi zai dang de lingdao xia yifa duli xingshi jianchaquan," 3.

Party Central document number sixty-four of 1979 stipulates that appropriate comrades should be carefully chosen from among cadres with a standing equivalent to that of members of the standing committee of the Party committee of the same level to serve as the leaders of public security, procuratorate and court organs. The system under which the public security, procuratorate and court organs of the next higher level cooperate with the local Party committee in the management and examination of cadres is thus restored. The local Party committee should obtain the agreement of the next higher level public security, procuratorate or court organ regarding the transfer of leading cadres of the public security, procuratorate and court organs,.[43]

According to Party policy, leaders of the procuratorial (as well as public security and court) organs were appointed and evaluated by the local Party committee in cooperation with the next higher people's procuratorate. Thus in July 1979, when Huang Huoqing (then president of the SPP) declared that his goal was to build procuratorial strength to 85,000 by the end of the year, it was to the Party committees, not to the people's congresses, that he addressed his order to transfer reliable cadres into the procuratorate.[44]

The relationship of the Party to the procuratorate can also be seen in the responsibilities of the procuratorial committees. As reconstructed in 1979, the procuratorial committee system was intended to decrease the power of the chief procurators. Before the Cultural Revolution, the chief procurators had the final say on issues on which the procuratorial committee could not reach a consensus. Now, such questions were to be referred to the standing committee of the people's congress of the same level for a decision. The purpose of this reform was to strengthen the principle of collective decision-making and to avoid the potential abuses that went with one-man leadership. But while the reforms of 1979 freed the procuratorate from one-man leadership, they were clearly not meant to free the procuratorate from the leadership of the Party committees. One of the fundamental responsibilities of the procuratorial committees remained to ensure that the Party's guiding principles and policies (*fangzhen, zhengce*)[45] were implemented in the work of the procuratorate.[46]

---

43. "Jiang Hua tongzhi zai Henan sheng gaoji renmin fayuan ganbu hui shang de jianghua," 13.

44. "Huang Huoqing tongzhi zai quanguo jiancha gongzuo zuotanhui shang de zongjie," 32.

45. As Harro von Senger has pointed out, *fangzhen*, or guiding principles, ". . . prescribe the course for a work or undertaking by regulating the basic aspects of this work or undertaking which are understood to be in a mutually dialectical relationship." *Zhengce*, or policies, on the other hand, are concrete measures and procedures laid forth by the Party for the realization of specific objectives. von Senger, "Recent Developments in the Relations Between State and Party Norms," 177-178.

46. Zhang Siqing, ed., *Zhonghua renmin gongheguo jiancha yewu quanshu*, 34-35.

For a practical example of the relationship between the procuratorate, the Party organization of the same level, the Party organization within the pro-curatorate itself and the procuratorial committee, we can look at the procuratorate of Dazu County. The Dazu County procuratorial gazetteer reveals that during the first half of the 1980s, seven men served on the Dazu county procuratorate's procuratorial committee. Of these seven, five were members of the procuratorate's Party cell. One of the other two was a member of the Party branch organization. One of the Party cell members who served on the procuratorial committee was also a member of the county Party Committee and a representative in the county people's congress. He and another member of the procuratorial committee held concurrent posts in the disciplinary inspection committee of the county Party organization. Five of the members of the procuratorial committee were Dazu natives.[47]

There is no evidence to indicate that the Dazu county procuratorate was necessarily corrupted by local influences; but the inter-locking structure of Party cell, procuratorial committee and county Party committee, in combination with the prevalence of local men in the procuratorial leadership shows an intertwining of state, Party and local interest such that corruption would be difficult to overcome if it was to occur. There is no reason to believe that Dazu county was exceptional in this regard. Indeed, given the shortage of resources and trained personnel, it is difficult to see how a complete national procuratorial system could be staffed by trained professionals without links to local Party and government organs, even if China's leaders desired to construct such a system.

THE PEOPLE'S COURTS

Like the people's procuratorates, the people's courts were established in 1949 on the Soviet model. The 1979 Organic Law of the People's Courts re-confirmed the basic structure: a unified hierarchy of base, middle and higher people's courts at the county, district (*di*) and provincial levels respectively. All courts came under the unified leadership of the Supreme People's Court in Beijing. Base level courts were responsible for the first hearing of ordinary criminal (and civil) cases and also for out-of-court resolution of minor civil and criminal cases and for supervising the people's mediation committees, whose task it was to mediate minor conflicts in order to prevent them from coming to court. The middle courts had initial jurisdiction over certain types of case regarded as being too serious or too difficult for the base level courts to handle: counter-revolution, offenses that might lead to life imprisonment or capital punishment, and cases involving

---

47. *Dazu xian jianchazhi*, 25, 108, 110-111.

foreigners. The higher people's courts were the courts of first instance for major criminal cases having an impact on an entire province.[48]The courts operated a two-trial (single appeal) system. Each court was itself divided into different sections, civil and criminal. The adjudication panel for any given case—the judge or judges who actually heard the case—would be organized from among the judges within the appropriate section of the court. All court business was subject to the leadership of the president of the court and the adjudication committee, a leading organ established within each court. In addition, each court was subject to the leadership of the people's court of the next higher level and of the people's government of the same level.[49]

As was the case with the public security organs and the procuratorate, the court system had to be expanded and strengthened in the early 1980s. New cadres had to be transferred into the system and material shortages overcome. In 1979 two thirds of the court personnel were said to have begun work during the Cultural Revolution and consequently to lack any real professional training. The other third consisted of cadres who had been working in the court system since the 1950s or early 1960s, but were either trained in the Soviet legal tradition or were without any formal training at all. Most judges had no practical experience in trying cases according to law. They were accustomed to a legal system that had operated—when it did operate—on the basis of policy and under the hands-on, day-to-day leadership of local party committees.[50]

The transfer of new cadres into the court system appears to have proceeded less smoothly than desired. It was carried out in the context of continued factional struggle—the aftermath of the Cultural Revolution and the reflection of the struggle then taking place between the factions of Deng Xiaoping and of Hua Guofeng. According to Jiang Hua, the details of this factional struggle, which extended from the base level up through the Supreme People's Court, were not entirely clear even to the court leadership. Nor were court cadres entirely clear on Party policy regarding the appointment of leading cadres of people's courts. As described above on page forty-six, the Communist Party Center had dictated, in document number sixty-four (1979) that leading cadres of the courts (and of public security and procuratorial organs) be appointed by the local Party committees with the agreement of the next higher people's court, and that leading cadres of the courts be managed and evaluated jointly by local party committees and the next higher people's court. Yet in his talk to cadres of the Henan higher people's court, Jiang Hua expressed doubts as to whether or not this document had actually been followed—or even read or seen—by base level court cadres. Suggesting that his

---

48. Criminal Law (1979), Articles 14-16.
49. Wu Lei, Zhongguo sifa zhidu, 81; Yang Chunxi, ed. *Xingshi faxue da cishu*, 404-405.
50. Jiang Hua, "Sifa renyuan zhifa yao xuefa," 211-219.

colleagues in Henan investigate the implementation of the new rules in their province, Jiang Hua reminded them "after all, this is stipulated by a central Party document!"[51]

It was hoped that the court system could expand its strength by 48,000 in 1979, but by the end of the year, only 29,000 new cadres had been transferred in.[52] In 1980, complaining about the number and the quality of cadres being transferred to the court system, Jiang Hua characterized his judicial cadres as "old and poorly educated." Requesting younger cadres, he remarked that "the courts are not nursing homes."[53]

Three years later in his report on an inspection trip to Sichuan and Yunnan provinces, Jiang Hua expanded on the theme of personnel shortage. In such a large and populous province as Sichuan, he found that there was only one judge for every 20,000 people. These judges were "politically reliable." Eighty-four percent were Party members. Only 4.6% of them had any formal training in law. Fifteen percent had educational levels of primary school or below, and a large proportion of these were illiterate. In Sichuan and Yunnan, and throughout the country, the lack of personnel made it impossible for courts to implement the Criminal Procedure Law. In some places in the southwest, a single judge would both hear cases and act as clerk. In other courts, clerks doubled as judges. In ethnic minority areas in Yunnan, 37% of the judges had educational levels of primary school or below. Translators—required by law in the trial of non-Chinese speaking minorities—were insufficient. Furthermore, those cadres being transferred into the system—many of them from the PLA—were untrained. In some cases, Jiang complained, PLA units used the transfer of cadres to the court system to rid their ranks of the old, the sick, and even the mentally ill.[54]

The personnel shortage was related to, and compounded by, shortages of material goods and of cash. The Party center and NPC, realizing the problems involved, allowed the courts to implement the Criminal Procedure Law in stages over the year 1980 rather than requiring that the law be followed to the letter from 1 January. One problem was the shortage of court-rooms. Drawing on Jiang Hua's report of his tour of the southwest in 1983, we find that over one hundred county courts and most intermediate courts had no court-rooms.[55] Many courts in both Yunnan and Sichuan province were forced to rent or borrow space from other

---

51. "Jiang Hua tongzhi zai Henansheng gaoji renmin fayuan ganbu hui shang de jianghua," 7, 13.

52. "Jiang Hua tongzhi zai quanguo gaoji renmin fayuan yuanzhang huiyi shang de jianghua," 225.

53. "Jiang Hua zai Henansheng gaoji renmin fayuan ganbuhui shang de jianghua." 13.

54. Jiang Hua, "Guanyu renmin fayuan zai ren, cai, wu fangmian de yanzhong kunnan qingkuang de baogao," 308.

55. In 1983 Yunnan province had a total of 116 county-level administrative units (96 counties, 19 autonomous counties, and one town (*zhen*) as well as 8 cities (*shi*) of county level. Minzhengbu xingzheng quhuachu, ed. *Zhonghua renmin gongheguo xingzheng quhua shouce*, 52.

work units, or even to hold court in the shade of a convenient tree. Office space and housing facilities were similarly in short supply.[56] Money problems also undermined the courts ability to implement the Criminal Procedure Law. In 1983, local governments were supposed to establish separate budgets for the courts, separating court expenses from the general administrative budget. In practice, according to Jiang Hua, only a few cities and provinces carried out this reform. Courts thus remained dependent on local governments for funds—which meant in practice that they were chronically under-funded. In Sichuan and Yunnan provinces, Jiang found that the annual budgets of the local courts were sufficient for less than six months. Taking Yunnan province as an example, calculating the average cost of trying criminal and civil cases in accordance with the law (five hundred and two-hundred yuan, respectively), Jiang Hua estimated that the court system's budgetary requirement for adjudication alone amounted to 3,160,000 yuan, while the amount allocated was only 1,760,000 yuan.[57]

The court system was also adversely affected because court cadres suffered from discrimination in regards to rank and income. In 1979 the Party Center had ordered that the presidents of people's courts at all levels should be chosen from among cadres of equal ranking with the members of the Party committee of the same level. Base-level court presidents should be equal in rank to county-level cadres, and ordinary judges equal in rank to district (qu) level cadres. According to Jiang Hua, this order was not followed. In practice, most county-level court presidents in China were treated as district-level cadres. This made it more difficult for court personnel to rise in rank, influenced their income and various benefits adversely, and made it more difficult for them to arrange jobs for their children.[58] As of the early 1990s, the low pay and low social status of judges were described as factors leading to corruption in the judiciary.[59]

While material and personnel shortages clearly had an adverse affect on the implementation of the criminal procedure law, so also did attitudes toward the administration of criminal justice. The Criminal Procedure Law, the Organic Law of the People's Courts, and later (in 1982) the Constitution of the PRC all enshrined the principle of judicial independence as a means of guaranteeing that the courts would apply the law as written, without falling under the undue influence of any individual, group, or social organization. In practice, the principle of judicial independence was limited by deep-rooted habits and attitudes regarding the role of the courts and of the Party committees, by the de facto need to combine

---

56. Jiang Hua, "Guanyu renmin fayuan zai ren, cai, wu fangmian de yanzhong kunnan qingkuang de baogao," 310.

57. *Ibid*.

58. *Ibid*.

59. Interview file 8.

judicial independence with Party leadership, and by the ambivalent and fundamentally contradictory, definition of judicial independence in the law.

Chinese judicial workers and Communist Party members alike had been accustomed to regard judicial independence as no more than a myth for the justification of bourgeois dictatorship; in fact, as judicial power was regarded in instrumental terms as a means for the imposition of the will of the ruling class on social reality, the judiciary could never be independent. In the practice of jurisprudence in revolutionary China, this abstraction was manifest in the hands-on leadership of the Communist Party. Prior to 1979, criminal cases were routinely passed on to Communist Party secretaries for review and approval.[60] This system not only concretely manifest Party leadership over the organs of justice, but also protected judges from being held responsible for making "incorrect" decisions.

As a part of the legal reforms, the system of Party secretary approval of cases was prohibited and the principle of judicial independence introduced into the law. The concept of judicial independence and its relation to Party leadership consequently had to be explained to those judges and Party members for whom it must have seemed strange and dangerous, perhaps even counter-revolutionary. In April 1979, Jiang Hua explained the relationship between Party leadership and judicial independence in the following dialectical terms:

Is there a contradiction between leadership of the Party committees and independent adjudication? Unity [of the two] is of primary importance; contradiction exists, but it is of secondary importance. Difference of opinion amounts to contradiction, doesn't it? When I say that unity is of primary importance, that is to say that the work of the people's courts is carried out under the leadership of the party committees of all levels. We must resolutely obey the leadership of the Party and implement the Party's principles and policies. Leading cadres of the courts are to be managed by the Party committees, while the courts of the next higher level assist the Party committees in this management. Concrete cases are to be handled by the courts; some cases are to be referred to the party committee for approval. Right now, capital cases are referred to the provincial party committees for approval, and ten types of capital case and criminal cases involving foreigners are brought together to the Supreme People's Court which reports them to the Party Center for approval. If they pass the criminal law and the criminal procedure law at the next National People's Congress, then capital cases will have to be heard or approved by the Supreme People's Court. In fact, the power to impose the death penalty resides with the Center, but in the law we

---

60. Leng and Chiu, *Criminal Justice in Post-Mao China*, 22-23.

have to write that they are heard or approved by the Supreme People's Court.[61]

The meaning of "judicial independence" as reflected in Jiang Hua's comments was limited. Certain cases were still to be referred to Party committees for review, and the source of the ultimate state power—the power of life and death—was understood as residing in the Party, not in the courts, the law, the State Council or the National People's Congress. In the vast majority of cases, however, the courts were to carry out the concrete work of adjudication and sentencing in accordance with the law and without the participation or the need to seek the case-by-case approval of the local Communist Party committee. In comparison with previous practice, this represented a major change.

Not surprisingly, there were theoretical objections and practical violations of this new judicial independence. The theoretical objection that judicial independence could undermine Party leadership was dealt with by pointing out that law was in fact the "concrete manifestation of policy" and that to follow the law was thus to follow the commands of the Party Center. The practical problem of getting judicial personnel and Party committees used to the new system was more difficult. In the talk referred to above, Jiang Hua suggested that judges not be arrogant or inflexible in the assertion of judicial independence. Party committee members would inevitably make suggestions. Some might be in accordance with the law, others might not be. Those that were should be taken into consideration; those that were not should be rejected, but not without explanation:

> In Zhejiang there was a county party secretary who wanted the court to include a criticism of Lin Biao and the "Gang of Four" in a written judgment. The president of the court said that won't do, a written judgment is not the place to make criticisms, so he [the party secretary] said you're "using law to resist the Party." You see, he didn't understand, so he slapped on that label, and that won't do, the president of a court can't take that! But on the other hand, we comrades in the courts shouldn't casually accuse people of interfering with judicial independence, because they won't be able to take it; the more fuss is made the more of a deadlock there will be, and that won't resolve the problem. We have to do propaganda instead; it's our responsibility to make a clear explanation to others.[62]

---

61. "Jiang Hua tongzhi zai bufen gao, zhongji renmin fayuan he junshi fayuan fuze tongzhi zuotanhui jieshu de jianghua," 197.
62. "Jiang Hua tongzhi zai bufen gao, zhongji renmin fayuan he junshi fayuan fuze tongzhi zuotanhui jieshu de jianghua," 198.

The principle of judicial independence in the new Chinese legal system was limited in another respect as well: it referred to the independence of the courts as a whole, not to the independence of the individual judge or judges trying a case. Inasmuch as the court system itself was hierarchically structured and inasmuch as leadership was provided within each court by the court president and the adjudication committee, the principle of judicial independence as understood in the Chinese legal system still left the possibility that those judges who heard the case would not actually pass judgment, while those who passed judgment did not actually hear the case.

According to the organic law of the people's courts, every court established an adjudication committee consisting of the president of the court and other members nominated by him and appointed (according to law) by the people's congress of the corresponding level. The legally mandated tasks of the adjudication committees were to summarize and draw practical lessons from work experience, to discuss important or difficult cases, and to address other problems related to adjudication. Meetings of the adjudication committee were presided over by the president of the court, and were attended not only by the members of the adjudication committee, but also by the chief procurator of the corresponding level.[63] In practice, the adjudication committees routinely discussed cases and passed judgment prior to the trial—a system known in Chinese legal circles as "first verdict, then trial." The rationale for this system—a rationale that need not be dismissed entirely—was that the quality of judges was so poor that it was necessary that the few trained, qualified or experienced members of a court exercise concrete leadership over the work of their less qualified colleagues.[64]

On the other hand, Chinese legal scholars criticized the role of the adjudication committees on a number of points. First, they pointed out that the practice of "first verdict, then trial" effectively nullified the already minimal significance of the defense lawyer. Under these conditions, the only meaningful defense could be one undertaken in private by a defense lawyer who enjoyed a good personal relationship with the members of the adjudication committee. Second, the practice of "verdict first" enabled judges to avoid the rules and procedures for withdrawal from a case due to conflict of interest because those rules and procedures (Art. 23-25 of the Criminal Procedure) were not written with the adjudication committees in mind. Third, the practice blurred the lines of responsibility. If the verdict of an adjudication committee, made in a closed meeting and subsequently announced in public trial were later to be found incorrect, then who would be held responsible?[65]

---

63. "Zhonghua renmin gongheguo renmin fayuan zuzhifa," Article 11.
64. Interview file 8.
65. These criticisms are raised in Wang Xinru, "Shenpan weiyuanhui dingan ying yu gaibian," 24-25 and Yang Yintang, "Xianpan, houshen yinggai gechu,"10-11.

While Chinese scholars did not say so, we can also assume that the adjudication committee would be able to implement Party policy both in respect to the general direction of the practice of adjudication (for example, heavier or lighter sentences as called for during campaigns) as well as the "correct" disposition of "important" or "difficult" cases, political cases as well as common criminal cases, in which the Party might take an active interest.

THE ORGANS OF CRIMINAL JUSTICE
AND THE POTENTIAL FOR CHANGE

As China entered the new era of reform and opening to the outside world, the law and the policies of the Communist Party made it clear that crime was to be defined by the criminal law and criminals identified, tried and punished by the organs of criminal justice in accordance with the criminal procedure law. The organizational structure of the three organs of justice, their relationship with each other (both according to law and in practice), the number, training, work habits and attitudes of their personnel, their material resources and their budgets formed the institutional context in which these two laws would be implemented over the coming decade.

Taken as a whole, the system certainly had its drawbacks. Shortages of material resources, from police equipment and uniforms to motor vehicles, offices, courtrooms and residential buildings militated against the timely and efficient implementation of the laws. Even those personnel who were already in place were often untrained and utterly unprepared for the tasks that would be required of them by the new laws. In 1979, for example, a Party document (not yet the law itself) gave county procuratorates the right to approve arrests under the condition that they filed reports on each case with the district (*diqu*) branch procuratorate. According to the report of a member of the Sichuan higher (provincial-level) people's procuratorate, the result, at least in his province, was chaos. County procurators did not know how to carry out the required paper-work, or attached little importance to it. In their reports, there would be arrest forms with no record of any review of the case files, no indication of any discussion of the case, and even no basis for the charges made. In other reports, there would be a conclusion, but no indication of the circumstances of the case or how the crime was committed. Cases involving two or more offenders were handled with no clear statement as to the identities of the main offender and the accomplices. In some cases, the county procurators had simply written "agree to arrest" or "do not agree to arrest" on the form.[66] When even the simplest of bureaucratic tasks presented such serious

---

66. Hao Qingshan, "Zuohao pibu gongzuo de beian shencha gongzuo," 216.

problems, one can only imagine the practical difficulty in implementing all the requirements of the criminal procedure law, simple as they might seem to a trained lawyer or judge.

Despite provision in the law for a high degree of cooperation between the three organs of justice in the criminal procedure and the system of "first verdict, then trial," procurators and judges also found it difficult to adjust to the concept of a public trial in which a defense lawyer might appear on behalf of the accused. Procuratorial staff appear to have been worried that their preparation would be insufficient and they would be caught in a mistake by a defense lawyer. When the system of defense lawyers was introduced with the new criminal procedure, the journal *People's Procuratorate* printed a number of articles urging procurators to overcome courtroom fright and arguing that the presence of lawyers might actually be a good thing, inasmuch as it would force the procurators to do a more conscientious job of investigation and preparation.[67] Some were evidently not convinced by this propaganda: in 1983 the academic journal *Developments in Legal Studies* quoted an unnamed "high-ranking cadre" in the Guangdong provincial procuratorate as saying that "it would be best if the lawyer system were done away with."[68] He need not have worried. In their annual reports to the NPC throughout the 1980s, China's chief procurators routinely reported that the procuratorates nationwide gained convictions in well over 90% of the cases that they brought to the people's courts.

While drawing attention to the weaknesses of the criminal justice system as it stood in 1979-1980, we should not fail to note its strengths. For advocates of the rule of law, whether in China or abroad, the reforms, limited though they might be, were certainly an improvement. As Tang Tsou, political scientist at the University of Chicago put it, the legal reforms represented one part of China's step back from totalitarianism.[69] The subsequent development of the criminal justice system during the anti-crime campaigns of the early to mid-1980s convinced many observers that this assessment may have been overly optimistic. But nonetheless, for the first time, the People's Republic had a criminal justice system that was, at least theoretically, to exercise the coercive power of the state in accordance with openly published laws and procedures. On paper at least, the new legal system put more emphasis on the protection of defendants' rights and the strict construction of crime (requiring both intent and behavior in the constitution of an offense) than was the case in the legal thinking reflected in draft codes of the late 1950s and early 1960s. The reconstitution of the procuratorate, the provisions for legal

---

67. For example, see "Huang Huoqing jianchazhang dao Hubei jiancha gongzuo yaoqiu jinkuai ba gexiang jiancha gongzuo quanmian kaizhan qilai," 59. Huang was quoted in this article as saying that "Court-room appearance work should continue to emphasize over-coming battle-shyness."
68. Gong Xiaobing and Liu Shuguang, "Jianli sifa xingzheng jiguan tiqing shenyi zhidu quyi," 2.
69. Tsou, "Back From the Brink," 73-74.

defense, and the institution of procedures for detention, arrest and trial at least held forth the possibility that the administration of criminal justice in the 1980s would be more formalized and less politicized than it had been previously.

Significant though it was, the reconstruction of the criminal justice system through the promulgation of new laws and the reconstruction of the public security, procuratorial and court organs was no more than the beginning of the development of the Deng regime's approach to the administration of criminal justice—a task that was seen as an essential part of the larger project of Chinese modernization, as it was crucial in the creation of the social and political stability and unity that Deng regarded as essential to the accomplishment of his goals. The real development of the Chinese criminal justice system would take place through the actual administration of criminal justice. As Deng Xiaoping put it in January 1980, little more than two weeks after the criminal and criminal procedure laws had gone into effect:

> If we are really going to consolidate stability and unity, we must of course rely primarily on measures that are positive and fundamental, on economic growth and the development of education and, at the same time, on perfecting the legal system. When our economic and educational work is proceeding satisfactorily and our legal system and judicial work are improved, the orderly progress of society as a whole can largely be guaranteed. But the legal system will be improved only gradually in the course of practice, and we can't wait for that. When we fail to mete out stern punishment to so many criminals, can we even speak of having a legal system? All those who undermine stability and unity in any way must be dealt with sternly, according to the merits of each case.[70]

---

70. Deng Xiaoping, "The Present Situation and the Tasks Before Us."

3

PREVENTION AND PUNISHMENT: THE PRACTICE OF CRIMINAL JUSTICE, 1979-1982

Throughout the past thirty years of judicial work in our country, there has been an ongoing struggle between two schools of thought: to reduce arrests and reduce capital punishments or to increase arrests and increase capital punishments. . . . some comrades, including a few comrades in leading positions, still believe that a life must be paid for with a life, so that all cases of killing, without distinction, should be punished by death. . . . I advocate reducing arrests and reducing capital punishments; I am against increasing arrests and increasing capital punishments, and I publicize this idea everywhere.

> Jiang Hua, June 1980, "Jiang Hua tongzhi zai Henan sheng gaoji renmin fayuan ganbu hui shang de jianghua," 8 -9

The thirty-year debate that Jiang Hua described in 1980 has its echoes in every country and in every time. What is the best way to deal with serious deviant behavior? To prevent it through education, indoctrination, and organization? Or to define it as crime and to arrest, detain, try and imprison or execute the deviants, thus removing them from society and offering a severe warning to those who would follow in their footsteps?

In China, this debate had its historical counter-part in the opposition between the ideas of Confucius and of the various philosophers who have been categorized as Legalists. While admitting that he was as good as the next man at hearing disputes, Confucius argued true social harmony could only be attained through the inculcation of moral virtue: "Guide them by edicts, keep them in line with punishments, and the common people will stay out of trouble but will have no sense of shame. Guide them by virtue, keep them in line with the rites, and they will, besides having a sense of shame, reform themselves."[1] Han Fei and other "Legalist" thinkers, on the other hand, believed that social stability could only be achieved if a strong central government were to promulgate detailed laws and to enforce them with severe punishments.[2]

The theory and the practice of Chinese regimes from the Han Dynasty onwards was to combine these two positions in a constantly developing Chinese legal system. In the traditional Chinese legal system, Confucian virtues were expressed in terms of law and backed up with punishments that could be quite severe. China's dynastic governments continued, at least rhetorically, to regard the law as a supplement to rule by virtuous example, proper organization and care of the people, and moral instruction. But in the concrete practice of government, hard decisions had to be made regarding the proper use of moral suasion and criminal punishment. Should preventive and punitive techniques be used in tandem or in sequence? If in sequence, then what was the proper sequence of their employment? On what basis should the ruler decide which approach to take toward deviant behavior?

During the Tang Dynasty an emperor posed just such questions to Bo Juyi, the Tang poet and official who was then serving on the Board of Punishments. Observing that the ancient sage kings had attained public order by correcting the people's evils with penal law, guiding their emotions with the rites and leading their human nature with the Way, the emperor asked: 'What do you think? Are these to be used singularly, or employed jointly? Regarding their suitability, is their a correct order as to which should come first and which should follow? Regarding their efficacy, are their differences between those that are superior and those that are inferior?" Bo replied that:

> the nature and emotions of the people are like the soil and the fields of the sovereign. When they are fallow and weed-choked, cultivate them with penal law. When they are opened, plant them with the rites. When they have been planted, harvest them with the Way. So it is that penal laws are implemented, and then the rites are established, and that after the rites have been established, then the Way springs to life.[3]

In order to exercise the power of moral transformation that would bring his people to a state of honesty and harmony, the ruler was enjoined to "observe the depth or shallowness of order and of chaos, and follow the sequence of penal laws and rites." Each served its functions, and each had its proper time. Although punitive

---

1. Confucius, *The Analects*, 61 (II:3).
2. Bodde and Morris, *Law in Imperial China*, 23-24.
3. Bo Juyi, "Xing, li, dao," 1352-1353.

techniques alone could not be relied upon to bring out the best that human nature has to offer, "when it comes to punishing evil, repressing immorality and putting people in a state of fearful admonishment, nothing is superior to penal law."[4] In so saying, Bo was, of course, echoing the words of an ancient text and its commentaries, *The Punishments of Lu*, in which it is stated that there are historical epochs in which penal laws may be lenient, and other epochs in which they must be heavy, with lenient punishments used to rule a newly established state, and severe punishments to bring under control a society that has declined into chaos.[5]

While they expressed themselves less eloquently than the Tang poet, China's leaders in the 1980s were concerned with a similar question: what is the most appropriate and effective state response to the problem of crime? As indicated by Jiang Hua, various members of China's Communist Party leadership and the Chinese legal community held fundamentally different views on the correct approach to social deviance in the late 1970s-early 1980s. Some advocated an emphasis on the use of heavy punishments in order to bring society under control. Others argued that the only fundamental solution to crime lay in attacking its social roots through reformative, preventive programs supplemented by criminal sanctions. It is hardly surprising, then, that Chinese policy toward crime and the implementation of the criminal and criminal procedure law during this period display an internal tension and that this tension became manifest in the emergence of two guiding principles (*fangzhen*): comprehensive management of public security (*shehui zhian de zonghe guanli*) and severe and rapid punishment (*congzhong congkuai*).

BRINGING ORDER OUT OF CHAOS

As the Chinese Party and state abandoned the policies of the Cultural Revolution in the late 1970s, the immediate task was represented in the slogan *boluan fanzheng*, four characters loosely translated as "bring order out of chaos" or "to turn from heterodoxy to the right path."[6] Translated literally, the slogan means "get rid of chaos, return to order." Thus the Chinese regime, as it moved away from the policies of the immediate past and toward an unknown future, sought legitimacy by claiming to be "returning" to the order of a mythical past—in this case, the 1950s.

In the field of criminal justice, the task of "bringing order out of chaos" involved the reassessment of all that had been done in the past ten years or more.

---

4. *Ibid.*
5. *Lu xing*, 135.
6. *Han ying cidian; Mathews' Chinese-English Dictionary.*

Cases (especially cases of counter-revolution) tried and punished during the Cultural Revolution had to be reviewed and re-tried when necessary. The violent verbal and physical attacks on allegedly "counter-revolutionary" people, things and institutions that had been considered normal, healthy revolutionary behavior from 1966 through 1976 now had to be reconsidered. At the same time, action had to be taken against current counter-revolutionary and other criminal offenses.

An important part of the supposed "return" to order was the review of cases from the Cultural Revolution. In 1978, the Communist Party Center ordered that cases from the Cultural Revolution be reviewed and that the verdicts in unjust, false and mishandled cases be revised as appropriate.[7] A document issued by the Party cell of the Supreme People's Court and approved and circulated by the Party Center described the types of case to be reviewed and corrected. These included cases of people sentenced for opposing Lin Biao and the Gang of Four or for protesting the unfair treatment of vice-premier Deng Xiaoping during the Cultural Revolution, those punished for making errors construed as counter-revolutionary in the writing of big-character posters, in idle doodling, or in the shouting of slogans, youth and children punished for having innocently written words construed to be counter-revolutionary, persons punished again during the Cultural Revolution on account of political problems for which they had previously been punished, mentally ill persons whose ravings had been construed as counter-revolutionary, and persons who had been punished regardless of the facts due to forced confessions or to the unquestioning issuance of a verdict without consideration of the facts of the alleged case.[8]

Review and rectification of these cases was difficult. Some courts and judges feared that improper revision of cases of counter-revolution might lay them open to charges of counter-revolution themselves. Sometimes, judges were assigned to review and correct the verdicts in cases that they had originally judged themselves. For some courts, the review of Cultural Revolution cases presented an overwhelming workload.[9] There were also other forms of opposition to the review of cases. At times, local Party committees ripped up "not guilty" sentences and declared them invalid. Judges who revised verdicts were accused of "rightism," and outraged Party members wrote letters and sent telegrams to the Party Center accusing the SPC of protecting criminals[10] Supreme People's Court president Jiang Hua gave talks to numerous base-level courts and took part in the review of

---

7. "Zuigao renmin fayuan, gonganbu, minzhengbu, guojia laodong zongju guanyu anzhi pingfan shifang hou wujia kegui renyuan de tongzhi," 205. The document refers to zhongyang (1978) 78 hao wenjian (central document #78, 1978).

8. "Zuigao renmin fayuan dangzu guanyu zhuajin fucha jiuzheng yuan jia cuo an renzhen luoshi dang de zhengce de qingshi baogao (jielu)," 191-193.

9. *Ibid.*

10. "Jiang Hua tongzhi zai Henan sheng gaoji renmin fayuan ganbu huiyi shang de jianghua," 10.

selected cases himself in order to push the work forward.[11] By the end of June 1980, sentences had been revised in 261,000 cases, including over 175,000 cases of counter-revolution.[12]

If cases of people unfairly accused of political crimes during the Cultural Revolution were to be reviewed and sentences revised, then what of those people guilty of beating, smashing and looting? A large number of people, after all, had participated enthusiastically in the violence of the Cultural Revolution. At the time, their conduct had been regarded as revolutionary. Now, it was subject to moral as well as political condemnation. In 1978, the Party Center took the point of view that the real culprits of the Cultural revolution were Lin Biao and the Gang of Four (Jiang Qing, Yao Wenyuan, Zhang Qunqiao and Wang Hongwen), and that the conduct of other individuals should be considered carefully in the historical context in which it occurred. Cases of homicide and cases in which persons formerly classified as landlord, rich peasant, counter-revolutionary and bad elements took advantage of the circumstances of the Cultural Revolution to carry out "class revenge" were to be pursued, as were serious cases of people having framed their enemies in order to get revenge and cases of those who were guilty of multiple counts of serious beating, smashing and looting.[13] The vast majority of the many cases of Cultural Revolutionary violence, however, were not to be pursued. As for those who had been victimized during the Cultural Revolution, the Party encouraged them to forgive their former attackers and to "concentrate all [their] anger on the persons of Lin Biao and the Gang of Four."[14]

The Party's purpose in all of this was to preserve social stability. As Hu Yaobang reportedly stated in 1980 in a letter to the Politico-legal affairs committee, even the arrest of a million youth for such Cultural Revolutionary crimes would not suffice to clear the books of such cases, but it would be enough to cause a national uproar with, in the words of Jiang Hua, foreseeable results: "Once you're in turmoil, you have no stability; then how can you do the four modernizations? Foreign countries won't be willing to do business with us, to invest, so no matter what, you won't get anything done."[15]

---

11. *Dangdai Zhongguo de shenpan gongzuo*, 148.
12. Leng and Chiu, *Criminal Justice in Post-Mao China*, 146.
13. "Zhonggong zhongyang guanyu shenzhong chuli 'wenhua da geming' zhong da, za, qiang wenti de tongzhi (jielu)," 21. Jiang Hua says that policy toward Cultural Revolution beating, smashing and looting cases was laid forth in Party Central document no. 48 of 1978. The number of the document referred to above is not given in *Falu guifanxing jieshi jicheng*, but it may possibly be document 48 to which Jiang Hua refers. See "Jiang Hua tongzhi zai Henan sheng gaoji renmin fayuan ganbu hui shang de jianghua," 7.
14. "Zhonggong zhongyang guanyu shenzhong chuli 'wenhua da geming' zhong da, za, qiang wenti de tongzhi (jielu)."
15. "Jiang Hua tongzhi zai Henan sheng gaoji renmin fayuan ganbu hui shang de jianghua," 7.

The decision to handle Cultural Revolution offenses "prudently" while focusing the nation's attention on the denunciation and trial of the Gang of Four may be understood, as a calculated attempt to reconstruct a sense of national unity and stability.[16] The justice of focusing blame for the Cultural Revolution on four individuals is of course questionable, but it was clearly successful. While an undercurrent of tension often persisted between victims and victimizers of the 1960s and 1970s as they continued to work and live together in the 1980s and 1990s, the cycle of violence that had characterized the Cultural Revolution was brought to an end.

IMPLEMENTATION OF THE LAWS

While the crimes of the Cultural Revolution were being forgiven, the criminal justice system was instructed to pay close attention to current counter-revolutionary and common criminal offenses. In international perspective, crime rates do not appear to have been high. In a talk delivered in October 1978, Zeng Hanzhou (an official of the SPC) stated that the number of criminal cases (including counter-revolution and common crime) tried by people's courts in the first half of 1980 had declined by 20% as compared to the same period in 1977. At the same time, there had been noticeable increases in common crime, and especially in serious offenses, in "some cities."[17] Nonetheless, China's crime rates per 100,000 of population for the years 1979-1982 (64.8, 76.3, 89.4 and 74) were much lower than the world averages for the same period.[18] According to official figures, 0.075% of the Chinese population was convicted of a crime from 1979-1981. In the United States of America, 5.22% of the population was convicted of a crime during the same period.[19]

While China's crime rates might seem to have been low when viewed in international perspective, they appeared to be quite high in terms of the Chinese leadership's view of recent Chinese history. The 570,000 criminal offenses recorded in 1980 compared unfavorably to an average annual number of cases of 290,000 from 1950 through 1965.[20] Rising crime rates in urban areas, and the fact

16. The "Gang of Four" (Mao Zedong's wife Jiang Qing, and former high-ranking Party members Yao Wenyuan, Zhang Qunqiao and Wang Hongwen were tried in the winter of 1980-81. For a short description of the trial, see Meisner, *Mao's China and After*, 461-463.

17. Zeng Hanzhou, "Zai quanguo xingshi shenpan gongzuo huiyi shang de baogao (jielu), 313. Zeng's comments indicate that the greatest decrease was in counterrevolutionary offenses—a decrease that may be more attributable to changing definitions of "counter-revolution" than to any change in social behavior.

18. Bakken, "Crime, Juvenile Delinquency, and Deterrence Policy in China," 50.

19. Scherer, *China Facts and Figures Annual 1984.*

20. Leng and Chiu, *Criminal Justice in Post-Mao China*, 131.

that roughly 70% of criminal offenders were youths (*qingshaonian* —generally defined as 25 years of age and under) were also worrisome, as were the activities of political dissidents and other counter-revolutionary offenders. The circumstances of the late 1970s and early 1980s seemed to call for a reconsideration of China's approach to the problems of crime prevention and of criminal justice.

As the leaders of the SPC saw it, the problem in 1978-79 was that the court system was placing too little emphasis on counter-revolution and other serious offenses while putting too much emphasis on the handling of common crime. As a result, the courts were imposing unreasonably harsh sentences on the large number common criminal cases handled. As Jiang Hua described the situation in talks delivered in March and April of 1979:

> Under the destructive interference of Lin Biao and the Gang of Four, there has come to exist in criminal adjudication work a tendency toward more executions, more sentences, and heavier sentences. The facts prove that we have truly sentenced many who should not have been sentenced, that more than a few who should have been given light sentences have been dealt heavy sentences, and that we have killed some who should not have been killed. Because they suffer from "Rightist-phobia," some comrades believe that the more sentences they hand out and the heavier the sentences are, the better. They think that this is "taking a firm stand" and that the more they execute, the more "revolutionary" they are. This is especially noticeable in the disposition of cases during movements.[21]

In contrast to this existing tendency to address the broad range of deviant behavior through the application of criminal sanctions, high-ranking court and party officials pointed to the need to make distinctions between different levels of offense. Crime was to be regarded as being, for the most part, a contradiction among the people, rather than a contradiction between the people and the enemy.[22] Youth crime in particular was to be attributed to the ideological and economic damage of the Cultural Revolution: on the ideological side, a general decline of moral standards and erosion of discipline, and on the economic side, the lack of employment and educational opportunities for young people.[23] The same thinking led Peng Zhen to declare that "When youths commit crimes, we can't say that they are innocent, but we must consider the social causes that produce youth offenders.

---

21. "Jiang Hua tongzhi zai liang ci bufen gao, zhongji renmin fayuan he junshi fayuan fuze tongzhi zuotanhui shang de jianghua," 175.
22. See, for example, Zeng Hanzhou, "Zai quanguo xingshi shenpan gongzuo huiyi shang de baogao (jielu)," 321.
23. "Zhonggong zhongyang zhuanfa zhongyang xuanchuanbu deng bage danwei 'guanyu tiqing quandang zhongshi jiejue qingshaonian weifa fanzui wenti de baogao' de tongzhi (jielu), 3-12.

These are indivisible from the poison of Lin Biao and the Gang of Four. The resolution of the problem of youth offenders is mainly a question of education."[24] Thus in the practice of and the debate on criminal justice from 1978 through 1980, we observe the use of both punitive and preventive techniques in the context of the transition from policy-based adjudication of cases to a criminal procedure that sought to apply the standards of the Criminal Law in accordance with the code of criminal procedure.

During this period of transition, counter-revolution continued to be regarded as the most seriously threatening form of crime. High-profile counter-revolutionary cases, including the case of Wei Jingsheng were tried. Wei, tried under the 1951 Regulation on Suppression of Counter-revolutionaries, was sentenced to fifteen years in prison for having allegedly revealed "military secrets" to a foreign reporter and for having criticized the socialist system and the dictatorship of the proletariat in articles published in his unofficial magazine, *The Search*.[25] Such cases were not, however, typical of counter-revolutionary offenses. A document issued by the Ministry of Public Security in 1981 states that in the first half of that year, approximately 60% of counter-revolutionary cases were those of people accused of sending "letters of contact" (*guagouxin*) to espionage organizations of the Nationalist regime on Taiwan. The incidence of persons sending such letters was said to have increased significantly (27%) since 1979 in response to Nationalist "psychological warfare" in the form of radio broadcasts. An unknown number of people were investigated for having written letters. Many such letters were judged to have been innocent requests for money, goods, help in emigrating or for pen-pals. Others allegedly contained offers to supply intelligence or to carry out secret missions.[26]

World-famous cases of counter-revolution such as that of Wei Jingsheng and the more common, unsung cases alike carried clear implications for the freedom of speech in China, as they established the boundaries of permissible political activity and expression of opinion. But the arrest, trial and punishment of common criminals was of more direct importance to the average Chinese person, and had a greater impact in terms of numbers of people affected.

As the criminal justice system did its part to "bring order out of chaos," the hand of the law fell heavily on persons accused of murder, rape, battery, robbery and theft. The Western press reported an increase in executions in 1979-1980.[27] Whether this apparent increase reflected, in fact, an increased number of

24. "Peng Zhen tongzhi zai quanguo jiancha gongzuo zuotanhui, quanguo gaoji renmin fayuan he junshi fayuanzhang de huiyi, di san ci quanguo yushen gongzuo huiyi shang de jianghua," 98.

25. Ladany, *Law and Legality in China*,

26. "Gonganbu guanyu jianjue daji xiang guomindang tewu jiguan xie xin guagou de fanzui fenzi de tongzhi," 294-95.

27. Leng and Chiu, *Criminal Justice in Post-Mao China*, 132.

executions or was simply a function of increased propagandizing of executions cannot be known without access to reliable statistics regarding the use of the death penalty. According to one report based on a perusal of the Chinese press and courthouse notices, at least 198 persons were executed in China in the year ending 30 June 1980.[28] These executions often followed very closely on the trial; in at least one case, the sentence was announced and the defendant executed in the presence of an audience of 6,000.[29]

As the public security organs, the courts and the procuratorates worked to improve public order through the arrest and trial of criminal offenders, they were also making the transition from policy-driven administration of criminal justice to law-guided administration of criminal justice. The Criminal Law went into effect on 1 January 1980. The organs of criminal justice thus had to begin defining criminal behavior in the terms laid forth in the law. Cases that the authorities were accustomed to referring to as "writing letters of counter-revolutionary contact," for example, now had to be analyzed and named as one of the counter-revolutionary offenses listed in the Criminal Law.[30]

The Criminal Procedure Law was originally to have taken effect on 1 January 1980, just the same as the Criminal Law. On 12 February of that year, in response to the request of the SPC and the SPP, the Standing Committee of the National People's Congress decided to allow the Criminal Procedure Law to be put into effect gradually over the course of the year. Cases placed on file but not yet sentenced before 31 December 1979 would be handled according to the former procedural policies and regulations. Cases placed on file beginning 1 January 1980 should be handled in accordance with the Criminal Procedure Law, but:

If there are too many cases and an insufficient number of personnel to handle them, so that they cannot be disposed of within the time limits established for investigation, prosecution, first trial, and appeal, then during the year of 1980, the standing committees of the provinces, autonomous regions and directly administered cities may approve extensions of the time limits for disposition of cases.[31]

---

28. *Ibid.*

29. Ladany, *Law and Legality in China*, 86.

30. "Zuigao renmin fayuan, zuigao renmin jianchayuan, gonganbu guanyu fan geming guagou anjian de zuiming, zuizheng wenti de tongzhi," 293-94; "Gonganbu guanyu jianjue daji xiang guomindang tewu jiguan xiexin guagou de fanzui fenzi de tongzhi," 294-95. The latter document states that depending on the circumstances, the offense of writing letter of counter-revolutionary contact might fall under the Criminal Law, article 17, para. 1, article 98, article 97 para. 3, article 100, or article 92.

31. "Diwujie quanguo renmin daibiao dahui changwu weiyuanhui di shisan ci huiyi guanyu xingshi susongfa shishi wenti de jueding," 676.

In April, the Standing Committee further instructed the Ministry of Public Security, the SPP and the SPC to formulate rules concerning such procedural matters as detention, arrest, criminal investigation, preliminary examination and procuratorial work.[32] Over the course of the year, the Ministry of Public Security, the SPC and the SPP issued a number of regulations of this nature, including the Ministry of Public Security's Rules for Investigation of Crime Sites (xingshi anjian xianchang zhencha guize), Rules for Preliminary Hearing (yushen gongzuo guize) and Rules for Criminal Technical Appraisment (xingshi jishu jianding guize), the procuratorate's Provisional Regulations for Criminal Procuratorial Work (xingshi jiancha gongzuo shixing xize) and the Provisional Courtroom Rules of the People's Courts of the People's Republic of China (Zhonghua renmin gongheguo renmin fayuan fating shixing guize).[33]

The promulgation of these and other rules and regulations regarding everything from the transfer and handling of files to the proper procedures to be followed when dissecting a human body point to a concentrated effort to institutionalize, to regularize and to professionalize the administration of the coercive power of the state through the criminal justice system. At the same time, however, this process of institutionalization and professionalization was not and should not be understood as a movement toward judicial independence or the autonomy of law. Indeed, the Provisional Regulations for Criminal Procuratorial Work stated clearly that among the principles that must be respected in procuratorial work was that the procuratorates must "under the leadership of the Party committee and the procuratorial organ of the next higher level, practice division of labor, mutual cooperation and mutual control with the public security organs and the people's courts."[34]

COMPREHENSIVE MANAGEMENT OF PUBLIC SECURITY

While the criminal justice system was being strengthened and the criminal and criminal procedure laws implemented, steps were also being taken to improve the authorities' ability to prevent crime from occurring in the first place. Arguments for prevention raised in 1979-1980 led in 1981 to the formulation of an all-round approach to crime prevention referred to as "comprehensive management of public security" (shehui zhian de zonghe zhili, hereafter referred to as "comprehensive management").

---

32. "Quanguo renmin daibiao dahui changwu weiyuanhui guanyu shishi xingshi susongfa guihua wenti de jueyi," 678-79.

33. In Zhonghua renmin gongheguo falu guifanxing jieshi jicheng, 797-799, 841-844, 801-803, 679-684, 1478-1479.

34. "Renmin jianchayuan xingshi jiancha gongzuo shixing xize," Article 4, para. 4, in Zhonghua renmin gongheguo falu guifanxing jieshi jicheng, 679.

While Jiang Hua used the term "comprehensive management of public security" at least as early as 1980,[35] Chinese observers trace its establishment back to the 1979 "Report Suggesting the Entire Party Emphasize the Resolution of the Problem of Youth Lawbreaking and Crime." Prepared at the request of the Communist Party Central Committee by representatives of eight units including the Central Propaganda Ministry, the Ministry of Education, the Ministry of Culture, the Ministry of Public Security, the National Labor Bureau, the National Labor Union, the Central Committee of the Communist Youth League and the National Women's Federation, this report described the problem of youth crime and suggested steps to be taken to resolve the problem.[36]

As the report described it, youth offenders were responsible for seventy to eighty percent of crimes committed in urban areas and sixty to seventy percent of crimes committed in rural areas. Research in the cities of Beijing, Tianjin, Shanghai, Xi'an, Nanning, Changchun and Jilin during the first quarter of 1979 revealed that students accounted for 40% of youth criminals apprehended, followed by young workers (19%), youth "waiting for employment" (15%), rusticated youth returned to the cities (8%) and "other" (11%). These shockingly high rates of youth crime—the overwhelming amount being committed by young students and workers—was partially attributed to the moral and the economic damage of the Cultural Revolution. These young people had grown up in an atmosphere of anarchic violence and consequently had failed to develop a strong moral sense of right and wrong. Now, they experienced extraordinary difficulty as they tried to advance through the educational system or find employment. Facing an uncertain future and living in poverty, some turned to crime.[37]

The youth crime problem could also be attributed in part to the failure of the Party itself to place sufficient emphasis on the recognition and the resolution of social problems leading to crime and on the education and assistance of troubled youth. "Some comrades," said the report "are unwilling to undertake the patient and painstaking work of education and reform, but instead take an attitude of detestation and rejection," dealing with school discipline problems by simply suspending, transferring or expelling the offenders. Teachers were alienating students not only through inappropriate disciplinary techniques, but also by teaching at a level designed to interest the most intelligent students while neglecting the needs of those who were less advanced, and by emphasizing the acquisition of knowledge while neglecting to carry out moral education. Some parents, too, were failing to educate their children properly, exercising no discipline or excessively rough discipline, or alternating between the two extremes

35. "Jiang Hua tongzhi zai quanguo gaoji renmin fayuan yuanzhang huiyi shang de jianghua," 222.
36. Wang Zhongfang, ed., *Zhongguo shehui zhian zonghe zhili de lilun yu shijian*, 8.
37. "Guanyu tiqing quandang zhongshi jiejue qingshaonian weifa fanzui wenti de baogao," 7-8.

without finding the middle ground. Finally, work units were at fault for failing to institute and maintain proper security measures, leaving raw materials, finished goods, and even weapons storerooms unsecured and loosely guarded.[38] All these weaknesses were identified as causes of increased rates of youth crime.

In order to address the problem of youth crime, the report suggested an all-round approach to the social factors contributing to crime. Ideological education in the schools and in society must be strengthened, young students' and workers' spare time should be organized and filled with healthy activities, employment should be found for those who needed it, efforts should be made to keep minor offenders in school or at work, rather than rejecting them, reform schools and labor reform and re-education institutions should be improved, and, while those who committed serious criminal offenses should be punished severely, the scope of punishment should be reduced as much as possible, while the scope of education should be expanded. In all of this, China should "carry out the leadership of the party committees, mobilize the entire Party, get the Party secretaries involved, depend on schools, factories, government organs, the army, street committees, rural production brigades and other base-level organizations, and all social forces to strengthen the education of youth."[39]

The holistic approach outlined in the report on youth crime was more fully and concretely articulated as a guiding principle of public security work in May, 1981 at the "Conference on Public Security of the Five Cities of Beijing, Tianjin, Shanghai, Guangzhou and Wuhan."[40] At the time, comprehensive management was not given a sophisticated theoretical basis. It was simply stated that because China's public security problems were multi-faceted, their resolution called for comprehensive efforts to reduce crime by addressing it many causes simultaneously. Since the vast majority of criminal offenders belonged to a work unit, it was assumed that the starting-point for crime prevention was to strengthen the management of work unit facilities and property and to get base-level Party organizations, labor unions, the Women's Federation , the Youth League and other mass organizations to do a better job of organizing the educational lives and spare-

---

38. *ibid.*, 8. These problems are also underlined in "Jiaoyubu, gongqingtuan zhongyang, gonganbu, guanyu zhuanfa 'Jinxi xian qiming zhongxiao xuesheng jiehuo daoqiang yumou sharen anjian de qingkuang diaocha' de tongzhi," 60-65.

39. "Guanyu tiqing quandang zhongshi jiejue qingshaonian weifa fanzui wenti de baogao," 8-11.

40. Wang Zhongfang, ed. *Zhongguo shehui zhian zonghe zhili de lilun yu shijian*, 8-9. According to *People's Adjudication* (a publication of the SPC), the guiding principles, policies and methods outlined at this conference were made on the basis of Party Central directives regarding political and legal work issued between December 1980 and May 1981. See "Shanyu yunyong falu wuqi yu fanzui fenzi zuo jianjue douzheng," 4. Comprehensive management was further established in the 1982 "Zhonggong zhongyang guanyu jiaqiang zhengfa gongzuo de zhishi" (Directive of the central committee of the Chinese communist party regarding the strengthening of politico-legal work). See Ma Jie, *Zhongguo shehui zhian zonghe zhili yanjiu*, 96.

time activities of young workers.[41] In effect, the principle of comprehensive management called for local Party organizations, local governments, work units and mass organizations to bring heretofore un-managed or badly managed things, places, people and time into formal organizational systems in which deviant behavior could be more easily detected and prevented. This approach to crime control developed over the next fifteen years and beyond, accruing both a more sophisticated theoretical basis and a formal bureaucratic structure as well as practical experience.

In terms of things and places, comprehensive management involved such steps as better accounting and tighter security for raw materials and other warehoused goods to prevent pilfering. It also involved better control over access to such unit facilities as cafeterias, bath-houses and dormitories.[42] One way of doing this was to set up "public security management responsibility systems." Under such systems, a task such as the security of a factory warehouse would be assigned to specific people whose political reputations and material interests would be tied to their success in preventing security problems.[43]

Other measures of comprehensive management called for Party organizations, public security bureaus and work units to identify potential criminal offenders and to prevent them from committing security offenses or crimes. As exemplified in the approach taken by a number of work units in Beijing, comprehensive management began with the organizational, personnel and security sections of the work unit carrying out an investigation of all workers, and particularly of new workers. By contacting authorities in a worker's former school, the place where he/she had been "sent down" to the country-side during the Cultural Revolution, the street committee of the area where he/she lived and so on, the investigators would try to establish the family background of each worker and his/her current behavior and state of mind. On this basis, the work unit could identify those workers who had the potential to be trained as cadres and those whose background revealed that they were potentially dangerous and thus deserved special investigation and reform through ideological work.[44]

The practice of comprehensive management involved both bringing people and their time into formal organizational frameworks and tailoring "help and education" to the specific needs of the individual. Successful cases of "help and

---

41. Hu Shiyou, "Gaohao shehui zhian de zonghe zhili," 17.
42. Gonganbu guanyu zhuanfa Beijingshi gonganju 'guanyu changkuang qiye danwei luoshi shehui zhian zonghe zhili qingkuang de diaocha baogao' de tongzhi." The appended investigative report of the Beijing public security bureau is dated 15 June 1982. In Xie Anshan and Yan Li, ed. *Zonghe zhili shehui zhian gongzuo shouce*, 44.
43. "Shiwei zhengfa weiyuanhui zhaokai zonghe zhili zhengdun zhian jingyan jiaoliuhui," 9.
44. Gonganbu guanyu zhuanfa Beijingshi gonganju 'guanyu changkuang qiye danwei luoshi shehui zhian zonghe zhili qingkuang de diaocha baogao' de tongzhi," 47.

education" were publicized in order that they might serve as examples of the correct approach. One example is the system for the management of students' vacation time employed by the schools of the city of Anqing in Anhui province. Under this system, primary and middle school students were issued "vacation notices" when they were released from school for the summer holidays. Each student was to report, bearing this notice, to his or her street committee. The street committees, in cooperation with the parents, would arrange for each student to spend his/her time in organized educational and sports activities. At the end of the vacation, a street committee official would write a comment on the student's behavior on his/her "vacation notice." On returning to school, the students would turn their "vacation notices" in to the school administration.[45]

Another example of comprehensive management in action is the case of Yang Qi, a young man from Zhangqiu County in Shandong province. Yang's father, it seems, was too old and feeble to look after him properly, and his mother suffered from mental illness. In consequence, Yang Qi had become a habitual petty thief. As a part of the comprehensive management of public security, a local cadre contracted to carry out "help and education" in an effort to prevent Yang from sliding any further into a life of crime. This cadre's "help and education" consisted of both care for Yang's "thought" and the resolution of his concrete material problems. The cadre thus not only talked to Yang about his life and his future, but also got together with the local street committee to arrange a job as a tractor driver, to help him build a house, and act as a match-maker to find him a wife.[46]

The management of Anqing schoolchildren's summer vacation time in 1986 and the "help and education" extended to Yang Qi in 1982 are not necessarily "typical" in the sense that they are experiences common to all or even a majority of Chinese who came into contact with programs for the "comprehensive management of public security." These examples of comprehensive management are, however, representative of the thinking behind the administration of comprehensive management and of the attempts made to carry it into practice. The theory of comprehensive management assumed that free time, particularly that of students and young workers, should be taken up with formally organized activities, and that each individual should be made to feel in concrete, material ways the warmth and care of the socialist state.

In practice, of course, it proved increasingly difficult to bring Chinese into the scope of comprehensive management programs. As economic reform added a capitalist sector to the Chinese economy, more and more persons came to live and work at the margins of or even outside of formal social organization. These included private entrepreneurs, contract workers, school drop-outs, the unem-

45. Anhui sheng gonganting, "Zhibiao zhiben yiqizhua," 25-26.
46. "Jinan shi gonganju, "Luoshi jiceng zhian baowei gongzuo de hao banfa," 19.

ployed, and the urban floating population. The growing numbers of such "free people" undermined the work-unit, street-committee based approach to the management of society and thus placed limits on the success of comprehensive management.

As the reform era progressed, however, attempts were made to develop a body of theory that would not only provide a conceptual basis for comprehensive management as a long-term crime prevention strategy, but also establish it as a nationally and internationally recognized field of study.[47] During the latter half of the 1980s, conference were held, articles and books were published, and attempts made to explain comprehensive management to Chinese and foreign audiences.

The work of the comprehensive management theorists did not comprise a single theory. It was, instead, an eclectic combination of a number of ideas. These included Marxism, Mao Zedong's theory of contradictions, concepts of disease drawn from Chinese medicine, systems theory, information theory and management theory.[48] Behind the apparent eclecticism, however, there was a certain logic. First, comprehensive management theory regarded crime as a systemic problem that could only be addressed by strategies that dealt with the whole life-circumstances of the offender and with the whole social milieu in which the offender existed. Second, comprehensive management had to be explained and justified in the context of the assumption that China, although a socialist state, was in the "primary stage of socialism." This idea both justified the continued existence of a market economy and made possible the explanation of crime as a by-product of the market economy and a result of the inability of the as-yet incomplete socialist system to address effectively the emerging conflicts of interest between different social groups in the overall context of economic backwardness.[49] The theory of comprehensive management thus envisioned the increasingly effective prevention of crime through the establishment and construction of ever-more coordinated, technologically advanced, centralized systems for the scientific management of people, places, things, time and information.

In their pursuit of this vision, theorists of comprehensive management put forth ideas whose complete implementation was far beyond the capacity of the Chinese state to achieve in practice. Jin Guangzheng, Zhu Zhongbao and Yue Maohua, writing in the respected *Tribune of Political Science and Law* suggested that:

---

47. Ma Jie, "Lun shehui zhian zonghe zhili de lilun jianshe," 92-93.
48. *Ibid.* 99-100, 108-109; Wang Zhongfang, ed. *Zhongguo shehui zhian zonghe zhili de lilun yu shijian*, 18.
49. Gu Yingchun, *Qingshaonian fanzui zonghe zhili gailun*, 59; Ma Jie, "Lun gaige yu shehui zhian zonghe zhili," 13.

In order to comprehensively manage public security, we must establish, with the goal of control, an information system dealing with certain major factors which may lead the individual in society to bring about socially dangerous consequences. These include: 1) sex, age, ethnic group, native place and other natural conditions; 2) political attitude; 3) educational level; 4) moral level; 5) strength of legal consciousness; 6) illnesses (especially illnesses affecting the nervous system); 7) degree of need for and reaction to alcoholic beverages.[50]

In the same vein, Gu Yingchun suggests that in order to realize the comprehensive management of youth crime, work units should:

Carry out a thorough and painstaking investigation of the personality , interests, hobbies, ideals, goals, work performance, family situation, previous crimes and misdemeanors, social contacts, romantic relationships, activities outside the factory, living habits, economic situation, political inclination, direction of development of behavior and so on, put them together to form a picture of the work unit as a whole, establish card files on young workers and keep constant track of the situation. These cards should be different from the staff and worker files; they are a reflection of a changing situation, and should be updated regularly, with the goal of predicting crime.[51]

The control systems envisioned in the writings of Gu Yingchun, Jin Guangzheng and others stands in sharp contrast to the reality of a China in which market forces, urbanization and geographic mobility led not to more, but to less, effective central control over Chinese society. They also stand in contrast to what we know of the more violent side of Chinese criminal justice in the 1980s—China's increasing reliance on criminal sanctions, campaign tactics, the wide-spread use of torture to obtain confessions, wretched prison conditions, and increasing reliance on the death penalty. This side of Chinese criminal justice is reflected in the second "guiding principle" of the 1980s: severe and rapid punishment.

SEVERE AND RAPID PUNISHMENT

Like comprehensive management, "severe and rapid punishment" was established as a guiding principle of criminal justice at the Five Cities Public

---

50. Jin Guangzheng, Zhu Zhongbao and Yue Maohua, "Lun shehui zhian de zonghe kongzhi," 63-64.
51. Gu Yingchun, *Qingshaonian fanzui zonghe zhili gailun*, 120.

Security Conference in May 1981.[52] The conference called for comprehensive management of public security to be combined with the application of severe and rapid punishment to particular offenses: homicide, robbery, rape, arson, setting explosions and "other serious criminal offenses."[53] Severe and rapid punishment was understood to mean that cases of the target offenses should be handled as rapidly as possible within the framework established by the Criminal Procedure Law and that the offenders should be dealt sentences at or near the maximum allowed by the Criminal Law.[54]

The articulation of the guiding principles of comprehensive management and severe and rapid punishment was followed by the initiation in May 1981 of a campaign to "Strike severe and heavy blows against serious criminal offenders." This campaign was to implement "severe and rapid punishment" in order to bring about a "fundamental turn for the better in public security."[55] The campaign was also the occasion for significant revisions to the Criminal and the Criminal Procedure Laws, for the introduction of practices of questionable legality into the criminal procedure, and for open, and at times publicly praised violations of the law on the part of the criminal justice system itself.

Changes to the Criminal Procedure and the Criminal Law in 1981 came in the form of three decisions of the Standing Committee of the National People's Congress.[56] The "Decision Regarding the Question of Approval of Cases Involving Death Sentences" transferred the power to approve death sentences in cases other than counter-revolution and corruption from the SPC in Beijing to the higher (provincial level) peoples courts. The "Decision Regarding the Handling of Offenders Undergoing Labor Reform or Labor Re-education Who Escape or Commit New Crimes" provided that escaped inmates might have their sentences

---

52. Xing Jianting, "Guanyu jinyibu guanche zhongyang guanyu zhengdun shehui zhian de zhishi de jidian yijian," 2. Xing states that severe and rapid punishment was defined in Party central document no. 21, but omits to mention of what year. He is apparently referring to "Zhonggong zhongyang pizhuan zhongyang zhengfa weiyuanhui zhaokai de 'jing, jin, hu, sui , han wu da chengshi zhian zuotanhui jiyao' he Peng Zhen, Peng Chong tongzhi zai zuotanhui shang de jianghua" (Central Committee of the Chinese Communist party approval and transmission of the 'summary of the forum on public security in the five major cities of Beijing, Tianjin, shanghai, Guangzhou and Wuhan' held under the auspices of the central politico-legal affairs committee and the talks of comrades Peng Zhen and Peng Chong at the forum), Central document 21 (1981) (zhongfa [1981] 21 hao wenjian) mentioned in Zhonggong zhongyang guanyu jiaqiang zhengfa gongzuo de zhishi, 1096. See also "Shanyu yunyong falu wuqi yu fanzui fenzi zuo jianjue douzheng," 4.
53. Hu Shiyou, "Gaohao shehui zhian de zonghe zhili," 17; Jin Mosheng, "Yifa congzhong congkuai zhengzhi yanzhong xingshi fanzui," 3; "Quandang dongshou, fadong qunzhong, zhengqu zhian qingkuang genben haozhuan," 1.
54. Ladany, *Law and Legality in China*, 86.
55. "Quandang dongshou, fadong qunzhong, zhengqu zhian qingkuang genben haozhuan.," 1
56. The Chinese text and English translations of these decisions may be found in *The Criminal Law and Criminal Procedure Law of the People's Republic of China*, Beijing: Foreign Languages Press, 1984.

increased by up to seven years and allowed for "increased punishment" (*jiazhong chufa*) for escaped inmates found guilty of new offenses. Although the term "increased punishment" was not defined in the NPC SC's decision, it was described by *People's Daily* as meaning that "the crime may receive a sentence of the next division higher than the highest degree of punishment normally provided by the law."[57] The "Decision Regarding the Question of Time Limits for Handling of Criminal Cases" allowed the extension of time limits for investigation, prosecution and adjudication of criminal cases "in remote areas for which transportation is inconvenient."

The campaign to strike severe and rapid blows against serious crime achieved immediate and spectacular results in terms of persons arrested, public trials, sentencing rallies and executions. During the summer of 1981, tens of thousands of spectators gathered in sports stadiums and other venues to witness the pronouncement of sentences in rape, robbery, and murder cases. Newspapers reported that large numbers of criminal offenders had surrendered voluntarily to the police and that large numbers of escaped labor reform and labor re-education prisoners had been apprehended. In major cities, criminal cases were said to have decreased by ten and even twenty-five percent. Special praise was given to particularly impressive examples of judicial efficiency such as the courts of the city of Wuhan, which adjudicated 204 criminal cases in twenty days.[58]

To achieve these results techniques that were of questionable legality, and some that were clearly in violation of the law, were brought into play. As a part of the campaign, the criminal procedure was speeded up by the institution of "collaborative work within the Party" (*dangnei lianhe bangong*). Xing Jianting, writing in *Beijing Jurisprudence* in 1982, stated that most areas employed some form of collaborative work. In some jurisdictions, collaborative work meant that the leaders of the public security, procuratorate and court organs would hold regular meetings under the auspices of the local Party committee. In these meetings, they would analyze the current public security situation, discuss the handling of difficult cases, formulate plans for public security work, and choose representative cases for public sentencing rallies. These meetings also served as a forum in which Party and judicial system leaders could discuss and come to agreement on the handling of cases of deviant behavior that, although not covered under the Criminal Law, seemed to deserve criminal punishment. Another form of collaborative work involved *ad hoc* meetings of the heads of the public security,

---

57. Wang Hanbin, "Daji xingshi fanzui, weihu shehui zhian," 1.
58. These events are described in Leng and Chiu, *Criminal Justice in Post-Mao China*, 134-135 and in Ladany, *Law and Legality in China*, 86-87.

procuratorial and court organs to plan the joint handling of particularly serious cases as they were detected.[59]

Regular consultation between the heads of the public security, procuratorial and court organs and joint handling of some cases by representatives of all three organs could both be understood as being at odds with the spirit, if not precisely the letter, of the Criminal Procedure Law, which specifically laid forth a three-stage procedure in which cases were to be transferred from one organ to the next. The call for severe and rapid punishment might also be interpreted as being at odds with the assumptions and the practice of comprehensive management. The regular appearance of articles arguing against just these points in such publications as *Tianjin Daily, Beijing Jurisprudence, Red Flag* and *China Legal System News* testifies to the difference of opinion in Chinese legal circles on these issues.

In the article mentioned above, for example, Xing Jianting argued that collaborative handling of cases under Party leadership in 1981 was fundamentally different from the joint handling of cases by public security, procuratorates and courts in 1958.[60] Other articles stated clearly and forcefully that the scope of severe and rapid punishment must be strictly limited to the target offenses and that it must remain within the confines of the law; the campaign should not be carried out in such a way as to increase the punishments for all offenders across the board, nor should the organs of criminal justice act on the assumption that "the more arrests the better" or employ such techniques as charging an offender with a similar, but more serious offense than that which he had actually committed in order to be able to give him a more severe punishment. On the contrary, the organs of criminal justice, in carrying out the campaign, should not forget also to implement party policies such as "leniency to those who confess" and "those who may either be killed or not be killed, should not be killed."[61]

While arguing that the law must be and could be followed, however, these articles did not (and could not) point to any formal institutional guarantee that this would in fact be done. Instead, they argued that the reason for the injustices perpetrated during the Cultural Revolution was the former Party Center's incorrect

---

59. Xing Jianting, "Guanyu jin yibu guanche zhongyang zhengdun shehui zhian de zhishi de jidian yijian," 3.

60. *Ibid.*, 9. Xing argues that while the "combination of offices for handling of work" during the Cultural Revolution eliminated the distinction between the three procedural stages (investigation, prosecution, adjudication), collaborative work under Party leadership in 1981-82 maintained the independence of the three vertically organized public security, procuratorial and court systems and that the role of the Party was to guarantee that the law was strictly followed. For a description of the joint handling of cases by work groups composed of representatives of all three organs of criminal justice in 1958, see Cohen, *The Criminal Process in the People's Republic of China*, 17-18.

61. Xing Jianting, "Guanyu jin yibu guanche zhongyang zhengdun shehui zhian de zhishi de jidian yijian"; Wang Guiwu, "Jianding zhengque di zhixing yifa congzhong congkuai fangzhen," 31-33; Si Song, "Yifa congzhong congkuai daji xingshi fanzui fenzi," 2.

assessment of China's social and political situation (*xingshi*), which led to incorrect policies, and thus to injustice. With a correct understanding of the "situation" and a correct political line in place, the Party of 1982 was now able to institute correct policies and thus to uphold legality.[62] In practice, the limited extent of the Party organization's ability—and its will—to do so is evident both in the conduct of the campaign itself and in some of the propaganda appearing during the campaign.

A vivid example of this may be found in the *People's Daily* newspaper of 25 June 1981. On page five there appears an essay in which Zhou Daoluan, Sun Changli and Zhang Sahan argue cogently the importance of restricting the campaign to its chosen targets, keeping it firmly within the limits of the law, and continuing to show clemency when it is deserved.[63] Opposite, on page four, there is an article praising the authorities in Nanjing for their efficient administration of criminal justice. There had been a killing in Nanjing; within eight days, the affair had been investigated, a suspect taken into custody, the case solved, an arrest made, the offender tried in court, his appeal filed (and rejected), and his execution carried out.[64] As was subsequently pointed out in two letters to the editor of the journal *People's Adjudication*, the Nanjing authorities' handling of this case was as illegal as it was rapid. The defendant had only been notified of the charges against him one day before the trial, rather than the seven days required by the Criminal Procedure Law.[65]

By January of 1982, the campaign to strike severe and rapid blows against serious criminal offenders had been carried out for more than half a year. The Criminal Law and the Criminal Procedure Law had both been fully implemented and subject to some revisions. The press was reporting significant decreases in crime. Public security organs throughout the nation had placed a total of 890,281 criminal cases on file in 1981, giving China a crime rate of roughly 8.9 offenses per 10,000 of population for the year. In its "Directive Concerning the Strengthening of Politico-Legal Work," issued on 13 January 1982, the Central Committee of the Chinese Communist Party applauded these accomplishments, but went on to state:

It has already been five years since the overthrow of the "Gang of Four": why has there not been a fundamental change for the better in the public security

---

62. Hu Shiyou, "Gaohao shehui zhian de zonghe zhili," 17; Zhang Kaisi, "Luetan congzhong congkuai yu zonghe zhili," 1.

63. Zhou Daoluan, Sun Changli and Zhang Sahan, "Yifa congzhong congkuai daji yanzhong de xingshi fanzui," 5.

64. "Nanjing panchu sharenfan Luo Wenxuan sixing," 4.

65. "Zenyang zhengque lijie yifa congkuai ban'an," 15; "Congkuai reng ying jianchi yifa banshi," 15-16.

situation? The root [of the problem] is the after-effects of the long period of destruction by Lin Biao and the "Gang of Four." Added to this, since implementing the policy of opening to the outside world, the corrosive influence of foreign bourgeois ideology and the infiltration of foreign enemy forces have directly and indirectly led to and induced criminal activity in society. These are the objective reasons. The Party committees and the governmental and politico-legal organs of all levels still underestimate the seriousness and the complexity of the public security problem; they are not adept in the use of the weapon of law, in thoroughly relying on the masses and in resolutely striking against, dividing and demoralizing criminal elements; the politico-legal organs are under-strength, and their political and professional levels are inadequate to the needs of the struggle. There is a lack of unified recognition of certain questions, some have tied their hands and feet, and some show themselves to be soft-handed: these are the subjective reasons.[66]

In order to address these problems and thus more effectively reduce crime rates, the Central Committee made a number of recommendations in its directive. The organs of criminal justice, particularly the public security organs, should be strengthened through the transfer of new staff while individuals who rose to power as factional leaders and followers of Lin Biao, Jiang Qing, Kang Sheng and Xie Fuzhi must be transferred out of leadership positions. Special emphasis should be placed on Beijing in order to make it the safest, most orderly city in China and a shining example of the superiority of the socialist system. Cadres of the public security, the courts and the procuratorates should maintain unity with the Party Center and be given effective leadership by the local Party Committees. And since the Party itself was "the leader and the organizer of the totality of social life," the key to attaining the goal of a clear turn for the better in public security in 1982 was to improve the Party work-style, and strengthen Party discipline.[67]

Of particular concern to the Party during 1982 was the problem of economic crime—a problem closely related to the ability of the Party to lead the criminal justice system in improving law and order, inasmuch as economic criminals were often Party members. Also in January 1982, the Party Center expressed concern about the prevalence of smuggling in Guangdong Province and throughout the nation, and the involvement of cadres—including senior provincial and central cadres—in smuggling activities. All areas were ordered to take measures against smuggling and corruption, and several cadres from the Party Center were dispatched to take urgent measures in the provinces of Guangdong, Zhejiang,

---

66. "Zhonggong zhongyang guanyu jiaqiang zhengfa gongzuo de zhishi," 1095.
67. *Ibid.*

Fujian and Yunnan.[68] In the following months, as the "Emergency Notice" was followed by a Central Committee symposium on economic crime in Fujian and Guangzhou and the Standing Committee of the NPC's "Decision Regarding the Severe Punishment of Criminals Who Seriously Undermine the Economy" on 8 March, this campaign against smuggling developed into a broader campaign to "Strike Severe Blows Against Serious Economic Crime."

The Standing Committee's "Decision" revised the Criminal Law in such a way as to increase the range of punishment for certain economic crimes. The first paragraph of Article 1 provided that "in particularly serious circumstances," the offenses of "seeking exorbitant profits through smuggling, speculative arbitrage, and speculation in Article 118 of the Criminal Law, the crime of theft in Article 152, the crime of sale of narcotics in Article 171, [and] the crime of stealing and exporting precious cultural relics in Article 173" were to be punished by ten years or more of fixed-term imprisonment, life imprisonment or death, as well as possible confiscation of the offender's property. State personnel were to receive heavy punishment (i.e. sentences at the upper end of the spectrum) if convicted of using their positions to engage in economic crime, and the punishment for accepting bribes was increased from "not less than five years imprisonment" to as much as life imprisonment or death.[69]

These revisions of the Criminal Law were followed on 13 April by the "Decision on Striking at Serious Economic Crimes." This document, issued jointly by the Central Committee and the State Council, referred to economic crime as a manifestation of class struggle and an issue upon which hinged the success or failure of China's modernization. In order to direct the campaign, the Party Central Disciplinary Commission sent 154 high-ranking cadres out to the provinces to participate in the handling of important cases and to investigate the work being done.[70] The SPC directed the courts to take immediate action and to "maintain absolute unity with the Party Center." Base-level, middle and higher people's courts were directed to communicate with each other as they adjudicated cases of economic crime, while major and important cases at all levels were to be reported

---

68. "Zhonggong zhongyang jinji tongzhi," 1092. See also Ma Qibin et al. ed., *Zhongguo gongchandang zhizheng sishinian*, 486.

69. "Decision of the Standing Committee of the National People's Congress Regarding the Severe Punishment of Criminals Who Seriously Undermine the Economy." Adopted by the 22nd session of the Standing Committee of the Fifth NPC, 8 March 1982. English translation and Chinese text in *The Criminal Law and the Criminal Procedure Law of China*, 229-240. Article 188 of the Criminal Law,. Dealing with serious smuggling, speculation and profiteering had originally prescribed a maximum sentence of ten years imprisonment, Article 152 a maximum of life imprisonment, Article 171 not less than five years fixed-term imprisonment, and article 173 not less than ten years of fixed-term imprisonment or life imprisonment. The original text of all four articles had already provided for confiscation of property as a supplementary punishment.

70. Ma Qibin et al., ed. *Zhongguo gongchandang zhizheng sishinian*, 490. The document is also discussed in Ladany, *Law and Legality in China*, 88-89.

to the SPC.[71] Further guidance was established in May, when the higher people's courts were ordered to compile all case materials for "major and important cases" and have them brought directly to the SPC in Beijing, which would work to ensure that sentences for major cases were standardized. Cases about which the SPC had unresolved questions or upon which its justices could not reach agreement would be referred to the Central Politico-Legal Affairs Committee, while "very large cases" and capital cases would all be "referred to the Party Center for review and approval."[72]

The results of the campaign against economic crime were decidedly mixed. Preliminary statistics indicated that by the end of 1982, over 164,000 cases of economic crime had been placed on file, of which 86,000 had been fully investigated and adjudicated, resulting in the sentencing of 30,000 offenders.[73] The poor results can be attributed to a number of factors. The April "Decision on Striking at Serious Economic Crimes" drew sharp limits on the scope of the struggle, emphasizing that current and important cases involving state organs, enterprises and institutions were the targets: ordinary citizens were not to be affected by the campaign, the method of "mass movements" was to be avoided, legal personnel were warned to beware of framed-up cases, and the campaign was to complement, rather than to oppose, the Party's liberal economic policies.[74] Legal scholars and workers found that the "Decision of the SC of the NPC Regarding the Severe Punishment of Criminals Who Seriously Undermine the Economy" was poorly drafted and thus "not only was unable to resolve doubts and clear up confusion for the judicial organs, but made the boundaries of economic crime more complicated."[75] For example, the "Decision" used the term "seeking exorbitant profits" and referred to "speculative arbitrage" (taohui). Neither term appeared in Article 118 of the Criminal Law, and it was unclear to many whether they constituted new offenses or were simply used to denote particularly serious cases of smuggling and profiteering.[76]

---

71. "Zuigao renmin fayuan guanyu jianjue zhixing quanguo renda changwei 'guanyu yanzheng yanzhong pohuai jingji de fanzui de jueding' de tongzhi," 6-8.

72. "Zhongyang jilu jiancha weiyuanhui, zhongyang zhengfa weiyuanhui guanyu panchu jingji fanzui anjian tongyi liangxing de tongzhi," 28.

73. Ma Qibin, ed., Zhongguo gongchandang zhizheng sizhinian, 490.

74. "Zhonggong zhongyang, guowuyuan guanyu daji jingji lingyu zhong yanzhong fanzui huodong de jueding," 1.

75. Chen Xingliang, ed. Jingji fanzui yian tanjiu, 5.

76. For discussion of these terms, see Zhang Shangzhou, Zhonghua renmin gongheguo xingfa gailun, 340; and Shan Zhanzong, Ouyang Tao, Zhang Sihan and Zhou Daoluan, "Tantan jingji lingyu zhong yanzhong fanzui anjian de dingzui he liangxing wenti," 11-12. Shan et al. argue that "speculative arbitrage" should be handled as smuggling if it involves cross-border operations, but otherwise as speculation and profiteering.

Finally, it seems that cadres did not understand the campaign or simply did not wish to carry it out with the enthusiasm expected. The relevant laws and regulations appeared to be too difficult to follow, and the vibrancy of the growing market economy meant the appearance of types of economic activity that had not been formally defined as legal or as illegal.[77] Even in clear cases of illegality, procuratorial cadres resisted when it came to investigating cases involving their friends or family members. When possible, well-connected persons guilty of economic crime would pull strings in order to have their problems handled by the Party disciplinary apparatus rather than by the criminal justice system. In some work units, the campaign simply wasn't carried out at all.[78]

CONCLUSION

In 1979-1982, the Chinese criminal justice system was reformed, its constituent organs, the public security, the procuratorate and the courts, were strengthened, and the exercise of the coercive power of the state brought under the guidance of law—in the form of codes of criminal and criminal procedure law—for the first time in the history of the People's Republic. As the Communist Party led China through the process of "bringing order out of chaos," the organs of criminal justice closed the books on the Cultural Revolution and its legacy of enmity and violence by revising old counter-revolutionary sentences, declaring the innocence of those now considered to have been unjustly sentenced, and by dealing circumspectly with those guilty of violent acts during the Cultural Revolution, focusing attention on show-trials of a chosen few scape-goats such as Jiang Qing and her co-defendants.

At the same time as the book was being closed on the Cultural Revolution, the public security, the procuratorates and the courts sought to address, under the leadership of the Communist Party, the new crime problems of the reform era. During the Maoist era, the organs of criminal justice had been primarily concerned with political offenses and, in cases of common crime, had considered not only the facts of the case, but also the class background of the offender. Now, the system was concerned overwhelmingly with common crime committed by young persons of working-class background and with economic crime—much of which was committed by Communist Party cadres themselves.

There were, as Jiang Hua's comments quoted at the start of this chapter indicate, differences of opinion within the Party and judicial system leadership

---

77. Ladany, *Law and Legality in China*, 89.
78. "Zuigao renmin jianchayuan guanyu jixu zhuajin zhuahao daji yanzhong jingji fanzui huodong de tongzhi," 202-206.

concerning the most effective approach toward the rectification of China's public security situation. Some preferred to place the emphasis on punitive techniques, while others, including (on the basis of his own remarks) Jiang Hua, favored an approach in which the scope of punishment (including the use of the death penalty) was limited while putting greater effort into the development of programs designed to address the moral, social and economic causes of deviant behavior.

The influence of both approaches is evident in the development of the theory and practice of criminal justice between 1979 and 1982. According to the statements of Gao Mingxuan, the new Criminal Law itself contained fewer provisions for the use of the death penalty and of life imprisonment than had previous drafts—a decrease in the proposed level of punishment that Gao justified by pointing out that most criminal offenders were youth who belonged to the category of "the people" rather than that of "the enemy."[79] The comments in 1979-1980 of leading cadres including Jiang Hua and Peng Zhen, as well as the "Report on Youth Crime" offered to the Party Center in 1979 indicate a concern with the understanding of the moral, social and economic causes of crime and the need for programs designed to address those root causes. This concern took on more concrete form with the articulation in May 1981 of the guiding principle of comprehensive management of public security and the institution of at least some practical techniques of crime prevention under the rubric of comprehensive management in the following years. The opinion that punitive measures should be limited in scope and applied strictly in accordance with the law was further expressed in much of the rhetoric—if not always the practice— surrounding the campaign to strike severe and rapid blows against criminal offenders and the campaign against serious economic crime.

On the other side, we have ample evidence of the influence of the point of view that a fundamental improvement in public security could only be accomplished through the increased use of arrests and punishments, including the increased use of the death penalty. The apparent increase, and certainly the enthusiastic propagandizing of capital punishment in the anti-crime campaigns of the early 1980s points to the influence of this position, as does the articulation of the guiding principle of severe and rapid punishment at the same time as that of comprehensive management. Faith in the usefulness of the death penalty was also reflected in the increase in the number of offenses punishable by death, from 28 in the Criminal Law as promulgated in 1979 to 34 as a result of the Standing Committee of the National People's Congress Regarding the Severe Punishment of Criminals Who Seriously Undermine the Economy.

As a whole, what emerged through the implementation of the Criminal Law and the Criminal Procedure was an approach to crime in which preventive and

---

79. Gao Mingxuan, *Zhonghua renmin gongheguo xingfa de yunyu he dansheng*, 23.

punitive techniques were combined and in which the leadership role of the Party both reconfirmed and further institutionalized. The leading role of the Party Center was evident in the drafting and the promulgation of the laws themselves, in the articulation of the guiding principles of comprehensive management and severe and rapid punishment and in the initiation and prosecution of the campaigns against serious criminal offenses and against serious economic crime. The Party Center continued to maintain guidance over the concrete handling of cases considered to be particularly important, including, as seen above, serious cases of economic crime.

At the same time, the guiding role of the local Party organizations, provided for in abstract form in the criminal and criminal procedure laws, took on more concrete form. The guiding role of the local Party committee was reconfirmed in internal rules and regulations such as the "Provisional Regulations for Criminal Procuratorial Work." In practice, the leadership of local Party committees was further institutionalized in the "collaborative work" or "joint handling of cases" by the public security, the procuratorates and the courts under the auspices of the party committee and by the continued practice of the organs of criminal justice consulting the local party organization concerning the handling of particularly serious or difficult cases.

4

STRIKE HARD!
THE ANTI-CRIME CAMPAIGN OF 1983-85

At present, the public security situation in many areas is still very bad, particularly in that serious and odious cases of a shocking nature continue to occur regularly. In many places, the arrogance of criminals still knows no bounds . . . The experience of the past few years fully proves that only if we resolutely organize a number of major battles in the spirit of "severe and rapid punishment, one fell swoop" and show absolutely no mercy in striking determined blows against criminal elements will we be able to strike fear into the hearts of criminal elements, to instruct and save the many young people who have been led astray, better implement the guiding principle of comprehensive management of public security and reverse the present abnormal situation.

> Central Committee of the Chinese Communist Party, "Decision Regarding Striking Hard Blows Against Criminal Activities." Party Central Document #31 [1983], dated 25 August 1983, in *Shierda yilai zhongyao wenxian xuanbian, shang*, 385.

In the latter half of 1982 and early 1983, the casual observer might have concluded that China's strategy for dealing with crime—preventive techniques under the rubric of comprehensive management combined with campaigns in which criminal punishment was dealt out (more or less) within the parameters established by the Criminal Law and the Criminal Procedure—had been reasonably successful.

Official statistics indicate that the public security organs placed 890,281 criminal cases on file in 1981, and 748,476 in 1982, and that the crime rate per 10,000 of population in those years was 8.9 and 7.4 respectively. *People's Daily* reported on 2 September 1982 that in the first half of that year, crime was 16.7%

lower than it had been in the first half of 1981, and down 13.9% in comparison with the last half of 1981.[1]

Provincial and local newspapers proclaimed similar successes. *Fujian Daily* reported on 24 November 1982 that crime in that province from January through October 1982 was 29.2% lower than during the same period in 1981. The *Shaanxi Daily* for 8 July 1983 stated that crime in Shaanxi for January through June 1983 was down 14.3% compared to the same period of the year before, with a 3.5% decrease in the number of major cases.[2] In May 1983 the head of the Shanghai people's procuratorate reported that the number of criminal cases occurring in Shanghai in 1982 was 34% lower than in 1980 and 33.5% lower than in 1981, with a 22.2% decline in serious criminal cases in 1982 as compared to 1981 and a 32.2% decline in youth offenses.[3] In these and other publications, crime continued to be characterized as being, for the most part, a matter of contradictions among the people, and comprehensive management was emphasized as the means by which to bring about a fundamental solution to the public security problem. In the words of the chief procurator of Shanghai:

> Inasmuch as the political situation in our country has undergone a fundamental transformation such that the absolute majority of law-breaking and criminal activities now fall into the category of contradictions among the people, then aside from meting out stern punishment according to law to those serious currently active criminals who severely threaten public security, the procuratorial organs may handle average criminal offenders as warranted by the situation as reflected in the relative severity of the offense and the degree of seriousness of the circumstances. Those who may either be arrested or not be arrested we must absolutely not arrest, [but instead] rely on the forces of society to educate and reform them."[4]

---

1. "Quanguo zhengdun shehui zhian shoudao mingxian chengxiao," 5.

2. Zhuahao jindong mingchun shehui zhian gongzuo," 1; "Yifa congzhong congkuai daji xianxing fanzui huodong," 1. In "Qieshi zhuahao jindong mingchun shehui zhian gongzuo," *Dazhong bao* reported that in January through October 1982, crime was down by 21.2%, with major cases declining by 7.5%. "Tianjin shi renmin jianchayuan gongzuo baogao," 3 reported that the crime rate for 1982 was 17.6% lower than for 1981.

3. Qin Kun, "Shanghai shi renmin jianchayuan gongzuo baogao (zhaiyao)," 8.

4. *Ibid.* See also "Jiaqiang he gaige gongan gongzuo baozhang guojia changzhi jiuan," 1. This story on the National Public Security Work Conference held in Beijing from 19-29 April 1983 under the auspices of the Politico-legal Affairs Commission of the Party Center similarly stated that the vast majority of crime was a problem of contradictions among the people, and that crimes of this nature (as opposed to crimes of the nature of a contradiction between the people and the enemy) had become China's major criminal problem.

These positive reports may indicate that the recently reconstructed criminal justice system and the Communist Party's approach to the problem of social deviance had been moderately successful. At the very least they show that in its publicly issued propaganda, the Party leadership was still interested in giving the appearance that it was committed to continue along the path of working with the legal system while at the same time putting greater emphasis on social-based crime prevention programs. But sometime in the winter or spring of 1983, in the context of this apparent decrease in crime, Party policy on crime control underwent a fundamental change. The extent of that change became apparent when the Communist Party leadership launched a new crackdown on criminal activities—the Strike Hard campaign. This campaign brought further revisions in the criminal law and record numbers of arrests—so many that the editors of *Forty Years of Rule by the Chinese Communist Party* state that "This concentrated attack [on crime] was that of the largest scale since the campaign to Suppress Counter-Revolutionaries in 1950."[5]

STRIKING HARD

In his work report to the National People's Congress on 6 June 1983, Zhao Ziyang described the public security situation this way:

There has been some improvement in recent years thanks to the efforts by various quarters, but public order is still not as good as in the best years after the founding of the People's Republic. Such criminal offences as murder, robbery, rape and larceny pose quite a problem in some places. The recent plane hijacking indicates that there are serious loopholes and defects in our system of management, that the public security, procuratorial and judicial departments have failed to perform some of their functions effectively as organs of dictatorship.[6]

Zhao's comments indicate that in spite of the overall decline in crime rates throughout the country, the Party leadership was concerned about the continued occurrence of serious, violent criminal offenses. There were certainly reasons for concern. Although there had been declines in the overall crime rate, the number of murder cases placed on file in 1982 (9,324) was not appreciably lower than that

---

5. Ma Qibin et al., ed. *Zhongguo gongchandang zhizheng sishinian*, 525. It is estimated that 800,000 trials of counter-revolutionaries took place in the first half of 1950. See Meisner, *Mao's China and After*, 81.
6. Zhao Ziyang, "Report of the Work of the Government," 4 July 1983, quoted in Leng and Chiu, *Criminal Justice in Post-Mao China*, 135-36.

in 1981 (9,576), and the number or reported rape cases had actually increased, from 30,808 in 1981 to 3,5631 in 1982.[7] The hijacking of a Chinese airliner to South Korea and the multi-provincial murder and robbery spree of two brothers from Liaoning province may have been particularly shocking to the Chinese leaders.

On a more individual (and less verifiable) level, the Hong Kong magazine *Contention* claims that robbers had attempted to hold up Deng Xiaoping's limousine as he rode through the hills above the sea-side resort of Beidaihe, prompting Deng, unharmed but outraged, to take a personal interest in the violent suppression of criminal activity.[8] Whatever the truth of that report may be, Deng Xiaoping's role in the planning of the campaign is attested to by his own remark, made in a speech to the Third Plenary Session of the Central Advisory Commission of the Communist Party on 22 October 1984: "Last year, I devoted myself to only one thing: a crackdown on criminal offenders."[9]

Concern with the public security situation was translated into plans for a new and more severe campaign against crime sometime in the winter or early spring of 1983. According to one interview source, Deng Xiaoping gave the task of coming up with an overall crime-reduction plan to the new Minister of Public Security, Liu Fuzhi. Liu's plan, according to this source, remained within the scope of the Criminal and Criminal Procedure laws, and was rejected by Deng as being too weak. A new plan, according to this source, was later hammered out at heated meetings in Beidaihe, during which Deng argued that it was necessary to "overcome chaos with severe punishments" (*zhi luanshi yongzhongdian*)[10] According to another account, the anti-crime campaign was the idea of Liu himself, who believed that only a strong campaign would re-establish in people's minds an authoritative image of the public security, the procuratorates and the courts. In this account, Liu first gained Peng Zhen's agreement. Then he and Peng convinced Deng Xiaoping of the need for a campaign, and Deng, who had been vexed by crime in some personal way, agreed.[11]

From our point of view as outside observers of these events, the Strike Hard campaign emerges from behind the walls of Zhongnanhai in July 1983. During the first week of July, initial instructions concerning the new campaign against crime were relayed from the Party Center to the provincial and then to the local level.

---

7. *Zhongguo falu nianjian, 1987*, 886-887.

8. Jin Zhong, "Suzhu yundong: Zhonggong daju zhenya fanzui," 50-51; Luo Bing "Deng Xiaoping yujie yu da daibu," 6-10.

9. Deng Xiaoping, "Speech at the Third Plenary Session of the Central Advisory Commission of the Communist Party of China," 55-56.

10. Interview file 6.b. The source may be said to have stood in a student-teacher relationship with Liu, and his account may therefore have purposely portrayed Liu in a positive light.

11. Ding Yichou, "Zhuanzheng xia de fazhi," 17.

First the Central Politico-Legal Affairs Commission held a telephone conference on public security affairs. Then the provincial Politico-Legal Affairs commissions held their own conferences. As reported in the openly circulated press, these conferences called for the usual "correct recognition of the situation," the strengthening of comprehensive management and for stronger coercive measures against crime, including more police patrols, inspection points and strengthened ideological indoctrination of the public security forces.[12]

The initial stages of the campaign may also have included the setting of quotas the arrest or detention of suspected criminal offenders. A person who worked in a provincial city procuratorate in 1983 described the setting of such quotas in his city. Before the campaign began, the municipal public security bureau called a meeting of the heads of the precinct stations, who were asked to give an estimate of the number of troublemakers in their areas. These estimates were added up to arrive at an estimated number of persons to be taken into custody around the city. When the campaign began, the numbers established by each precinct station served as quotas for which each station was responsible. Each precinct station made a sweep of its own area, bringing in the requisite number of persons for "shelter and investigation."[13]

The campaign began in earnest in late July and early August. In preparation for the campaign, county level public security offices, procuratorates and courts were brought under the overall leadership of "command posts" that coordinated action and oversaw the "joint handling of cases" (*lianhe ban'an*) which enabled the three organs of criminal justice to coordinate their efforts and to speed up the handling of criminal cases.[14] When preparations were complete, the authorities then carried out mass detentions and arrests of criminals and suspected criminals.

The "resolute measures" taken by the public security organs of the city of Tangshan (Hebei Province) served as an initial experiment and example of the type of action that was expected. As reported in the *People's Daily* of 14 August, six hooligan gangs led by ex-convicts released from labor reform and labor re-education camps had been terrorizing the city for a year, robbing, harassing women in public, and carrying out gang-fights in the streets. On 19 July an incident took place on a public bus in which six hooligans assaulted three women. A passenger who tried to intervene was stabbed to death. In response, the public security office arrested 106 individuals on charges of hooliganism in the next ten days, thus breaking up six hooligan gangs.[15]

---

12. *Zhongguo fazhi bao* (China legal system news), Beijing: 8 July 1983, 1; Shen Qingyun, "Sheng zhengfa weiyuanhui zhaokai dianhua huiyi," 1.

13. Interview file 6.a. The use of quotas was also reported in "Quota Means Death Penalty for Petty Offenders," *South China Morning Post*, 20 September 1983, 1.

14. For short descriptions, see *Hengtai xianzhi*, 528; *Wushun xianzhi*, 383.

15. "Yanli daji xingshi fanzui huodong,"1; "Tangshan shi yiwang dajin liuge liumang tanhuo," 1.

Similar mass arrests took place in other jurisdictions around the country during the first weeks of August. On August sixth, the public security forces of Beijing conducted a major sweep of the city. According to a report published in Hong Kong, 3,000 persons were detained for questioning and police entered houses and apartments to detain persons who had records of previous law-breaking.[16] In Dazu County in the province of Sichuan, the initial crackdown was carried out between August tenth and twentieth. Sixty-nine arrests were made during this period—eight more than the total number of arrests made in Dazu County during the entire year of 1982.[17]

The point of this "first battle" of the campaign was to take as many real and potential criminal offenders as possible off the streets and into detention centers, re-education through labor facilities and labor reform camps. In order to prevent undesirable elements already in labor reform or labor re-education from returning to society, the labor reform and re-education camps were simultaneously ordered to put an immediate, although temporary, halt to the return of prisoners to society upon completion of sentence. While the paperwork of their release was still carried out, prisoners who had served their terms and were scheduled for release were forcibly retained at their labor reform or re-education units.[18] Over 28,000 persons were thus retained between the issue of this order on 19 August 1983 and 9 December, when another document was issued allowing limited numbers of prisoners to be released to rural, small-town, and suburban areas.[19]

The Strike Hard Campaign, now started, was explained to the general public and to the Communist Party on 25 August. In a work report given on that day, Minister of Public Security Liu Fuzhi noted that crime rates had not yet been brought down to the record lows of the late 1950s; the state had not been forceful enough. Hooliganism in particular remained a problem, he said, and the people were right to criticize the public security organs for "letting the tiger return to the mountain."[20]

Liu's formulaic call for stronger measures against crime and his reference to hooliganism in particular were given more concrete form in a document entitled

---

16. Jin Zhong, "Suzhu yundong," 50; Luo Bing, "Deng Xiaoping yujie yu da daibu," 6.

17. Dazu renmin jianchayuan, ed. *Dazu xian jianchazhi*, 57.

18. "Sifabu, gonganbu, zuigao renmin jianchayuan, zuigao renmin fayuan guanyu dui fanren xingman he laojiao qiman renyuan zanting fanghui shehui de jinji tongzhi." This document (dated 19 August 1983) suspended two documents of 4 and 5 May of the same year regarding the return of prisoners and labor re-education personnel to society on completion of their terms of sentence.

19. "Sifabu, gonganbu, renmin jianchayuan, zuigao renmin fayuan guanyu jiang yibufen xingman he jiechu laojiao de zanliu renyuan fanghui shehui tongzhi"; "Guowuyuan bangongshi guanyu zuohao fanren xingman shifang hou luohu he anzhi gongzuo de tongzhi." According to this document dated 16 July 1984, strict control was still to be exercised over the return of released prisoners to Beijing, Tianjin and Shanghai.

20. "Yifa congzhong congkuai chengchu yanzhong xingshi zuifan," 1.

"Decision of the Central Committee of the Chinese Communist Party Regarding Striking Hard Blows Against Criminal Activities" (Party Document 31, 1983). This document, also issued on 25 August, laid forth in vehement language and in practical terms the reasons and the goals of the Strike Hard campaign, the general plan of action, the targets of the campaign, and the relationship between criminal punishment and the preventive techniques of comprehensive management. Substantial excerpts from sections one through three and section five are reprinted in *Selected Important Documents Since the Twelfth Congress, Volume One*, while excerpts from section four appear in the *Dazu County Procuratorial Gazetteer*.

Explaining the need for a new and stronger crackdown on criminal activity, Document 31 pointed to the failure of the criminal justice system and of comprehensive management to bring about the desired "fundamental turn for the better" in public security. The Party leadership understood this as a failure of strength, the major reason being that the guiding principle of "severe and rapid punishment" had not truly been carried out and thus "blows against criminal elements have lacked force."[21] Furthermore, the Party Center argued that the crime problem (which it ascribed to the lingering influence of Lin Biao and the Gang of Four and to the influx of foreign ideas since opening to the outside world in 1979) posed a threat to the moral tenor of Chinese society and thus to the ability of China to achieve modernizing economic growth:

> Without going through this great struggle, we will be unable to improve public security, a fundamental improvement in the social atmosphere will not be possible, and socialist construction also will not be able to progress smoothly. At the same time, it is only in this way that as we open to the outside world and revitalize the domestic economy and step by step promote economic prosperity, we may avoid the incurable disease of rampant crime, social unrest and moral degeneracy that afflicts the capitalist countries . . .[22]

China, as opposed to the unfortunate capitalist countries, would be able to achieve this fundamental improvement in public security and in social morality because "In our country, criminal elements do, after all, comprise a small minority of the population . . . "[23]

The method by which the Party proposed to deal the decisive blow that would rapidly and permanently lower crime rates was to carry out a three-year campaign consisting of three battles in which criminals would be apprehended "in one fell

21. "Zhonggong zhongyang guanyu yanli daji xingshi fanzui huodong de jueding (jielu)" (A), 387
22. *Ibid.*, 385-386.
23. *Ibid.*, 387.

swoop." Explaining this phrase, the Party Center noted that it did not mean that new criminals would not appear, but simply that all persons recognized as being criminal elements should be punished without exception, and that the same should be done to any future criminals. Such punishment should, the Party stressed, be meted out in accordance with law, but ". . . [we] absolutely must not stiffly interpret the implied meaning of the text of the law or the scope of punishment in ways that are beneficial to criminals and detrimental to the people."[24]

The main targets of the campaign were identified as: 1) hooligan gang elements (*liumang tuanhuo fenzi*); 2) serial offenders; 3) murderers, arsonists, bombers, poisoners, drug traffickers, rapists, robbers and persons guilty of serious theft; 4) traffickers in women and children, criminals who force, lure or shelter women in prostitution or criminals who produce, reproduce, or sell publications, pictures or recordings of reactionary or pornographic content; 5) members of reactionary secret societies currently engaged in wrecking activities; 6) persons escaped from labor reform camps, persons released from labor reform or labor re-education who commit new crimes and other persons under warrant of arrest for criminal activities; 7) active counter-revolutionary elements who write counter-revolutionary slogans and pamphlets, write letters of counter-revolutionary contact or anonymous letters, and other remnants of Lin Biao and the Gang of Four currently engaged in wrecking activities.[25]

This rather long list of targets reveals a variety of concerns. Notably absent from the list of were economic offenses and other offenses that tend to involve Party and state cadres, such as illegal detention and interrogation under torture. As for the targeted offenses, some were clearly legacies of the past. The concern with followers of Lin Biao and the Gang of Four points to unresolved tensions stemming from the factional struggles of the Cultural Revolution, while the reference to "secret society elements" points to the re-emergence of a problem that had originally been dealt with during the 1950s. Counter-revolution was, of course, a constant concern, as were violent or major offenses such as homicide, rape, robbery and large-scale theft. Other targets indicate the Party's awareness of the newly emerging problems that were to become a part of the Chinese scene of the 1980s—transient, serial offenders, narcotics, the trade in women and children, prostitution, pornography and recidivism.

---

24. *Ibid.*, 388.
25. "Zhonggong zhongyang guanyu yanli daji xingshi fanzui huodong de jueding—jielu" (B), 132.

Out of this list of targets, which included twenty-four types of behavior coming under seventeen different articles of the Criminal Law[26], the Party singled out one group of offenders for particular attention: hooligan gang members:

> These hooligan gang elements are new dregs of society produced under the new historical conditions, elements of the underground society. By killing and impermissible behavior, by raping women, hijacking airplanes and boats, setting fires and explosions and other such cruel means they cruelly injure and kill the innocent masses. They hate socialism and pose an extremely great threat to public security. We must recognize the nature of hooligan gangs . . . Hooligan gang elements must be taken in one fell swoop, hooligan leaders must be resolutely killed off . . . [27]

With these strong words about hooligans and other criminal offenders targeted in the campaign, the Communist Party made it clear that at least for the moment, crime was no longer regarded as a "contradiction among the people" to be dealt with by means of prevention and reform where possible. Nor were criminals to be understood as the victims of the moral vacuum caused by Lin Biao and the Gang of Four. Hooligans were not apolitical rowdies, but vehement haters of socialism; the struggle against crime was "a severe struggle between the enemy and ourselves in the political arena."[28]

The new, more politicized characterization of crime explicitly refuted the idea that youth offenders were in some way victims of their socio-economic environment. "There are some people," wrote commentator Chong Fa in the *Beijing Daily*, "who think that criminals commit offenses because 'contradictions among the people were not handled well and became antagonistic,' or because 'no solution could be found for their personal problems.' A few even ascribe serious criminal offenses to the offenders' 'not having work' and so on. These points, to sum them up, give people the impression that 'crime is justified.'" Chong proceeded to argue that crime was nothing but the conscious and wilful behavior of the criminal and that in China, where the people were the masters of the country and thus had open to them legitimate channels for the resolution of their problems,

---

26. These articles include: 61 (recidivism); 64 (multiple offenses); 97 (writing letters of counter-revolutionary contact and anonymous counter-revolutionary letters); 99 (reactionary secret societies); 102 (writing counter-revolutionary slogans and pamphlets and, by analogy, reactionary publications); 105 and 106 (arson, bombing and poisoning); 132 (homicide); 139 (rape); 140 (forcing women into prostitution); 141 (trafficking in women and children); 150 (robbery); 152 (theft); 160 (hooliganism); 161 (escape from labor reform); 169 (luring or sheltering women in prostitution); 170 (pornographic publications). Being a "Lin Biao/Gang of Four element" would presumably be some form of counter-revolution.
27. "Zhonggong zhongyang guanyu yanli daji xingshi fanzui huodong de jueding—jielu" (B), 133.
28. "Zhonggong zhongyang guanyu yanli daji xingshi fanzui huodong de jueding (jielu)" (A), 385.

there could be no excuse for crime: every individual must therefore be held fully accountable for his or her own actions.[29]

With crime now understood as a struggle between the people and the enemy and criminals as fully responsible individuals who must be dealt with by harsh punitive measures, the "guiding principle" of comprehensive management and the relationship between prevention and punishment required further elucidation. Propaganda from 1981-1982 had suggested that only comprehensive management could effectively address the crime problem at its roots. Now, the Central Committee declared that: "Use of dictatorial measures to mete out severe punishment to criminals according to law is the first item of comprehensive management."[30] Punishment was the first link, the essential precondition without which the preventive, reformative techniques of comprehensive management would not be able to get off the ground. Thus while comprehensive management and harsh punishment of criminal offenders were regarded as being complementary, preventive methods were now understood as being supplementary to punitive means.[31]

After the Strike Hard campaign had been going on for more than a month, the Standing Committee of the NPC supplied it with a legal basis by passing two decisions: the "Decision Regarding the Severe Punishment of Criminal Elements Who Seriously Endanger Public Security" and the 'Decision Regarding the Procedure for Rapid Adjudication of Cases Involving Criminal Elements Who Seriously Endanger Public Security."[32] The former decision, adopted on 2 September 1983, revised the Criminal Law to allow for punishment up to and including death for the offenses of leading a hooligan group, causing intentional injury, injuring state personnel or civilians who expose or arrest criminals, leading a group engaging in the abduction and sale of people, illegal manufacture, trade, transport or theft of weapons or explosives, organization of sects or secret societies, the use of superstition to carry out counter-revolutionary activities, and luring, forcing or sheltering women in prostitution. The "Decision" also created a new offense of imparting criminal methods, to be punished by anywhere from less than five years of fixed-term imprisonment to life imprisonment or death, depending on the circumstances. The increased range of punishment provided for

---

29. Chong fa, "Bo fanzui youli lun," 3.
30. "Zhonggong zhongyang guanyu yanli daji xingshi fanzui huodong de jueding (jielu)" (A), 388.
31. This redefinition was made not only in Document 31, but also in the Party Central propaganda bureau's propaganda outline (*xuanchuan tigang*) for the Strike Hard campaign. See Wang Zhongfang, ed. *Zhongguo shehui zhian zonghe zhili de lilun yu shijian*, 9.
32. The Chinese text and English translation of these two decisions are printed in *The Criminal Law and the Criminal Procedure Law of China* (Beijing: Foreign Languages Press, 1984), on 241-245 and 246-249, respectively.

in the "Decision" was to be applicable to all criminal cases adjudicated after its promulgation.

The "Decision Regarding the Procedure for Rapid Adjudication of Cases Involving Criminal Elements Who Seriously Endanger Public Security" (also passed on 2 September) stated that in serious criminal cases the people's courts need not be bound by the requirements of Article 110 of the Criminal Procedure Law, which provided that the defendant must be notified of the charges made against him seven days prior to trial and that defendants, witnesses, defense lawyers and interpreters be summoned or subpoenaed at least three days prior to trial. The decision also shortened the time limit for filing an appeal from ten to three days.

THE RESULTS OF THE STRIKE HARD CAMPAIGN

The precise schedule of the campaign varied somewhat in different jurisdictions. Overall, the first and most aggressive period was from August 1983 through early 1984. In early 1984, evidently in response to the overly aggressive way in which the campaign had been carried out, or perhaps reflecting a shift in the balance of power among the Party leadership, the Central Committee added the character for "accuracy"(*zhun*) to the campaign slogan. The Strike Hard Campaign thus continued, although at a significantly lower level of ferocity, through late 1986 or early 1987. The campaign had an immediate and profound effect on the administration of criminal justice in China. Record numbers of Chinese were detained, tried and punished for law-breaking during the first six months of the campaign. The short-term and the long-term effects of the campaign on Chinese crime rates, however, turned out to be highly debatable.

One of the most fundamental changes brought about by the campaign was that as procuratorates and courts investigated and tried criminal cases, they were encouraged to look beyond the objective facts of the crime to give more weight to factors such as the subjective intention of the criminal offenders and the authorities' interpretation of the degree of harm done to "public security." The internally circulated professional journal *Beijing Jurisprudence*, for example, suggested that in handling cases, judicial personnel ". . . must not one-sidedly emphasize that the direct goal of the crime was not attained, or that the consequences 'were not serious' (for example, attempted murder, theft of goods whose value was not great, attempted rape etc.), while neglecting the criminal motive, purpose, circumstances, means, time, place and other such factors and the severe harm done to the present public security situation."[33]

The vehemence with which the Strike Hard campaign was carried out between late July 1983 and January 1984 was certainly related to the practice of giving more weight to the subjective factors of the crime and to the underlying assumption that all criminal activity, attempted or successful, represented a serious threat to "public security". The ferocity of the campaign was also related to the fact that the major target—"hooligan gang elements" guilty of gang fighting, harassment of women, rape and a host of other offensive behavior, was a rather broad category.

In the Criminal Law (Article 160), the offense of hooliganism was defined as assembling a crowd to have brawls, stir up fights and cause trouble, humiliate women, or "engage in other hooligan activities, undermining public order." In legal theory and practice, "other hooligan activities" was understood to include not only sexual assault and harassment of women, but also sexual promiscuity—consensual sexual relations between unmarried men and women, group sex, and homosexual activity. The concept of "undermining public order" was understood not simply to mean disorderly public behavior, but also deviant behavior (i.e. behavior violating the principles of order and morality) even when that behavior was carried out in private.[34]

A practical example of the effect of the campaign on the way criminal cases of hooliganism were adjudicated is provided by the description in *Democracy and the Legal System* of the Shanghai Middle People's Court's handling of a hooliganism case in late August-early September 1983.[35] The facts of the crime were as follows: on the evening of 8 June, some sixty members of two rival gangs engaged each other in a fight in the area of Hotien Road and Zhonghua New Road in Shanghai, blocking traffic and causing public buses to be re-routed. Weapons including knives, swords, sticks and spades were employed in the brawl. Twelve of the gang members were wounded, and eight youths were arrested.

Prosecution was initiated in this case on 17 August. Three leading members of the two gangs were sentenced to death and deprivation of political rights (a standard auxiliary punishment) on charges of hooliganism under Article 160 of the Criminal Law and Article 1 of the "Decision Regarding Severe Punishment of Criminal Elements Who Seriously Endanger Public Security." Of the remaining five defendants, three were sentenced to death and deprivation of political rights for hooliganism and robbery under Articles 160 and 150 of the Criminal Law and Article 1 of the "Decision Regarding Severe Punishment . . . " One was sentenced

---

33. Li Cheng and Tang Huayong, "Qiantan yifa congzhong congkuai yanzheng yanzhong fanzui de wenti," 29.
34. Liu, "Hooliganism," 57.
35. "Shouyao fenzi bei panchu sixing," 39.

to life imprisonment and deprivation of political rights for hooliganism and robbery, and the last to ten years imprisonment for hooliganism and six years for robbery, the sentences to be served concurrently. The executions were carried out on September thirteenth.

Commenting on this case, a legal analyst for *Democracy and the Legal System* (who applauded the strict sentences meted out) noted that prior to the Strike Hard campaign and its attendant changes to the criminal law, this case of gang-fighting would not have been considered to have been so serious. The fight had not resulted in any deaths and no bystanders had been injured; the injury of twelve of the gang members would have been considered as being little more than what they deserved. A probable sentence prior to August 1983 would have been fifteen years fixed-term imprisonment for the leaders and seven years for the other defendants.[36] The severe sentences meted out were not illegal, but they are evidence of the effects of the Party Center's admonition not to interpret the law in ways beneficial to the defendant and the accompanying encouragement to give greater emphasis to subjective factors including the very subjective assessment of the "harm done to public security" rather than to the objective facts of the case.

The hooliganism case discussed above also reveals another characteristic of the Strike Hard campaign—the application of the policies and laws introduced in July-September 1983 to offenses committed before that time. The legality of retroactive application of the law was not in question: the "Decision Regarding the Severe Punishment of Criminal Elements Who Seriously Endanger Public Security" (Article 3) stated explicitly that "In adjudicating the above criminal cases [i.e. those offenses for which severe punishment had been provided in the Decision] after the promulgation of this Decision, this Decision is to be applied." Some legal scholars argued—reasonably enough given its wording—that the retroactive force of the "Decision" was limited to those cases that had occurred prior to 2 September 1983 but which had not yet been tried or in which verdict and sentence had not yet been delivered by that date.[37]

In practice, the retroactive force of the "Decision" appears not to have been limited. Not only were new crimes and crimes prosecuted after 2 September tried and punished under the new rules, but cases previously tried and sentenced were brought up for reconsideration and revision of sentence during the campaign. Indeed, as is revealed in a document issued by the SPP, it was possible for offenders previously sentenced to punishments other than the death penalty to have their cases reconsidered and be re-sentenced to death during the campaign. The SPP ordered that such revisions of sentence be confined to cases in which "there was great public outrage, the crime deserved the death penalty, [and the of-

---

36. Wei De, "Zhezhong fanzui huodong ying zai yanli daji zhi li," 39.
37. Ke Gezhuang and Gu Xiaorong, "Guanyu 'jueding' de sujili wenti," 19-20.

fender's] behavior during incarceration has been very bad." Those offenders who, although guilty of heinous crimes, had shown themselves willing to reform, were not to have their sentences changed.[38]

During the campaign it was also possible for instances of deviant behavior that had previously not been considered as criminal and had thus punished by administrative sanction to be hauled up again for reconsideration under the criminal law. Such was the case of a twenty-year old man by the name of Liu Cai of Jiange County, Sichuan province. On his way home from a militia cadres' meeting on the afternoon of 16 May 1983, Liu noticed a sixteen-year old young woman whom he found attractive. Hiding by the side of the road until she passed by, Liu came up behind her, patted her on the shoulder, and suggested: "Come on, let's go to bed." When the young woman told him that he was shameless and that she was going to report him, Liu turned and left. On 15 July, the county public security bureau punished Liu for his hooligan behavior with seven days of administrative detention. But on 29 August, Liu was arrested on a charge of attempted rape for which he was tried, convicted and sentenced to two years in prison. Fortunately for Liu, the middle and higher people's courts reviewed his case and instructed the Jiange county court to revoke its original verdict and declare him innocent.[39]

One might expect that the sudden introduction of rapid adjudication procedures and unusually severe sentences might prompt protests from defense lawyers and an increase in the number of appeals. In an adversarial legal system, this would very likely have been the case. But in the Chinese system, the Strike Hard campaign was accompanied by further limitations on the functions of the defense lawyer and significant decline in the number of appeals. The ability of a lawyer to prepare a defense, already limited by the provision of the Criminal Procedure Law that a lawyer could only be retained seven days before trial, was further constrained by the NPC SC "Decision on Rapid Adjudication." This Decision provided that in the cases of "criminal elements on whom death sentences should be imposed" for the serious offenses targeted in the campaign, the courts need not be bound by the regulation in Criminal Procedure Law (Article 110) which provided that defendants be informed of the charges against them and advised of their right to retain a defense lawyer at least seven days prior to trial. The campaign technique in which the public security, the procuratorates and the courts worked on cases together under the leadership of the Party committee also placed the function of the defense lawyer in question.

Under such conditions, what could a defense lawyer do? The Ministry of Justice addressed this question in its "Notice on Giving Full Play To the Function

---

38. "Zuigao renmin jianchayuan guanyu gaipan 'sixing' anjian de jidian yijian (jielu)."
39. Xin Ru and Lu Chen, ed. *Zhonghua renmin gongheguo falu lifa sifa jieshi anli daquan*, 985.

of Lawyers During the Campaign to Strike Hard Blows Against Criminal Offenders." Lawyers, the Ministry instructed, should defend their clients as required, pointing out any mitigating circumstances in accordance with the Criminal Procedure Law; but if there were no mitigating circumstances, the defense lawyer should not raise the question of a light or reduced sentence. If lawyers discovered additional perpetrators who had not been brought to justice, major circumstances that had been over-looked, or errors in the application of law, they should bring these issues up as the case was being handled jointly under the auspices of the Party or work with the procuratorate and the court to clear the matter up before trial. If a lawyer had problems with important facts and evidence or with the application of policies or laws in cases in which the death penalty might be used, he/she should not raise these issues directly with the public security, the procuratorate or the court, but should report them to the local organs of justice, whose leaders would discuss these sensitive issues directly with the politic-legal affairs commission of the local Communist Party committee.[40]

As the function of the defense lawyer was further limited, so too did the rate of appeals decline. Citing research carried out by the Supreme People's Court, a scholar at People's University reports that while 22% of criminal cases were appealed in 1981, only 10% were appealed after the beginning of the Strike Hard campaign in August 1983.[41] This does not mean that criminal defendants or their lawyers accepted the justice of their trial and punishment during the Strike Hard campaign. They simply realized that an appeal would be useless, if not dangerous.

It is difficult to know precisely how many people were arrested, tried and punished during the campaign. The *China Law Yearbook* of 1987 reports a total of 610,478 criminal cases placed on file by the public security offices in 1983 (for comparison, the number of cases placed on file in 1982 and in 1984 were 748,476 and 514,369 respectively).[42] The *Yearbook* does not, however, break these cases down by type of offense, as it does for all other years. In this respect, the statistical record itself seems to have been a casualty of the campaign. In order to get some idea of the number of criminal cases investigated and criminal offenders punished during the campaign, we must look at whatever local and national statistics are available and then draw some tentative conclusions.

Arrest, prosecution and trial statistics from twenty-six local (county and city) jurisdictions seem to indicate that the number of arrests made and the number of persons prosecuted for the offenses of rape, hooliganism and theft were substantially higher during the campaign than in the years immediately before or after. In Hougang city, for example 73 rape offenders were sentenced in 1982, 134 in

---

40. "Sifabu guanyu yanli daji xingshi fanzui huodong zhong chongfen fahui lushi zuoyong de tongzhi."
41. Sun Fei, *Woguo xingshi susongfa di er chengxu lun*, 28-31.
42. *Zhongguo falu nianjian, 1987*, 886-887.

1983, and 122 in 1984. In Huma county, 33 rape cases were adjudicate in 1982, and then 71 in 1983. In Yuanan County, there were 11 rape cases and no hooliganism cases in 1982, but 43 and 70 cases, respectively, in 1983.[43]

On the national scale, it is clear that the Strike Hard campaign resulted in the arrest of record numbers of persons charged with criminal offenses. In 1984, Amnesty International estimated that tens of thousands of arrests and several thousand executions took place in the first three months of the campaign (August-October).[44] A Ministry of Justice document dated February 1984 states that up to that time (six months into the campaign), the labor reform and labor re-education facilities had taken in 563,000 new inmates, pushing the total reform system population up to 1,260,000. The Ministry of Justice estimated that another 500,000 prisoners would enter the system as the first battle of the campaign progressed.[45] As of January 1984, there were, in addition to those in labor reform and labor re-education facilities, 170,000 persons being held in detention centers, 55,200 of them already tried and sentenced, 31,700 under investigation, 42,200 awaiting sentence, and 8,000 whose cases were being handled independently by the courts, the procuratorates or the Ministry of State Security.[46] This sudden influx of large numbers of prisoners caused serious over-crowding and the spread of infectious disease among the prisoner population.[47]

According to *Forty Years of Rule by the Chinese Communist Party*, the Central Politico-Legal Affairs Commission reported on 31 October, 1984 that in the first battle of the Strike Hard Campaign, 1,027,000 criminals had been arrested on charges of homicide, arson, robbery, rape, and hooliganism. 975,000 had been prosecuted, 861,000 had been sentenced, including 24,000 sentenced to death—a figure that seems to include persons sentenced to death with a two-year reprieve. 687,000 new prisoners entered the labor reform system and 169,000 labor re-education.[48] Citing these figures, the editors of *Forty Years of Rule by the Chinese Communist Party* add that this was the largest crack-down on criminal offenders since the 1950 Campaign Against Counter-revolutionaries.[49]

Looking at the campaign from the perspective of 1988, Luo Feng reports that from the beginning of Strike Hard in August 1983 through the end of 1987, China tried 692,955 criminal cases in which 2,047,839 criminal offenders were

---

43. *Yuanan xianzhi*, 518, 520; *Huma xianzhi*, 341; *Hougang shizhi*, 600.

44. Amnesty International, *China: Violations of Human Rights*, 54-55.

45. "Sifabu guanyu di, shi chouban laogai, laojiaochang de baogao."

46. "Zuigao renmin fayuan, zuigao renmin jianchayuan, gonganbu, sifabu guanyu zhuajin shencha chuli kanshousuo ya renfan de tongzhi."

47. "Sifabu guanyu di, shi chouban laogai, laojiaochang de baogao."

48. If these figures are accurate, then it appears that of the 24,000 persons sentenced to death, 5,000 were sentenced to immediate execution, while 19,000 were sentenced to death with two year reprieve and thus entered labor reform.

49. Ma Qibin et al.,ed. *Zhongguo gongchandang zhizheng sishi nian*, 525.

sentenced. Of these defendants, 38% were sentenced to punishments ranging from five years fixed-term imprisonment to life imprisonment or death, 61.2% to under five years fixed-term imprisonment, detention, control or no punishment, and .07% were found not guilty. Of these, 45.47% (931,093) were found guilty of one of the seven target offenses laid forth by the NPC SC.[50] In the originally projected campaign period of three years (August 1983-December 1985), the Chinese courts tried over 112,000 criminal cases, sentencing over 1,395,000 persons, of whom 51% were found guilty of one of the seven target offenses.[51] *China Today: Public Security Work,* calculating the Strike Hard Campaign as lasting from August 1983 through the end of January 1987 reports that during this period the public security organs broke 1,647,000 criminal cases, made 1,772,000 arrests, sent more than 322,000 persons to labor re-education facilities and over 15,000 minors to reformatories.[52] Some foreign scholars estimate that as many as 10,000 persons may have been executed between 1983 and 1986.[53]

In assessing the results of the Strike Hard campaign, it is important to note that the statistical increases in criminals arrested, tried, and punished do not necessarily indicate that there had been a corresponding increase in the actual commission of such criminal acts. Some of the increase was very likely due to the retroactive enforcement of the Standing committee of the NPCSC "Decision Regarding Severe Punishment," including the possible re-sentencing of cases that, after August 1983, were considered to have been punished too leniently. Wang Xiansheng, a judge during the Strike Hard campaign, recalls that 43% of the rape cases handled by his county court during the campaign had occurred before 1982.[54] Some of the increase is also attributable to the authorities prosecuting as rape, attempted rape or hooliganism cases that would formerly have been handled (and in some cases actually had been handled) as lesser offenses or even not regarded as crimes. Beverly Hooper and Zhou Huai both describe an atmosphere in the late summer and fall of 1983 in which young men might be accused of attempted rape or hooliganism for even brushing against a woman on a public bus.[55] Similarly, claims that the campaign brought about a substantial reduction in crime must be regarded with skepticism.

---

50. Luo Feng, "Fanzui xianxiang gaishu," 144-45.
51. *Ibid.*, 145.
52. *Dangdai zhongguo de gongan gongzuo,* 37.
53. Hood, *The Death Penalty,* 74-75.
54. Wang Xiansheng, "Shenli qiangjian anjian ruhe fangcuo de tihui," 24-25.
55. Hooper, *Youth in China,* 121; Zhou Huai, "Beijing zheng zai saodong," 12.

A FUNDAMENTAL TURN FOR THE BETTER?

Discussing the Strike Hard campaign in his "Work Report of the Government" delivered to the second session of the Sixth National People's Congress on 15 May 1984, Premier Zhao Ziyang had this to say:

> The results have been highly gratifying. The average monthly crime rate has dropped, and our actions have protected the interest and safety of the people and educated and redeemed a good number of youth juvenile delinquents . . . Though it has already been extremely successful, it will go on as a part of the comprehensive effort to improve public order.[56]

After a campaign, and especially after such a significant, large-scale national campaign as Strike Hard, a public declaration of victory was only too predictable. But just how effective were the aggressive anti-crime measures of the Strike Hard campaign in achieving the goals enunciated by the Communist Party in Document 31?

The initial results of the campaign seemed to be encouraging. Guangzhou's *Southern Daily* reported in November 1983 that 'Guangzhou municipality has won the first battle in its fight against criminal activities . . . criminal cases have shown a clear decline.'[57] The Shanghai periodical *Politics and Law* carried a story in April 1984 stating that from September through December 1983, the number of cases of robbery and violent hooliganism was about 80% lower than in the previous four months of the year, while hooligan street-fights, trouble-making, and harassment of women in public places had been virtually eliminated. If the struggle against crime were to continue without wavering, the editors concluded, it was certain that Shanghai could return to the record low crime rates enjoyed during the late 1950s and early 1960s.[58] On the national scale, Minister of Public Security Liu Fuzhi stated in an interview with the editors of *Democracy and the Legal System* that the incidence of criminal cases for 1983 was 18.4% lower than for 1982, and that the decline for the months of September through December was even greater, with the monthly average number of criminal cases reduced by 44.7% compared to the figure for the first eight months of the same year. As a result, said Liu, "there has been a clear turn for the better in pubic security, and the masses have an increased feeling of safety."[59] National crime statistics published in the *China Law Yearbook, 1987* and in *China Today: Public Security Work* indicate that the

---

56. Zhao Ziyang, "Work Report of the Government," 7.
57. Liu Jun, "Guangzhou Municipality's Public Security Shows Clear Improvement," 51.
58. "Yanli daji xingshi fanzui huodong, wei shixian shehui zhian de genben haozhuan er douzheng," 1-2.
59. "Gonganbu buzhang Liu Fuzhi da benkan bianjibu wen," 2.

number of criminal cases placed on file in 1984 (514,369) was approximately 42.2% lower than the number of cases placed on file in 1981 (890,281) and 31.3% lower than the number of cases in 1982 (748,476).[60]

As the campaign continued, the optimism displayed in the fall of 1983 and early 1984 began to be replaced by a more sober assessment of its achievements. In August 1984, *Southern Daily* suggested that although certain heartening results had been attained, they should not be cause for over-estimation nor for blind optimism.[61] This echoed statements made at a national conference of heads of higher and some middle people's courts held in Beijing in August 1984, at which judges were reminded that "the development of the struggle has been uneven, the achievements already made are not stable, the abnormal public security situation has not been fundamentally altered [and] the distance from a fundamental turn for the better in public security is still great."[62]

Reservations about the success of the Strike Hard campaign and the possibility of bringing about a permanent improvement in public security, to say nothing of the much-touted "fundamental turn for the better" mounted as time went on and as crime rates began to climb again in 1985 and the following years. In 1985, two years into the Strike Hard Campaign, Xue Guanghua, president of the Beijing Higher People's Court, cited figures compiled by the Beijing Public Security Bureau to describe the "unstable" nature of the decrease in crime. The rate of incidence of major criminal cases in 1984 was 44.4% lower than in 1983, but the rate for March 1985 turned out to be 15.2% higher than for the same month in 1984, and that for April 1985 57.1% higher than for April of the previous year.[63] Similar "instability" was demonstrated in Liaoning province, where initially heartening decreases in crime had given way to 21% increase in the number of homicide cases in 1985 (as compared to 1984), a remarkable increase in theft cases, in which those classified as "serious" rose by almost two times, and small increases in rape and robbery (particularly robbery of guns and of cars).[64]

In the long run, the Strike Hard Campaign appeared to have brought about a fundamental decrease in hooligan gang offenses—that is, the open violation of public order, public harassment of women and street-fighting that seems to have been a problem peculiar to China's cities in the years following the Cultural Revolution. But as this problem was resolved (and one can speculate that the resolution of the hooligan problem might have been related to the enlivening of the market economy as well as to the Strike Hard Campaign), other problems

---

60. *Zhongguo falu nianjian, 1987*, 887; *Dangdai zhongguo de gongan gongzuo*, 37.
61. Su Zhongheng, "Jixu guanche yifa congzhong congkuai fangzhen, shenwa yincang yanzhong xingshi fanzui fenzi," 4.
62. "Quanguo fayuan yuanzhang zuotanhui zai jing zhaokai," 3.
63. Xue Guanghua, "Jianchi guanche zhixing yifa 'congzhong congkuai' fangzhen," 6.
64. Lu Dong, "Jixu gaohao 'yanda,' di sanzhanyi, zhengqu shehui zhian wending haozhuan," 3.

increased or arose anew, including theft, narcotics offenses, prostitution and recidivism.[65]

The problem of mounting recidivism—the commission of new offenses by persons released from labor reform and re-education facilities—during the later years of the campaign and afterward pointed to another, unintentional result of the Strike Hard Campaign. Record numbers of criminal offenders were imprisoned during the campaign. Many of them were minor offenders for whom a "severe " sentence was two to ten years of fixed-term imprisonment. During their terms of imprisonment, it was expected (at least in theory) that these criminal offenders would be reformed. The first step of the process of reform was for the prisoner to confess his or her crime and accept the justice of his or her criminal sentence. In this respect, the Strike Hard Campaign appears to have had a detrimental effect on the reform process. In the wake of the campaign, resistance to reform, including refusal to admit wrong-doing, violation of labor camp discipline, the commission of new offenses while serving time, escape attempts and prisoner riots were all linked by Chinese observers to the way in which the Strike Hard Campaign had been carried out, and particularly to prisoners' perception that their heavy sentences were unjust because they had been unlucky enough to be arrested and tried during instead of before or after the campaign.[66]

Offenders' attitudes toward campaign-style justice may also be discerned from changes in the rate of appeals of criminal cases. While criminal appeals dropped to a rate of 10% during the initial phases of the campaign, they began to increase again as the intensity of the campaign declined in 1984-85.[67] Courts and procuratorates were now faced with the task of reviewing cases that were said to have been mishandled or inappropriately sentenced during the campaign. There were certain limits placed on the type, and possibly the number of Strike Hard cases in which sentences could be reduced on the grounds that they had been unreasonably severe. A person who worked in a provincial procuratorate during the latter stages of the campaign recalls that Qiao Shi had ordered that no full-scale review of such cases should be undertaken.[68]

In Shanxi province, the provincial procuratorate issued explicit instructions regarding the review and revision of sentences. According to this document, the relatively large proportion of campaign-related cases coming through the criminal appeals process was indicative of mistakes of fact, incorrect verdicts, and inappropriate sentencing. Procuratorates were instructed to immediately correct

---

65. "Jixu guanche 'yanda' fangzhen," 9; Bi Xiaonan, "Queyou mingxian haozhuan, mianlin xin de wenti," 10-11.

66. Li Yuqian, "Dangqian yunei fanzui huodong xin dongxiang ji qi duice," 138; Sifabu yanjiusuo yunei anjian ketizu, "Jin shinian lai quanguo yunei anjian de tedian ji jinhou duice yanjiu," 12.

67. Sun Fei, *Woguo xingshi susongfa di er chengxu lun*, 28-31.

68. Interview file 6.a.

any cases in which there had been errors of fact and to make appropriate revisions of sentence in cases in which the original sentence had been "obviously too light or too heavy." If the sentence appeared to be somewhat too heavy, but still within the legally mandated range of sentence allowed for the offense in question, then no change would be made.[69]

Another unintentional effect of the Strike Hard campaign was its effect on China's image in the West, and particularly in the United States. Under the conditions of opening to the outside world, the Chinese leadership was faced with a dilemma. What might seem to the Party leaders, and perhaps to the Chinese people as well, to be reasonable and effective ways of propagandizing the state's efforts to control crime could be interpreted in a very negative light in the Western media. The Party attempted to address this dilemma by ordering that propaganda concerning the Strike Hard campaign be tailored and targeted in such a way as to distinguish between Chinese and foreign audiences. In a document concerning the Party Center's guidelines for propaganda during the campaign, the Ministry of Justice reminded its provincial-level organs of the need to distinguish between propaganda aimed at Chinese and propaganda that might be seen by non-Chinese in cities open to foreign travelers: "In open cities, announcements of executions should be posted internally [i.e. in areas and buildings not accessible to foreigners], propaganda display cases should pay attention to the distinction between Chinese and foreigners; do not post photographs of executions in propaganda display cases visible from the street."[70]

Despite the Party leadership's awareness of the contradiction inherent between internal and external propaganda, foreign reporters and travelers did, of course, see much that they were not intended to see. For foreign legal scholars, it seemed as though policy had decisively gained superiority over law, and that this represented a major step back from China's commitment to construct a modern legal system.[71] For the general public, the Western mass media undermined the Deng regime's image with reporting on the Party's ability to manipulate the legal system, the campaign tactics, the public parading of shaven-headed criminals, the mass sentencing rallies and public executions.

Chinese leaders clearly considered this sort of publicity to be a problem. After *Newsweek* magazine printed photographs of an execution and Amnesty International criticized China for violations of human rights during the campaign, the Party leadership issued a document in which it banned the public parading of

---

69. Shanxisheng gaoji renmin fayuan, Shanxisheng renmin jianchayuan, "Guanyu yanli daji xingshi fanzui huodong yilai panchu de xingshi anjian tichu shensu de jidian yijian."
70. "Sifabu guanche zhongxuanbu 'guanyu daji xingshi fanzui de xuanchuan wenti de jidian yijian' de tongzhi."
71. "Concepts of Law in the Chinese Anti-Crime Campaign," 1903.

prisoners and the carrying out of executions in public areas.[72] Nonetheless, the Chinese criminal justice system continued to be dogged by unfavorable coverage in the Western media and by Western human rights organizations which regularly condemned China for torture, for the extensive use of the death penalty, for the imprisonment of political offenders and for the violation of the basic human rights of common criminal offenders and political prisoners alike.

---

72. "Zhonggong zhongyang xuanchuanbu, zuigao renmin fayuan, zuigao renmin jianchayuan, gonganbu, sifabu, guanyu yanfang fandong baokan liyong wo chujue fanren jinxing zaoyao wumie de tongzhi."

5

UNCIVIL SOCIETY: CRIME AND CRIMINALS

Beginning in May 1985, criminal cases in our country began to increase distinctly . . . such a large-scale increase in crime rates has rarely been seen, not only in the past ten years, but ever since the founding of the People's Republic. Moreover . . . the trend of increase in our country's crime rates will not change in the short term.

Kang Shuhua, ed., *Fanzuixue tonglun*, 98-99.

In her discussion of criminal justice in nineteenth-century France, Michelle Perrot observed that: "The statistics of crimes and offenses furnish the facts and figures of a two-fold obsession: property and sexuality."[1] National and local criminal statistics in China similarly demonstrate the "obsessions of the state." Although they must be analyzed with care, the statistical record and other sources reveal that the Chinese Communist regime was more concerned about certain types of offense than others, and that in consequence, the brute force of the law fell more severely on certain types of offenders. The organs of criminal justice protected private and state property, but much more effectively in cases of theft than of economic crime. Violent offenses such as rape, injury and homicide were subject to severe punishment while the employment of violence during the interrogation of suspected criminal offenders was subject to relatively mild punishments, even in cases in which death resulted. Moral offenses including "hooliganism" and prostitution were pursued vigorously, but with more importance attached to the offenses of women than to those of men.

---

1. Perrot, "Delinquency and the Penitentiary System in Nineteenth-Century France," 223.

While giving us some insights into the public security concerns of the Chinese leadership, criminal statistics and other sources also reveal the weakness of the state. They reveal a regime that expressed in strong language its commitment to equality before the law and yet found itself more able to mete out severe punishment to Chinese citizens of humble peasant and worker background than to Communist Party cadres and their family members. They reveal a government powerful enough to employ the most severe punishments in its drive to rectify public security, but at the same time not powerful enough to achieve its stated goal of reducing crime, or even to prevent significant increases in the crime rate. Under Deng Xiaoping, the Chinese Communist Party did not preside over a "fundamental turn for the better in public security" or the construction of a new spiritual civilization. Instead, it witnessed the development of an increasingly uncivil society and of a growing criminal underclass.

STATISTICS

Our understanding of the number and type of criminal offenses committed in China during the reform era comes from a variety of sources: openly published national criminal statistics, isolated numbers appearing in openly and in internally published documents, articles and books, local statistics appearing in county gazetteers, and local statistics generated as a part of internally published research. Inasmuch as crime statistics were (and still are) regarded as sensitive information, raw numbers were not always published at all; even in some internally published collections of judicial interpretations, sensitive numbers were replaced with large X's. As observers, we must look at as many sources as possible and see what sort of a picture emerges.

The most complete criminal statistics available for the 1980s and early 1990s are those published annually in the *China Law Yearbook*. These include figures for the number of criminal cases placed on file by the public security organs nation-wide, the number of cases prosecuted by the procuratorates, and the number of cases tried and sentenced by the courts. Chinese scholars of criminal law believe the openly published national criminal statistics to be roughly accurate. These (and, by extension, all other statistics), however, are said to be influenced both by under-reporting and by over-reporting of cases. In some instances, public security bureaus are said to have purposely under-reported the number of criminal cases received in order to "prove" that they have successfully reduced the incidence of crime.[2]

---

2. Shao Daosheng, "Qiwu qijian de fanzui fazhan qushi ji duice," 17; He Bingsong, "Woguo de fanzui qushi, yuanyin yu xingshi zhengce, shang"; Li Zenghui, "dangqian minzhe diqu xingshi fanzui de tedian qushi he duice," 18.

The national statistics for cases put on file by the public security organs indicate an overall increase in crime during the 1980s and early 1990s. The number of criminal cases declined somewhat from 1981 through 1984, with a very sharp 36% decrease in fall 1983-through spring 1984 associated with the Strike Hard Campaign.[3] From 1985 onwards, however, crime increased steadily, with a particularly rapid increase in 1988 and 1989, when crime rose by 45.1% and by 138% respectively.[4] At the same time crime rates per 10,000 of population held steady at 5.0 to 5.2 from 1984 through 1986, but rose from 5.4 in 1987 to 20.1 in 1990 (see tables 1-A and 1-B on pages 108-109).

There are several points worth noting in regard to the distribution of crime and the rate at which individual offenses were committed. The first is that property crimes, led by theft, accounted for the greatest single increase in the number of crimes committed. In 1981, theft accounted for 83.6% of the total number of criminal cases placed on file, with robbery and swindling accounting for 2.5% and 2.09% respectively. Theft cases increased from 744,374 in 1981 to 1,860,793 in 1990. Rape, which accounted for the second-largest number of offenses placed on file in 1981 had declined to fourth place in 1990, surpassed in number by both robbery and swindling. Also increasing were the number of cases classified (on the basis of the degree of violence used and the value of the goods involved) as "serious."

"Serious" cases (including 'serious theft,' homicide, robbery, assault and battery, and rape) were found by Chinese criminologists to have begun their increase in 1984—before the general trend of increase that began in 1985. By 1988, cases of robbery and serious theft had risen 59.9% and 75.8% as compared to 1987, while homicide and assault and battery posted increases of 11% and 7.8% respectively (see tables 2 and 3 on page 110). Criminologists writing in the 1980s and early 1990s predicted correctly that the increase in serious offenses would continue.[5] By 1993, the rate of commission of serious crimes was reported to be seven times that of 1983.[6]

---

3. Li Tianfu, Yang Shiqi and Huang Jingping. *Fanzui tongjixue*, 147.
4. Liu Dalin, ed. *Zhongguo dangdai xing wenhua: Zhongguo liang wan li "xing wenming" diaocha baogao*, 617.
5. Kang Shuhua, *Fanzuixue tonglun*, 216; Zi Junyong, "Guanyu daoqie anjian shangsheng de yuanyin he duice," 10; Tao Liqiang and Luo Xiaopeng, "Dangqian nongmin fanzui de tedian yuanyin ji fazhan qushi,"18; "Sha Zhengxin, "Xiangzhen qiye qingshaonian fanzui chutan," 164-165.
6. "Chinese Leaders Call for Stability." Beijing: U.P.I., 24 December 1993.

TABLE 1-A. Number of criminal cases placed on file by the public security bureaus, 1981-1985

year	1981	1982	1983	1984	1985
total	890,281	748,476	610,478	514,396	542,005
homicide	9,576	9,324	n.d.	9,021	10,440
injury	21,499	20,298	n.d.	14,526	15,586
robbery	22,266	16,518	n.d.	7,273	8,801
rape	30,808	35,361	n.d.	44,630	37,712
theft	744,374	609,481	n.d.	395,319	431,323
serious theft	16,873	15,462	n.d.	16,340	34,643
swindling	18,665	17,707	n.d.	13,479	13,157
counterfeiting	1,649	1,763	n.d.	707	491
% solved	73.1	77.4	n.d.	76.9	78.8
rate per 10,000 of population	8.9	7.4	6.0	5.0	5.2

Sources: 1981-1986, Zhongguo falu nianjian, 1987, 886-7; Zhongguo falu nianjian 1988, 820; Zhongguo falu nianjian 1989, 1084; Zhongguo falu nianjian 1990, 996; Zhongguo falu nianjian 1991, 942.

TABLE 1-B. Number of criminal cases placed on file by the public security bureaus, 1986-1990

year	1986	1987	1988	1989	1990
total	547,005	570,439	827,594	1,971,901	2216997
homicide	11,510	13,154	15,959	19,590	21,214
injury	18,364	21,727	26,639	35,831	45,200
robbery	12,124	18,775	36,318	72,881	82,361
rape	39,121	37,225	34,120	40,999	47,782
theft	425,845	435,235	658,683	1,673,222	1,860,793
serious theft	42,192	58,661	122,042	277,147	295,418
swindling	14,663	14,693	18,857	42,581	54,719
counterfeiting	497	436	500	865	1,398
% solved	79.2	81.3	75.7	56.4	57.07
rate per 10,000 of population	5.2	5.4	7.7	18.1	20.1

Sources: *Zhongguo falu nianjian, 1987, 886-7; Zhongguo falu nianjian, 1988,820; Zhongguo falu nianjian, 1989, 1084; Zhongguo falu nianjian, 1990, 996; Zhongguo falu nianjian, 1991, 942.*

TABLE 2. Number of serious crimes reported in China, 1980-1988

1980	50,000
1981	67,000
1982	64,000
1983	decrease, but no data
1984	60,000 (approximately)
1985	80,000+
1986	97,000
1987	122,000
1988	205,000

Source: He Bingsong, "Woguo jinnianlai fanzui gaikuang," 19.

TABLE 3. Incidence of serious crime in China, 1988,
with rates of change as compared to 1987

offense	# of offenders arrested	% change over 1987
homicide	1,204	11% increase
robbery	43,829	59.9% increase
assault and battery	25,084	7.8% increase
serious theft	38,784	75.8% increase
rape	30,112	14.1% decrease

Source: He Bingsong, "Woguo jinnianlai fanzui gaikuang," 19.

SAPA and local criminal statistics confirm the general trends demonstrated in the national crime statistics. Statistics in the 1987, 1988, 1989, and 1990 editions of the *China Law Yearbook* indicate that SAPA offenses increased by 75% from 1986 to 1990, while the rate of offenses rose from 11.7 to 17.8 per 10,000 of population. As in the criminal statistics, theft accounted for the greatest single number of SAPA offenses committed in the years 1986 through 1988. Property offenses in general (including theft, swindling, grabbing and looting, and the use of superstition to swindle) accounted for 33% of the total offenses committed over the five-year period. Also apparent from the figures for SAPA offenses are an increase in violent offenses, including the use of weapons, and a decline in the efficacy of the household registration system. Assault and battery cases rose by 74% over the five-year period, and there was a 668% increase in violations of the regulations concerning knives and guns. Violations of the household registration system rose by 228%.[7]

Local statistics indicate that these national increases in crime rates disguise significant regional differences. The rapidly developing provinces of the southeast, including Guangdong, Fujian and the Guangxi Zhuang Autonomous Region showed rates of increase higher than the national average. According to Public Security Bureau statistics cited by Li Zenghui, crime in Fujian province increased every year at an average yearly rate of 22.04% from 1982 through September 1989, with the only decrease being in 1984. Statistics for Zhejiang revealed an average annual increase of 31.21% from 1986 through September 1988. In 1988 crime in both provinces was approximately 70% more than in 1987, an increase much greater than the national rate of increase of 45.1% reported for that year. At the same time, the rate at which criminal cases were being solved was found by researchers to fluctuate, with the actual number of criminal cases far greater than those investigated and put on file by the public security organs.[8]

Research undertaken by Chinese criminologists at the local level indicated that while rural areas did have lower crime rates than seen in the cities, the Chinese country-side also experienced increased crime during the 1980s. As in the urban areas, a decline in hooliganism was accompanied by increases in theft and in swindling. The nature of theft itself changed as the rural economy developed: by the late 1980s, rural thieves were no longer stealing grain, farm animals and

---

7. *Zhongguo falu nianjian, 1987*, 887; *Zhongguo falu nianjian, 1988*, 820; *Zhongguo falu nianjian, 1989*, 1085; *Zhongguo falu nianjian, 1990*, 997; *Zhongguo falu nianjian, 1991*, 942.

8. Li Zenghui, "Dangqian minzhe diqu xingshi fanzui de tedian qushi he duice," 18. According to Li, "big cases" and "very big cases" increased at even greater rates—a yearly rate of 44.44% from 1982-September 1988 in Fujian and of 51.68% of 1985-September 1988 in Zhejiang. Similar rates of increase were seen in Hunan, in which "big cases" increased by 40.7% in 1987 as compared to 1986 and increased by 81.4% in January through November 1988 as compared to the same period in 1987. See Luo Bingzhong, "Dangqian xingshi da an shangsheng de yuanyin ji duice" (Reasons and counter-measures for the current increase in serious criminal cases), *Fanzui yu gaizao yanjiu* 3 (1989), 26.

tools, but instead were taking money, consumer goods, motorcycles, and electronic goods from the homes of wealthier rural families and semi-finished and raw materials from local industries. Also on the rise were disputes related to land and water rights, crimes related to arranged marriage and bride-price, trafficking in women, and female infanticide.[9]

THEFT AND ECONOMIC CRIME

The offenses of economic crime and theft were closely related, with the category of economic crime sometimes defined in such a way as to include theft. The *Encyclopedia of Criminal Sciences* defined economic crime as "Instances of the purposeful violation of laws and regulations regarding the management of the national economy in order to gain illicit economic benefit, thus undermining economic order and posing a threat to the smooth development of the national economy or instances of illegally taking possession by various and sundry means of legitimate public or private property, undermining legally protected social economic relations, deserving of criminal punishment."[10] The *Encyclopedia* included in this category virtually every non-violent offense committed with the intention of gaining a profit: smuggling, profiteering (*touji daobazui*) tax evasion, resisting taxation (*kangshuizui*), counterfeiting the national currency, undermining collective production, counterfeiting trademarks, illegal felling of trees or denuding of forests, theft, swindling, corruption, producing and trafficking in spurious medicines, trafficking in drugs, theft and illicit export of valuable cultural relics, bribery, and the acceptance of bribes.[11] In practice, this unwieldy concept of economic crime was divided so that theft was distinguished from economic crime. The definitions of these terms were not, however, clearly stated in the law. Instead, they were worked out in practice and expressed in policy documents, in the writing of legal scholars, and in judicial interpretations.

The Criminal Law, for example, did not say what it meant by "theft." The term was defined in a judicial interpretation issued by the SPC and the SPP in 1984 as "the act of secretly taking a relatively large amount of public or private money or goods with the goal of illegal possession."[12] The Criminal Law did, however, make

---

9. Ge Tingfeng. "Zhuanzhe shiqi de nongcun fanzui wenti," 45-50; Li Baoguo. "Qiantan shangpin jingji yu shehui fanzui," 9; "Nongcun qingnian fanzui weihe zengduo," 3; Tao Liqiang and Luo Xiaopeng. "Dangqian nongmin fanzui de tedian ji fazhan qushi," 15-18.

10. Yang Chunxi et al, ed. *Xingshi faxue da cishu*, 267.

11. *Ibid.*

12. "Zuigao renmin fayuan, zuigao renmin jianchayuan guanyu dangqian banli daoqie anjian zhong juti yingyong falu de ruogan wenti de jieda", in *Zhonghua renmin gongheguo falu guifan xing jieshi jicheng*, 345. According to this document of 2 November 1984, the term "relatively large amount" should be interpreted to mean above two to three hundred yuan in most areas, or above four-hundred

the act of theft punishable by anywhere from control to various terms of imprisonment to death, depending on such circumstances as the amount of goods involved,
the use of violence, and resistance to arrest.[13] Heavier sentences were also
provided for the theft of "a relatively large amount" or a "huge amount" of public
or private property, with the latter made punishable by sentences up to and
including death by the Standing Committee of the NPC "Decision Regarding the
Severe Punishment of Criminal Elements who Seriously Endanger Public
Security."

While the definition of theft was relatively clear, the same could not be said
for economic crime. In March, 1983, the Standing Committee of the NPC's
"Decision Regarding the Severe Punishment of Criminals Who Seriously
Undermine the Economy" included certain types of theft including "theft of articles
of state property" and "theft and sale of precious cultural relics" under the rubric
of "economic crime." But in January 1989, the National Politico-legal Work
Conference was reported to have explicitly excluded the offense of theft from the
category of "economic crime."[14] Even so after ten years of enforcement of the
criminal law and several campaigns against economic crime, legal scholars could
state in 1990 that "To date, there is no standard definition of economic crime . . ."[15]
However, if we follow the lead of most writing about economic crime and of
various published collections of economic crime cases, we may understand the
concept as it operated in the 1980s to have included the offenses of smuggling,
speculation, speculative arbitrage, profiteering, extortion, misappropriation of state
funds, and the acceptance of bribes.

Both economic crime and theft increased substantially during the 1980s. In
the case of theft offenses, this increase is reflected in the number of cases placed
on file by the public security organs. For the years of 1981 through 1990,
excepting 1983 (for which there is no data), 8,090,924 cases of theft (including
serious theft) were recorded by the public security organs, the yearly number of
cases having declined from 761,247 in 1981 to 411,659 in 1984, but then rising
to 780,725 in 1988 and 2,156,211 in 1990. (See tables 1-A and 1-B) This made
theft the most common offense of which Chinese citizens were accused during the
1980s.

---

yuan in areas that had experienced faster economic development, while a "huge amount" would begin
at 2,000 to 3,000 yuan or, in economically advanced areas, 4,000 yuan. As of 1984, cases of theft by
a single individual of money or goods worth 30,000 yuan or more was considered sufficiently serious
to merit the death penalty. Provincial-level procuratorates and courts were to establish concrete figures,
based on these guidelines, in consultation with the provincial-level public security organs.

13. Criminal Law, 1979, Arts. 151, 152, 153.
14. Xie Baogui, "Jingji fanzui de gainian," 25.
15. *Ibid.*

Figures on criminal cases heard by the people's courts are not broken down by specific offense, but by the categories of offense dealt with by the seven chapters of the special provisions of the Criminal Law. It is therefore difficult to determine whether or not the increase in theft cases placed on file by the public security offices was matched by similar increases in the number of theft cases heard by the courts. Legal publications such as *People's Adjudication* and *China Legal System News* do not, however, indicate that theft cases were particularly difficult to adjudicate, nor do they say anything to indicate that the increase in theft cases put on file by the public security organs was not matched by an increase in theft cases transferred to the courts for trial. Such problems were, however, characteristic of economic offenses.

From the beginning of the period of economic reform, economic crime, in particular smuggling, corruption, illicit transfer of state funds, and bribery represented a peculiar challenge to the criminal justice system. By 1980, economic crime was said to have become far more serious than at any prior time in the history of the People's Republic. In Guangdong Province—a hot-bed of economic crime, including—profiteering cases increased by 29% from 1980 to 1981, while smuggling, corruption and bribery offenses rose at similar rates.[16] The problem, Deng Xiaoping, predicted, would continue at least until China had achieved the Four Modernizations.[17]

As if to prove Deng was right, the number of economic criminal cases was reported to have increased by 3.9 times between 1980 and 1988.[18] The increase in economic crime was variously attributed to the adverse ideological and moral effects of the Cultural Revolution, the "destructive corrosion" carried out against China by "foreign and domestic class enemies," the backward, incomplete, and, according to some, undemocratic nature of China's enterprise management, its social administrative systems, and its legal system, and in the growing opportunities for corruption present in a growing economy, and in the nature of the market economy itself.

One problem posed by the concept of economic crime was that of how to handle borderline cases. For example, if a peasant arranged with cigarette factories to sell their over-stocked cigarettes in return for a commission, and did so, was this an honest business deal or a case of profiteering and speculation? If the same peasant, having earned his commission, acceded to the demands of the county-run sugar, tobacco and spirits company and of his commune enterprise department that

---

16. Ouyang Tao, "Dangqian woguo jingji lingyu jizhong fanzui de tedian," 1-2.
17. Deng Xiaoping, "Combat Economic Crime," 381.
18. He Bingsong, "Woguo jinnian lai fanzui gaikuang," 20.

he give them a part of his profits, was he guilty of bribery?[19] If a photographer took pictures of the entire range of electronic goods available on the market and used them to compile a price index, was he a clever entrepreneur, or was he guilty of illegally expanding the scope of his business beyond that for which he was originally licensed? It was only through years of experience that the boundaries of "economic crime" could be determined. In the meantime, unknown numbers of entrepreneurs were accused and found guilty of criminal offenses by criminal justice personnel who were accustomed to believe that anyone who made large amounts of money must be guilty of *something*.[20]

While some people were being found guilty of economic crime for no better reason than having demonstrated their business acumen, others were committing serious economic offenses without being brought to court at all. During the 1980s, officials in the court system sometimes found that although instances of economic crime were on the rise, the number of cases actually brought to court not only failed to increase, but even declined. The Beijing Higher People's Court complained in 1982 that while twice as many economic crimes were detected in 1980 as in 1979, and 1.8 times as many were detected in the first quarter of 1981 as in the first quarter of 1980, and while the amount of money and goods involved in these crimes had likewise increased significantly, only four out of every one-thousand persons implicated in economic crime cases in 1980 was sentenced in court. In the first half of 1981, only one person was punished for an economic criminal offense.[21] The Hunan Higher People's Court similarly found in 1985 that while economic crime was increasing rapidly in its jurisdiction, the number of cases brought to the courts in the first nine months of the year fell by 26% as compared to the first nine months of 1984.[22] Other jurisdictions reported similar difficulty in bringing cases of economic crime to court.[23]

This problem was not confined to particular jurisdictions. In a talk delivered in October 1988, SPC vice-president Lin Zhun observed that during the first half of 1988, economic crime cases of the first instance received by the people's courts

---

19. Shan Zhanzhong, Ouyang Tao, Zhang Sihan and Zhou Daoluan, "Tantan jingji lingyu zhong yanzhong anjian dingzui he liangxing wenti," 16-17. In the case described here, the defendant was found not guilty of speculation and profiteering only after heated debate among the judges.
20. "Zhengque zhangwo jingji fanzui yu zhengdang jingji huodong de jiexian," 21-22. This article discusses the cases of the photographer and several other entrepreneurs in the same county town in Zhejiang province who were labeled "kings" on account of their business successes and found guilty of economic crime during the campaign against economic crime in 1982, only to be declared not guilty on reconsideration in 1984.
21. Shi gaoji renmin fayuan jingji shenpanting, "Dui dangqian touji daoba anjian de fenxi," 10.
22. Hunan sheng gaoji renmin fayuan yanjiushi, "Dui jingji fanzui huodong daji buli de xianxiang bixu yinqi zhongshi," 12.
23. Tianjin shi gaoji renmin fayuan bangongshi, "Dakai jumian, yanzheng jingji fanzui," 3; Guangdong sheng gaoji renmin fayuan yanjiushi, "Jingji fanzui changjue, fayuan shouan xiajiang de qingkuang, yuanyin ji duice," 3.

throughout the country had declined by 3.5% as compared to the first half of the previous year and were 23.7% lower than the same period of 1987, despite an increase in the incidence of economic crime.[24] An editorial comment in *People's Adjudication* revealed that economic cases (excluding theft) received by the people's courts in 1987 were 32.3% fewer than in 1986, and that the number of cases received continued to drop in the next few years, declining by 19.8% in 1988, and with the number of cases received in January through May 1989 11.7% less than in the same period of 1988.[25]

The reasons for the difficulty in bringing cases of economic crime to court were manifold. Certainly one of the fundamental reasons was that the majority of persons accused of economic crime were Party and state cadres, factory and enterprise managers and the like. These people were well-connected and therefore in a position to resist investigation and prosecution. Communist Party members accused of economic crime could arrange to have their cases handled as disciplinary cases within the Party rather than as criminal cases. The ability of some cadres to have cases handled in this manner was probably made easier by the degree of leadership that local Party committees exercised over the legal system.

Structural peculiarities of the legal system and of its relationship to the Communist Party and to the industrial and commercial control organs (*gongshang guanli bumen*) of provincial and local governments were also related to the difficulty in bringing economic crimes to trial. Many economic crimes were detected and handled by the industrial and commercial control bureaus, not by the public security organs. In such cases, the accused persons would be subject to a fine and possibly confiscation of goods taken in evidence and then be released. These cases were not transferred to the procuratorate for prosecution, and thus were never tried in court.

This substitution of fines for criminal punishment was inadvertently encouraged by the rules regarding the disposition of money and goods recovered from criminals. The position of the courts was that all goods and money confiscated as evidence in criminal cases should be transferred to the courts for use in trial. To support this position, the courts could point to the law and to a long-standing Party directive to the effect that goods and money taken in fines or confiscated should all be transferred to the national treasury. According to law, units that handled criminal cases were not to take a percentage of confiscations or fines for their own use.[26]

In practice, the situation was more complicated than these regulations might indicate. Regulations issued jointly by the General Office of Industrial and

---

24. Xing Yi, "Qi sheng shi fayuan shenli jingji fanzui anjian zuotanhui zai jing zhaokai," 6.

25. "Ganyu xia dayu" (Dare to 'rain hard'), *Renmin sifa* (People's adjudication) 9 (1989), 2.

26. Shi gaoji renmin fayuan jingji shenpanting, "Dui dangqian touji daoba anjian de fenxi," 11; "Yifa yanzheng jingji fanzui fenzi quebao zhili, zhengdun jingji zhixu shunli jinxing," 12.

Commercial Control (*gongshang xingzheng guanli zongju*) and the Ministry of Finance (*caizhengbu*) in 1980 stipulated that "Twenty percent of the fines taken in each case solved should be taken as a reward fund; of this amount, fifty to seventy-five percent should be given to the person who revealed the case and to work units assisting in the handling of the case, while the remaining portion should be turned over to the district (city) industrial-commercial control bureau."[27] In December 1987, a document issued by the Ministry of Finance allowed the public security, procuratorate and court organs to take thirty percent of fines and confiscations as a "supplementary case fee."[28] Such regulations contradicted the law. They also gave the industrial and commercial control bureaus a positive incentive to handle those cases which they discovered by levying fines themselves, rather than transferring them to the criminal justice system.

The lack of a clear legal definition of "economic crime" and the law's employment of language such as "serious circumstances" also offered the industrial and commercial control bureaus legal grounds for determining on their own what level of seriousness was required for the constitution of a crime. The Guangdong Higher People's Court pointed out in 1989 that in a judicial interpretation, the SPC and the SPP had defined the threshold of criminal responsibility in crimes of speculation and profiteering in terms of the amounts of money involved, but that "comrades in other legal organs" did not recognize the authority of documents issued by the SPP and the SPC. Those organs—in particular the industrial and commercial control bureaus—therefore continued to decide on their own authority just what constituted a crime and to handle what they determined to be non-criminal cases through the imposition of fines.[29]

Some economic crimes were simply not viewed as crimes, either by the persons who committed the acts, by the authorities, or at times by both. Certainly, the arrest, prosecution, and then the re-trial and declaration of the innocence of entrepreneurs convicted of economic crime during the campaign of 1982 points to a contradiction between the popular conception of economic crime and the understanding of local-level police, procuratorate and court officials. Another difference in understanding is evident in the attitude toward credit card fraud. Knowing that the victims of credit card fraud were foreign credit card companies (Chinese banks not yet having issued credit cards), some local authorities believed that credit card fraud not only did not pose a social danger, but was good for the country, and thus should not be prosecuted.[30]

---

27. Shi gaoji renmin fayuan jingji shenpanting, "Dui dangqian touji daoba anjian de fenxi," 1.

28. Guangdong sheng gaoji renmin fayuan yanjiushi, "Jingji fanzui changjue, fayuan shouan xiajiang de qingkuang, yuanyin ji duice," 3.

29. *Ibid.*

30. Song Lei, "Sheji xinyongka de zhapian fanzui yingdang yinqi zhongshi," 6.

VIOLENT CRIME

The difficulties involved in law enforcement and the uneven application of the law that we observe in the handling of theft and economic crime were also evident in the definition and the handling of violent offenses. We will consider these difficulties as seen in the offenses homicide (Criminal Law Arts. 132, 133), injury (Arts. 134, 135), the use of torture to obtain confessions (Art. 136), illegal detention (Art. 143), and the abduction and sale of people (Art. 141).[31]

As reflected in the statistics of the public security bureaus, homicide cases increased from 9,576 in 1981 to 21,214 in 1990, while cases of injury rose from 21,499 to 45,200 (see Tables 1-A and 1-B). The incidence of injury appears to have responded to the 1983 Strike Hard Campaign, falling from 20,298 cases in 1982 to 14,526 in 1984. The campaign appears to have had less effect on the incidence of homicide, of which 9,324 cases were placed on file in 1982 and 9,021 in 1984. The impression communicated by these figures is confirmed by the comments of Lin Zhun, then a vice-president of the SPC, who indicated in an interview published in early 1987 that after the three-year, three-battle Strike Hard Campaign, the number of homicide cases had not been reduced.[32]

Chinese criminologists ascribed the increase in cases of injury and homicide in the 1980s to economic and social factors. As the urban and rural economies became more marketized, disputes over resources such as land and water increased. Failure to resolve these disputes peacefully through mediation or through civil litigation was linked to increases in violence leading to injury and homicide.[33] Violent crime, and specifically homicide, was also linked to the status of women and to the continued prevalence of arranged marriage in China, particularly in the country-side. These factors were reflected in an analysis of the cases of 154 rural criminal offenders sentenced to immediate execution in Anhui Province from January 1980 through May 1982.[34] Slightly over 5% of the death sentences were for the commission of homicide due to disputes over land, farm animals, water resources and so on, while 18% were for murders arising from disputes between family members or between neighbors over issues such as the support of elder family members, division of inheritance, and division of grain

---

31. Rape (including statutory rape, Art. 139), while classified as a violent offense, was explained largely in moral terms, and will be discussed below in the context of moral offenses.

32. "Jixu guanche 'yanda' fangzhen—benkan jizhe zoufang zuigao renmin fayuan fu yuanzhang Lin Zhun," 9.

33. *Ibid.*; Luo Bingzhong, "Dangqian xingshi da'an shangsheng de yuanyin ji duice," 27; Guo Xiang, "Zhongguo dangqian de baoli fanzui he yufang duice," 6.

34. Anhui sheng gaoji renmin fayuan yanjiushi, "Cong panchu sixing anjian zhong kan jin jinian lai nongcun fasheng zhongda xianxing fanzui de xin qingkuang," 3-6. The 154 death sentences discussed in this article are said to have represented 73.7% of the 209 persons sentenced to immediate execution throughout the province during the period in question.

rations.[35] Research carried out on women prisoners in Sichuan and in Hebei provinces in the late 1980s similarly indicated that of the over 45% who were guilty of homicide, most had committed murder as a result of extra-marital affairs, either their own or their husbands, with their victims being husbands, mothers-in-law, children and other close relatives or friends.[36]

While the most common serious offense for which Chinese women were imprisoned was homicide, women were more likely to be the victims rather than the perpetrators of violent crime. Violent crimes of which females were the victims included female infanticide, rape, and trafficking in women. Of these offenses, female infanticide was clearly considered the least significant by the criminal justice system. Infanticide was recognized as a negative phenomenon which should not be reported in the openly published press, as that would have a negative effect on China's image abroad.[37] The act of killing an infant was not, however, expressly prohibited in the Criminal Law, and the question of whether or not it even constituted a crime was matter for debate in legal circles in the mid-1980s. There was a tendency to regard infanticide as a family matter that did not pose a threat to society. In judicial practice it appears that infanticide did not constitute a crime, but that in rare cases in which the means employed were considered to have been particularly cruel or the circumstances odious, the act could be prosecuted as intentional homicide.[38]

The offense of trafficking in women, like female infanticide, was related to the strong desire, particularly among rural people, to have sons to carry on the family name. The practice of trafficking in women, which had virtually disappeared during the first two decades of rule by the Communist party, reappeared in the late 1970s and increased rapidly in the 1980s.[39] Although the business of trafficking in women is said to have involved virtually all provinces, cities and autonomous regions, certain patterns emerged, with the larger part of this illicit trade bringing women by force or by trickery from the poorer western provinces, particularly Sichuan and Gansu to certain areas of the eastern provinces of Shandong, Anhui

---

35. *Ibid.*
36. Hu Congshun, "1,269 ming zaiya nufan fanzui tedian de fenxi," 31-32; Wang Hongxing and Lang Qingrong, "150 ming nuxing zuifan diaocha," 35. Similar reasons were found to underlie the problem—more common in the rural areas—of women committing bigamy. See Liu Cuiying, "Nuxing weifa fanzui de shehui xinli tedian ji yufang cuoshi," 11-12; Dai Zihong, "Wunianlai nuxing weifa fanzui de jiben qingkuang,' 25-6; Kang Shuhua, *Fanzuixue,* 269. For a study on the continued prevalence of "feudal" marriage customs, including arranged marriage and two families trading a bride for a bridegroom, see Zhang Hua, "Nongcun hunyin zhong de lifa chongtu yanjiu" Zhang attributes the strength of tradition to the continued prevalence of traditional family-centered agricultural production and to its attendant "sub-culture."
37. "Ruhe jielu xiaoji yin'an de dongxi," 12.
38. Wang Chun, "Sifa shijian zhong jige you zhengyi wenti de tantao qingkuang zongshu," 1-5.
39. This and the following paragraph draw on material from Ge Tingfeng, "Zhuanzhe shiqi de nongcun fanzui wenti," 47 and Pang Xinghua, "Qita leixing de fanzui," 343-346.

and Henan. The areas to which women were sold were typically rural areas in which the standard of living had risen enough to give single men (or their families) some disposable income, but in which living conditions were relatively worse than the wealthy eastern and southeastern coastal areas in which economic reform and opening to the outside world led to rapid economic growth. Because of their relative proximity to areas of more rapid economic development, poor counties in Shandong, Anhui and Henan saw a deficit of marriageable women. The problem was exacerbated by a peculiarity of the household registration system: upon marriage, a woman's household registration could be transferred to her husband's place of residence but not vice-versa. Women thus tended to marry out of their poor rural home villages into wealthier areas. The resulting deficit of marriageable females in certain rural areas of the east, in combination with the pressures of over-population, rural unemployment and under-employment and poverty in the western provinces provided the basis for the business of trafficking in women.

The scope of trafficking in women is difficult to determine. Complete statistical studies have not been published, and the offense of trafficking in people is not included in the breakdown of types of criminal case put on file by the public security organs that appear in the *Law Yearbook of China*.

Pang Xinghua cites incomplete statistics from Sichuan's Zhongjiang county to provide an idea of the extent of the trafficking at the local level. Between 1974 and 1979, 2,016 women and children either left or were sold from Zhongjiang county, for an average of 336 a year. From 1980 to 1986, 4,826 left or were sold, an average of 689 a year, with the peak coming in 1980-1982, when an average of 1,369 women and children a year left or were sold. Slightly over half (51.72%) were married women, with the rest being unmarried women (32.97%), teenage girls (7.98%), and children (7.34%). On the receiving end, in the three areas of Shandong province in which the sale of women was most prevalent, 1,489 cases of the sale of women and children were uncovered between 1978 and 1988, involving 336 criminal groups with a total of around 1,000 members. Most of the women sold in these areas of Shandong were unmarried and in their twenties.[40]

Methods of trafficking in women varied from the lone criminal, sometimes acting on the spur of the moment and dealing in one or a few women at a time, to the organized group with members in both the exporting and importing areas and dealing in tens or hundreds of people. Women who left their home areas on their own to seek their fortune elsewhere might be accounted for as having been kidnaped and sold, while women who were forcibly sold might eventually give in, accept their fate, and obtain a legal marriage license. Women who were the victims of traffickers might be deceived with promises of jobs or entertainment or kidnaped by force. Often, they were raped by their abductors.

---

40. Pang Xinghua, "Qita leixing de fanzui," 343.

Once sold to a man, the victims faced rape and beatings. The man's family would prevent them from escaping, locking them in the house when necessary. If a woman proved to be an unsatisfactory wife, she might be resold. These circumstances led some women to commit suicide or to attack and sometimes kill their tormentors. The authorities, however, found that trafficking in women was a particularly difficult crime to solve and prosecute. The family and the village communities of a man who had spent good money to purchase a wife tended to rally to his defense. Even local Communist Party cadres would refuse to cooperate in the investigation of cases of the sale of women in their villages. Attempts to free such women sometimes led to fights between police and villagers.[41] Once apprehended, however, persons involved in trafficking in women were subject to heavy punishment.

While homicide, injury and kidnaping and sale of women were subject to severe punishment, the same could not be said about acts of violence perpetrated by the police. The Criminal Procedure Law stated that: "The use of torture to coerce statements and the gathering of evidence by threat, enticement, deceit or other unlawful methods are strictly prohibited."[42] Under the Criminal Law, the use of torture to coerce statements was punishable by a maximum of three years of fixed-term imprisonment. However, if a person's injury, disability or death was caused, the offender was to be handled under the crime of intentional injury. This could bring a punishment of up to seven years of imprisonment in cases of serious injury and from seven to twenty years imprisonment if death resulted.[43] Despite these legal prohibitions, beatings and torture were commonly used to elicit confessions, particularly from persons held under administrative detention (such as shelter and investigation) and during the preliminary hearing stage of the criminal procedure.

Chinese analysts typically attributed the stubbornness of the problem of torture to China's "feudal" legal tradition and to the Cultural Revolution.[44] There are some grounds for both explanations. Traditional Chinese legal practice put such great emphasis on confession that it was impossible to make a conviction without the confession of the accused.[45] The use of torture to obtain confessions (and other testimony) was legally sanctioned.[46] In practice, county magistrates employed not only the legally prescribed tortures, but others as well.[47]

---

41. *Ibid.*, 346.
42. Criminal Procedure Law, 1979, Art. 32.
43. Criminal Law, 1979, Arts. 136, 134.
44. For instance, Chen Zixian, "Yanjin xingxun bigong weizhe yifa chengchu," 4-6.
45. William Jones, translator. *The Great Qing Code*, 402.
46. Van der Sprenkel, *Legal Institutions on Manchu China*, 68.
47. Extralegal tortures are described in Jin Liangnian, *Kuxing yu Zhongguo shehui*, 53-71.

In the Cultural Revolution, beatings and other torture were also used by police and others to force their victims to confess. During the more violent phases of the Cultural Revolution, bands of Red Guards took the law into their own hands, imprisoning, beating, and even killing suspected "class enemies." In 1979, in an address at a national conference of public security bureau chiefs, Peng Zhen tried to dissociate police beatings, which he described it as an aberration of the Cultural Revolution from the "tradition" of the public security forces. He advised public security officers who had beaten people during the Cultural Revolution to regard themselves as having been misled and to apologize to their victims.[48]

Whether it had its roots in the traditional Chinese legal system or in the Cultural Revolution, it is clear that coercion of testimony under torture was a fundamental, though illegal, part of the practice of criminal justice in China during the 1980s. One reason for the prevalence of torture may have been that police found it to be the easiest way to get a quick confession and thereby solve a case. Another reason appears to have been that the authorities, including those at the Party center, took a caring and forgiving attitude toward the police because of the physically demanding nature of police work.[49] Sentences imposed on public security cadres found guilty of the offense of coercion of testimony, and even of beating suspects to death during questioning, seem generally to have been relatively lenient. Of seven torture cases included in an internally published collection of cases protested by the procuratorates, the average sentence of actual prison time (counting suspended sentences as zero) was 1.8 years on the first hearing, which increased to 4.6 after procuratorial protest brought about a second hearing. The heaviest sentences passed were of eight years in prison each for two public security cadres who beat a man to death. Eight years imprisonment is only one year above the minimum for the offense of intentional injury leading to death in Article 134 of the Criminal Law. These relatively light sentences stand in contrast to the "severe punishment" being meted out to common criminals and hooligans for much lesser offenses during the Strike Hard Campaign.[50]

While it is safe to assume that the vast majority of torture cases in the 1980s were the work of public security cadres, it should be noted that the use of torture to extract confessions was not limited to the police. Ordinary citizens occasionally took the law into their own hands, detaining, questioning, and sometimes even torturing suspected criminals. The same collection of cases referred to above includes four cases of illegal detention carried out by citizens (three peasants, two Party branch secretaries, and one assistant manager of an enterprise). In all four cases, the defendants were found guilty of illegal detention and of eliciting

48. "Peng Zhen tongzhi zai quanguo gongan juzhang huiyi shangde jianghua," 123.
49. Interview file 8.
50. These cases appear in Sun Peifeng and Liu Xiuhua, ed. Kangsu anli xuanbian.

confessions under torture. In two of the cases, the offenders made tape-recordings as they carried out illegal interrogations. Two of the victims were beaten to death, and two committed suicide. The average sentence of real prison time in these cases on first hearing was 1.4 years, and on second hearing, 3 years.[51]

RAPE, SEX CRIMES, AND PUBLIC MORALITY

Under the criminal law, the offense of rape was punishable by penalties up to and including death.[52] The offense itself was defined in a judicial interpretation of 26 April 1984 as "employing violence, coercion, or other means to force sexual relations on a woman against her will." The same judicial interpretation also stated in unequivocal terms that a reputation for sexual promiscuity (*zuofeng baihuai*) and the presence or absence of "signs of resistance" on the part of the victim were both irrelevant to the determination of guilt in rape cases.[53]

Understood strictly in terms of this definition, the law against rape functioned to protect the personal sexual rights of women. Certainly this was an aspect, arguably the most important aspect, of the law on rape. The explicit recognition that the object of the law was to protect the personal rights of women distinguished the law of the People's Republic from that of traditional Chinese law. In the Qing dynasty, for example, the law of rape was concerned with the protection of women's chastity rather than with the protection of women themselves.[54] However,

---

51. *Ibid.*
52. Criminal Law, 1979, Art. 139.
53. "Zuigao renmin fayuan, zuigao renmin jianchayuan, gonganbu yinfa 'guanyu dangqian banli qiangjian anjian zhong juti yingyong falu de ruogan wenti de jieda' de tongzhi." In this legal interpretation, "Violence" is defined as (1) striking; (2) tying up; (3) throttling; (4) holding down; (5) applying other means which threaten the victim's physical safety or freedom, or which render her incapable of resistance. "Coercion" is defined as threatening to physically attack the victim in future, threatening to reveal secrets or to harm her family; scaring the victim; using superstition, fraud, relationships of subordination or guardianship or professional powers to isolate the victim and put her in a state in which she accedes and does not resist. "Other means" is explained as including the offender taking advantage of serious illness or sleep, using alcohol or drugs to render the victim incapable of self-defense, or using the excuse of curing or pretending to cure illness. The "Explanation" defines "especially serious circumstances" as (1) the use of cruel and vindictive means; (2) raping or having illicit sexual relations with many women or underage girls or violating one victim numerous times; (3) being the leader in a gang rape of women and especially of underage girls; (4) rape leading to the victim's suicide, mental illness, or other serious consequences; (5) holding up and raping a woman in a public place; (6) multiple incidents involving pornography, "dark-room dances" (dances at which the lights are turned out) or other methods to attract and then rape young women. According to the law, the presence of any one of these "especially serious circumstances" calls for a punishment from a minimum of ten years' fixed-term imprisonment to a maximum of death. Taken in conjunction with the stipulations of Art. 139, this means that in rape cases, the courts, according to their evaluation of the "circumstances" of any given case, exercise their discretion in determining a sentence of somewhere between three years' imprisonment and capital punishment.
54. Ng, "Ideology and Sexuality: Rape Laws in Qing China," 57-70.

the theory and practice of Chinese rape law of the 1980s existed in a the context of a legal system and a field of legal and criminological theory in which sex within the confines of monogamous, state-licensed marriage was regarded as being legitimate, all other sexual acts were regarded as illegitimate and possibly criminal, and in which the policing of public morality and of the "cultural marketplace" was regarded as essential for the prevention of rape and other sexual offenses. The continued link between the law of rape and the protection of a broadly conceived public morality, rather than simply the protection of women's personal rights, was evident in certain aspects of the definition of rape and in the theoretical understanding of the causes of rape.

One aspect of the moral aim of China's rape law may be seen in the difference between the legal definition of rape and the popular understanding of the offense. The definition of rape offered in the "Explanation" referred to above was more broad than the common understanding of the offense of rape in Chinese society. A study in Hunan showed that those prosecuted for rape who had posed as a lover, used superior-subordinate relations in order to coerce the victim, taken advantage of the victim's intoxication, or seduced girls or mentally ill women generally did not regard their behavior as a criminal offense. "Rape," to them, meant waylaying a woman on the road or otherwise using violent force to have sexual relations.[55] In this sense, the law was expanding the definition of rape to include various ways, non-violent as well as violent, in which a woman might be forced, tricked, or manipulated into engaging in sexual relations against her will.

But at the same time, it must be noted that in the law and in the practice of the law, there were exceptions to the definition of rape as having sexual relations with a woman against her will. First, the law did not recognize violent sexual behavior within marriage as rape. Legal scholars argued that the prevalence of arranged marriages and trafficking in women (and thus of sex within marriage but against the woman's will) meant that to prosecute rape within marriage would be unrealistic and would alienate people from the legal system.[56] Second, violent or non-violent sexual acts occurring without the prior consent of the woman and outside of marriage but within the context of a long-standing relationship, and particularly within a serious courtship (that is, a relationship which the male party sincerely intended should lead to marriage) were, in practice, subject to lesser

55. Yue Hua, "Qiangjian fa'an weishenmo jiangbuxialai?" 22.
56. Jiang Rentian, "Dui qiangjianzui zhong 'weibei funu yizhi' wenti de zai renshi," 40; Li Hong and Huang Chi, "Lun qiangjianzui de waiyan," 25. Li and Huang also argue that the character (*jian*) in *qiangjian* (rape) itself refers to sex outside of marriage, thus to refer to *qiangjian* within marriage would be contradictory.

degrees of punishment.[57] Similarly, relationships that had begun with a rape, but in which the victim then continued on other occasions to voluntarily engage in sexual relations with her former attacker were not generally prosecuted as rape. The apparently voluntary nature of the ongoing relationship was assumed to represent a fundamental change in the will of the woman who had initially been a victim.[58]

The moral dimensions of the law of rape were also evident in the way in which legal scholars explained the offense. The causes of rape were found, not in the propensity of the rapist for violence in general or the desire to commit violent acts against women, but rather in a libido uncontrolled by morality: rape was understood as the result of an unhealthy desire for sex.[59] The existence of this unhealthy degree of sexual desire and the failure of rapists to channel sexual desire into the socially acceptable format of state-licensed marriage was attributed to the continued influence of "backward" or "feudal" ideas such as arranged marriage, to the detrimental effects of the Cultural Revolution on the moral tenor of Chinese society, and to the influx of Western bourgeois culture, including pornography. Not only rape, but also sex offenses falling under the category of "hooliganism" were linked in the minds of Chinese experts to the same set of causational factors: bad character, an inordinate desire for sex, lack of concern for others, backwardness, and low educations levels.[60] Rape was, in the final analysis, regarded as a particularly serious manifestation of a broader category of deviant behavior: hooliganism.

Article 160 of the Criminal Law defined hooliganism as assembling a crowd to "have brawls, stir up fights and cause trouble, humiliate women, or engage in other hooligan activities, undermining public order, when the circumstances are odious . . . "[61] The offense itself can be traced back to Soviet law. In the legal practice of the Soviet Union, the authorities used the offense of hooliganism in

---

57. The sincerity of such relationships can be a serious issue. One school of opinion held that the existence or lack of a sincere courtship of a woman with whom a man has had sexual relations within such a relationship was the key to determining whether or not the sexual behavior should be viewed as rape after the couple had parted ways. If the relationship had been sincere, then sexual acts performed within that relationship could not have been rape; if the relationship had not been sincere, then the man would be guilty of rape, even if his girlfriend had been willing at the time, because her willingness had been the result of a deception. See Li Zhongfang, *Xing yu fa*, 189. This point of view, though it may have reflected social mores, was not in line with the provisions of the "Explanation," (art. 3, para.1) which classified such deceivers as hooligans, rather than as rapists.

58. "Zuigao renmin fayuan, zuigao renmin jianchayuan, gonganbu yinfa 'guanyu dangqian banli qiangjian anjian zhong juti yingyong falu de ruogan wenti de jieda' de tongzhi," Art. 2, para. 2, The idea that consent could be given after the fact was also present in traditional Chinese law. See Meijer, *The Introduction of Modern Criminal Law in China*, 89.

59. Fang Qiang, *Fazhi xinlixue gailun*, 102-113.

60. See Liu Dalin et al., ed. *Zhongguo dangdai xing wenhua*, 617.

61. Criminal Law, 1979, Art. 160.

order to punish drunken, rowdy behavior, random violence, and, on occasion, political offenses.[62] In Deng's China, the offense was similarly used to punish the gang-fighting and random street violence that had been among the targets of the Strike Hard campaign. But in addition to dealing with these violent offenses, the law of hooliganism in China was written and interpreted in ways that allowed it to be used as a weapon in the Party's effort to guide the development of Chinese "spiritual civilization" by punishing a variety of moral offenses.

Under the rubric of "other hooligan activities," the criminal offense of hooliganism included a variety of sexual behavior not expressly prohibited by law: homosexual acts, extra-marital sex, promiscuity, group sex, and prostitution.[63] All these were regarded as "sex crimes," a term that did not appear anywhere in the Criminal Law, but was defined by one Chinese criminologist as "criminal behavior in sexual relations, undermining social order, offending public decency, poisoning the social atmosphere, destroying socialist relationships, and infringing upon citizens' rights of the persons, causing harmful consequences and deserving punishment by law."[64]

Both men and women were prosecuted for sex crimes. But while male criminal offenders were overwhelmingly guilty of theft, other property offenses, and violent crimes, sex offenses accounted for the largest proportion of women criminal offenders and law-breakers (i.e., women sentenced to labor reform for criminal offenses or to labor re-education for SAPA violations). Research on women prisoners in Sichuan and Zhejiang provinces indicated that the ratio of homicide offenders[65] to those guilty of less serious crimes varied as the targets of the criminal justice system shifted. During the Strike Hard Campaign of 1983-84, relatively larger numbers of sex offenders were prosecuted on criminal charges and sentenced to fixed-term imprisonment. The percentage of homicide offenders in the women's prisons decreased accordingly.[66] In Zhejiang, by 1988, sex offenders had dropped to 32.76% of women criminals, from a high of 72.03% in 1983. At the same time, sex offenders accounted for 94.89% of women in labor reeducation. If both labor re-education *and* prisoner populations are taken into account, then, even in the late 1980s, sex offenses appear to have remained the

---

62. Chalidze, *Criminal* Russia, 76-79, 91; Zeldes, *The Problem of Crime*, 12.

63. Zhang Zhehui, *Woguo xingfa zhong de liumang fanzui*, 158-61, 176-77, 256-58.

64. Li Xiaoying, "Shaonu xing zuicuo de chengyin," 30.

65. Homicide being the most common serious offense for which women were incarcerated, as opposed to theft for men.

66. Chen Yu, Tang Guofang, Xu Shiying and Chen Xiuping, "Yanda hou xinshou nufan de qingkuang he tedian," 198; Zhao Rongguo, "yanda tougai de nu shaonian zhong chuxian de xin qingkuang," 212.

single greatest reason for which women were punished, whether in Zhejiang itself, or in China as a whole.[67]

In addition to being charged with "hooligan promiscuity," female sex offenders were often charged with prostitution. In the definition and the handling of the offense, however, contradictions were evident between the Criminal Law, the SAPA, and social practice. The Criminal Law did not make the act of exchanging sex for money or other favors illegal. It did criminalize the acts of forcing, luring or keeping women in prostitution for the purpose of reaping profits in Articles 14 and 169). The tenor of the Criminal Law, then, was to cast the prostitute as a victim and the prostitutor as the offender. The SAPA, however, made the act of selling sex itself punishable by up to fifteen days of detention, a warning, a maximum fine of five-thousand yuan or, in "serious" cases, labor re-education.

In practice, the criminal justice system and some criminologists reacted to the rapid increase in prostitution in the 1980s by holding women who engaged in prostitution morally and even criminally responsible for their actions. Extensive and well-publicized campaigns against prostitution were carried out periodically throughout the 1980s, as women involved in the sex trade were rounded up for compulsory re-education and medical treatment.[68] The customers of prostitutes, although they could theoretically be punished for the offense of hooligan promiscuity, were rarely touched by the law.[69]

---

67. Dai Zihong, "Wunianlai nuxing weifa fanzui de jiben qingkuang," 261. Nanjing shi sifaju zhengce yanjiushi laogai laojiaochu Yangmeitang laojiaosuo, "Dangqian nu qingshaonian fan zuicuo de tedian," 190 states that 77% of women labor reeducation inmates surveyed were serving time for hooliganism (i.e. "sexual promiscuity"—see below); Zhao Rongguo, "'Yanda' tougai de nu shaonianfan zhong chuxian de xin qingkuang," 211 reports that of all juvenile (14-17) women in Jiangsu's reform schools, 96.5% were guilty of hooligan promiscuity; Zhang Li, "Dangqian nu qingshaonian laojiao renyuan de zhuyao tedian," 219 finds that 82% of woman labor reeducation prisoners surveyed were guilty of hooliganism; Huang Siyuan, "Jue buke hushi nu qingshaonian weifa fanzui," 21, finds that of women labor reeducation inmates 15-20 years old surveyed, 60.2% were guilty of hooliganism; Pang Xinghua "Shaonu xing zuicuo yanbian guocheng yu xinli tedian," 28 finds that 80% of juvenile prisoners surveyed were guilty of sex crimes.

68. "Zuigao renmin fayuan, zuigao renmin jianchayuan, gonganbu guanyu maiyin piaosu anchang anjian ying ruhe chuli de yijian" ; "Guowuyuan guanyu jianjue quti maiyin huodong he zhizhi xingbing manyan de tongzhi"; "Gonganbu guanyu yange yifa banshi, zhixing zhengce, shenru kaizhan chu 'liuhai' douzheng de tongzhi." The language employed by these documents is as instructive as the measures called for. The wording is very strong, exuding a hollow confidence, with the leadership calling for prostitution to be "eliminated," as the Party cells of the Women's Federation and the Ministry of Public Security declared: "we must grasp the problem to the very end, and absolutely not allow this hideous social phenomenon to be reborn and continue to spread." See "Zhonggong zhongyang bangongting zhuanfa gonganbu quanguo fulian liangdangzu guanyu jianjue quti maiyin huodong de baogao."

69. In discussions regarding a draft law on prostitution, members of the NPC, the Women's Federation and the Ministry of Public Security suggested that this hypocritical situation be remedied and that not only prostitutes, but also their customers, be taken in for re-education. See "Quanguo renda falu

128

CRIMINALS

If we take them as a whole, we find that China's criminals in the reform era were overwhelmingly young men of worker and peasant background. This is not unusual. Young men almost always commit crimes at higher rates than do middle-aged men, old men, or women. But during the 1980s, Chinese authorities detected an alarming increase, not only in the number, but also in the proportion, of crimes committed by youth (*qingshaonian*, defined in Chinese as persons aged fourteen through twenty-five). In the 1950s, both the rate of youth crime and the proportion of youth crime to total criminal offenses were substantially lower than they became in the 1980s. Accompanying the increase in youth crime was an overall decrease in the average age of youth offenders.

The greatest number of youth crimes in the late 1980s were property offenses—theft, swindling, looting, profiteering and smuggling, the most common being theft. Together, these accounted for approximately 75% of the total.[70] Other commonly committed offenses included violent crime (assault, rape, and homicide) and sex crimes. Overall, youth crime in the 1980s appears to have been character-ized by an increase in violent crime, a large increase in theft, and a peak rate of sex crimes in 1983-84 associated with the anti-crime campaign.[71] Other characteristics included the development of narcotics offenses, an increasing sophistication and maturity on the part of youth offenders, a rapid increase in the rate of offenses among young women, and an increase in recidivism, from 5% in the 1950s to 10% in the 1980s, and in some areas, as high as 15% in the early 1990s.[72] In addition, a large proportion of youth offenses were committed by members of "hooligan groups." Counter-revolutionary offenses accounted for only 1% of the total number of youth offenses.[73]

---

weiyuanhui dui 'guanyu yanjin maiyin piaochang de jueding (caoan' shenyi jieguo de baogao," 51. Statistics on customers of prostitutes apprehended in Guangzhou showed that 23.7% were farmers, 19.6% private entrepreneurs, 21.5% white and blue collar workers, 5.5% cadres, 16.5% transients, and 8.2% other mainland Chinese. Men from Hong Kong and Macau, Overseas Chinese, and foreigners together accounted for 5%. See Zhang Shaoquan and Deng Juncai, "Dangqian maiyin piaochang huodong de tedian ji qi duice," 7.

70. Kang Shuhua, ed. *Fanzuixue*, 208.

71. *ibid.*, 209-210; Xinxiang diqu zhongji renmin fayuan, "Guanyu qingshaonian fanzui qingkuang de diaocha fenxi" (Investigation and analysis of the youth crime situation), *Sifa* (Jurisprudence) 7 (1985), 16; Heilongjiang sheng renmin jianchayuan nenjiang fenyuan, "Guanyu qingshaonian fanzui wenti de diaocha baogao," 27.

72. Kang Shuhua, *Fanzuixue*, 210-215. See also Cao Manzhi, *Zhongguo qingshaonian fanzuixue*, 39; Heilongjiang haerbin shi zhongji renmin fayuan, "Dui qingshaonian fanzui de qingkuang, tedian, he yuanyin de chubu fenxi," 2-3.

73. Kang Shuhua, *Fanzuixue*, 208, 211.

A small number of criminals were identified as sufferers of mental illness. In the late 1980s it was estimated that 2.1% of the population suffered mild forms of mental illness, while 1.1% were seriously afflicted. The rate of serious mental illness appeared to be increasing, having been .27% in the 1950s and .54% in the 1970s. According to these figures, there were over 10 million people suffering from serious mental illnesses in the 1980s, of whom about 7% were said to present a social danger. In Shanghai alone, the authorities estimated approximately 80,000 mentally ill, of whom 10,000 were a threat to public security.[74] The mentally ill were reported to commit a number of crimes, from homicide to terrorizing train passengers to standing on the railway tracks and disrupting train traffic.[75]

Women represented a small but rapidly increasing proportion of criminal offenders. In 1987, 12% of total criminal offenses were committed by women, and women comprised 3.6% of the total criminal offenders serving prison terms.[76] The trend of the 1980s and early 1990s, however, was one of almost continuous increase in the rates of crime and law-breaking by women, a decrease in the average age of offenders, and a growing variety of the type of offense committed.[77] In 1985, women accounted for 13.3% of the total criminal offenders arrested, and for 18.64% of total youth (*qingshaonian*) offenders. Research in one unidentified province suggested that the rate of criminality among young women increased by a factor of six in the period 1985-1986. At the same time, male youth offenses increased by only two times.[78]

Criminals were considered to be dangerous, not only for the acts which they might perpetrate on others, but also because their presence in society was said to pollute the social atmosphere and to lead others into lives of moral dissolution and crime. While male and female criminals were understood to pose this broader social danger, women, and particularly women sex offenders, were seen by some criminologists as exercising an especially strong corrupting influence on others. In the words of one criminologist who wrote on women hooligans: "the main danger of their crimes was a spiritual danger, that is, they polluted the [social] atmosphere, disseminated poisonous germs, corrupted others, and adversely

74. "Woguo jingshenbing huanzhe yida 1000 wan," 1; "Woshi jingshenbing guanzhi gongzuo xiaoguo hao," 3; "Dazhong chengshi ying jinkuai jianli jingshenbing guanzhi yiyuan," 1; "Jiaqiang dui jingshen bingren de jianhu gongzuo," 1; Shanghai gongan nianjian bianjibu, ed., *Shanghai gongan nianjian (1988)*, 22-23; Chen Zhongshun, "Daxue jingshen weisheng," 92-94.
75. Wang Fusen, "Jingshen bingren ganrao tielu yunshu riyi yanzhong," 3; "Jingshen bingren fanzui de yiban tedian," 3; "Jingshen bingren weihai zhian riyi tuchu," 1.
76. Kang Shuhua, *Fanzuixue*, 213.
77. Chen Yu, Tang Guofang, Xu Shiying and Chen Xiuping, "Yanda hou xinshou nufan de qingkuang he tedian," 197-98; Pang Xinghua, "Shaonu xing zuicuo yanbian guocheng yu xinli tedian," 28; Lu Xiaoying, "Shaonu xing zuicuo de chengyin," 30.
78. Kang Shuhua, ed. *Fanzuixue*, 213.

affected social stability."[79] Promiscuous women were regarded as encouraging law-breaking by men who sought their favor and as having "a stronger power to affect others and greater powers of enticement than males."[80] They were also seen to exercise a bad influence on other young women, "pulling them into the water" and to function as the social nexus through which men and women with hooligan tendencies became acquainted with each other and formed some of the loosely organized "hooligan groups" that were a main target of the 1983-84 Strike Hard campaign.[81]

Criminologists located the fundamental causes of criminality in the social, educational, and family environment of the criminal offender. In the early 1980s, criminologists and Party leaders alike found the causes of crime in the moral and economic results of the Cultural Revolution. As time went on and crime rates continued to rise, the explanatory power of the Cultural Revolution faded. Instead, criminal behavior came to be linked to unemployment, under-employment and to disparities in the distribution of wealth. Research on crime rates in the late 1980s, for example, found a correlation between increases in rural crime, surplus labor in the rural areas, and the shrinkage of the job market.[82] Increases in theft and in serious theft in rural and urban areas, and the problem of theft committed by migrants searching for work in urban areas were clearly linked on the one hand to increased standards of living and on the other to the increasing disparity in the distribution of wealth as China abandoned egalitarianism to allow some people to get rich first.

Unemployment and regional disparities in the distribution of wealth were clearly implicated in the increased incidence of trafficking in women and in prostitution. The net flow of women was from poor and/or heavily populated western provinces such as Sichuan, Gansu and Shaanxi to areas of eastern provinces such as Shandong and Anhui that were, although poor relative to the boom areas of Guangdong and Fujian, relatively better off than the more backward western areas. Studies of prostitution in the urban areas of the eastern coastal areas, too, revealed that the women involved were predominantly unemployed, uneducated rural women who had migrated to the cities in search of work.

---

79. Zhao Rongguo. "'Yanda' tougai de nu shaonianfan zhong chuxian de xin qingkuang," 215.

80. Zhang Zhehui, *Liumangzui*, 111-113. This evaluation of the relatively greater danger posed by female criminals may also be found in nineteenth century European criminology. Charles Lucas, a French criminologist, stated that "the criminality of women is more dangerous than men, because it is more contagious, just as their morality is more expansive." Quoted in Michelle Perrot, "Delinquency and the Penitentiary System in Nineteenth-Century France," 183-84.

81. Zhao Rongguo, "'Yanda' tougai de nu shaonianfan zhong chuxian de xin qingkuang," 212; Lu Xiaoying, "Shaonu xing zuicuo de chengyin," 30; Zhang Li, "Dangqian nu qingshaonian laojiao renyuan de zhuyao tedian," 220; Heilongjiang sheng renmin jianchayuan Nenjiang fenyuan, "Guanyu qingshaonian fanzui wenti de diaocha baogao," 26.

82. Tao Liqiang and Luo Xiaopeng, "Dangqian nongmin fanzui de tedian ji fazhan qushi," 17-18.

Research on prostitution in Guangdong found that women engaging in prostitution in that province were overwhelmingly from Sichuan, Hunan, and Liaoning: Sichuan because its large population and dire poverty forced women to regard prostitution as a means of survival, Hunan because of poverty in combination with proximity to Guangdong, and Liaoning because its large, money-losing state industries were unable to pay wages and sometimes even fired workers.[83] The shortage of jobs for women in particular and the tendency for women to be the first to be dismissed from their jobs during period of economic restructuring were also factors contributing to prostitution.[84]

Problems in the educational system were also linked to the increase in crime. One problem was, of course, the lack of adequate schools, particularly in the poorer rural areas, but also in urban centers. Criminologists pointed to drop-out figures and youth crime rates and argued that as millions of young Chinese discontinued their education in primary or junior high school, they formed a large pool of potential criminal offenders.[85] For example, about one third of the juvenile offenders arrested in Beijing in the early 1980s were school drop-outs. In the late 1980s, this figure had increased to two thirds.[86] Another source reports that in the cities of an unidentified province which had a 3% junior high school drop-out rate, 39% of the drop-outs had committed either law-breaking or criminal behavior.[87]

Another aspect of the problem was the lack of opportunities for advancement within the school system, even for those who wanted to continue. For instance, even in Beijing in 1987, there were 80,000 junior high school students who weren't able to advance to senior high school for lack of places. Criminologists regarded these students, along with drop-outs, as a possible source of youth

---

83. Interview file 13.
84. Pi Yijun, "Maiyin xianxiang de chengyin tantao," 28; Liu Shengrong and Zhi Jun "Yantai shi maiyin anjian de diaocha," 11; Wang Shaolan, "Maiyin funu weifa xinli qianxi," 22; Cao Yi, "Guangzhou shi maiyin funu qingkuang poxi," 44; Da Dan. "Dui 203 ming maiyin renyuan bijiao fenxi," 44; Liu Dalin, ed. *Zhongguo dangdai xing wenhua*, 613. Pi Yijun also finds prostitution related to the concentration of wealth and power in the hands of men in a "patriarchal society," pointing to such cultural phenomenon as the use of women's bodies in advertising, arranged marriage, the commonly accepted practice of exchange of large amounts of money and goods as an essential part of "love marriages," and the exchange of sex in return for job transfer, change of household registration, approval of emigration, or as a means of gaining admission to the Youth League or to the Communist Party, and concluding that: "What those who sell sex do is merely to take the motivations accumulated in the social consciousness and express them in a more extreme form." Pi Yijun, " Maiyin de chengyin tantao," 31.
85. Wu Kaiyi, "Liushisheng fanzui chengyin qianxi," 27; Shao Daosheng, "Qiwu qijian de fanzui fazhan qushi ji qi duice," 8.
86. Kang Shuhua, *Fanzuixue*, 211.
87. Deng Youtian and Deng Xiuming, "Dangqian zhongxiaoxue shisheng weifa fanzui de zhuangkuang yu tedian," 12. See also Huang Jingxiang, "Shenzhenshi qingshaonian fanzui zhuangkuang ji tedian," 21. According to Huang, school drop-outs from other areas who came in search of jobs but failed to find them were a major source of youth crime in Shenzhen.

crime.[88] Similarly, officials in Keshan County, Heilongjiang Province, saw a connection between a 4% youth crime rate and the lack of opportunity for fifteen and sixteen year-olds to advance to senior high school.[89]

While lack of education or failure to be in school was identified as one cause of crime, certain characteristics of the school system itself, even in the wealthier urban areas, may have contributed to increased youth crime. Within the school system, schools were classified into "key schools," which catered to the most gifted students or those whose parents had the necessary connections and/or money to get their children registered, average schools, and what teachers referred to as "bottom-of-the-pocket schools" (*doudi xuexiao*). Key schools, of course, got the best teachers and facilities and better funding. Even within the schools, students were divided into fast and slow classes. In the words of one writer, the result was that "all kinds of contradictions are accumulated in the 'bottom-of-the-pocket' schools and in the slow classes. When the 'two-bad' students [those who have both bad grades and bad behavior] are grouped together, they influence each other. They feel that their prospects are bleak, so they don't study hard. Students who were originally just poor in their studies learn all sorts of bad habits. This creates a large number of drop-outs, some of whom go down the road to law-breaking and crime."[90]

The failure of some parents to correctly raise their children was also cited as a cause of the youth crime wave of the 1980s. An article that appeared in the *Beijing Legal System News* in October, 1990 provides an example of this sort of argument.[91] The author, Shi Po, states that family problems are a major cause of youth crime and adds that "in comparison to education in school and in society, education in the family remains a weak link . . ." As the family is the first unit of socialization, and as the head of the family must take the primary responsibility for the moral instruction of his children, then the results of socialization within the family "depend on the character of the head of the family himself, on his moral and cultural level."

According to this argument, the parents of youth who become criminals themselves have low moral and educational levels. Parents of young criminal offenders were blamed for spoiling their children, particularly younger or only children, or for demanding complete obedience, setting unrealistically high goals,

---

88. Liu Guangren, "Dangqian Beijingshi weichengnianren weifa fanzui ji yufang," 33.
89. Heilongjiang sheng renmin jianchayuan Nenjiang fenyuan, "Guanyu qingshaonian fanzui wenti de diaocha baogao," 28.
90. Beijingshi zhongxiaoxuesheng liushi yu weifa fanzui lianhe diaochazu, "Buke hushi de yige yanzhong shehui wenti," 28.
91. Shi Po, "Qingshaonian fanzui yu jiating jiaoyu," 2.

and using inappropriate disciplinary measures such as scolding, severe beatings, or even eviction from the household.[92]

There is a common theme running through the various explanations of crime. That theme is the alienation of the individual from the group and his/her consequent failure to develop a healthy moral sense. The unemployed worker, the student who has left or been forced out of school, the "two-bads" student who has been relegated to the bottom of the class, and the disobedient youth thrown out of the house by his/her angry parents are all deprived of the nurturing atmosphere that is regarded as essential not only for one's physical, but also for one's moral development. In the criminological literature, even victims of crime are portrayed as finding themselves suddenly thrust beyond the pale of society and thus deprived of the social context that is essential for the continuous nurturing of a healthy moral sensibility. Thus women who have been the victims of seducers or rapists and have lost their chastity are portrayed as having given up all hope of living a normal life in a society in which the greatest importance is attached to a woman's reputation for virtue. In their despair, they pursue a dissolute life of hooliganism and prostitution because no alternative is left to them. Similarly, a casebook published by the SPP described some victims of theft being forced into prostitution because they had no other means of supporting themselves.[93]

While law-breaking behavior and criminality were associated with various social and economic factors, the Criminal Law, criminology, and the statements of the Communist party leadership reflected a strong commitment to the principle that the individual, no matter what his or her social, economic, or family circumstances, is morally responsible for his or her own actions.[94] From the Central Committee of the Communist Party's characterization of hooligans as "dregs of society" to a high-ranking procuratorial official's description of thieves

---

92. For examples and discussion of youth being thrown out of, or leaving home and finding refuge with similarly rejected youths in street society, see: Zhang Fanshi and Wang Ya'nan, "Fanzui shaonian renji guanxi diaocha yanjiu," 13-23; Heilongjiang sheng renmin jianchayuan nenjiang fenyuan, "Guanyu qingshaonian fanzui wenti de diaocha baogao," 28; Liu Cuixiao, "Faxuejie dui qingshaonian fanzui de yuanyin he tedian taolun de zongshu," 5; Wu Kaiyu, "Liushisheng fanzui chengyin qianxi," 26. Wu Kaiyu characterizes the networks of human relations which form among lawbreakers and criminals as "ice-cold," presumably in contrast to the "warmth" of human relations within a family or mainstream society.

93. Ouyang Tao, ed. *Daoqiezui, guanqiezui*, 27.

94. There are exceptions: persons under the age of sixteen (or under the age of fourteen for killing, serious robbery, arson, habitual theft or other crimes seriously undermining the social order) were not to be held criminally liable, although they could be given shelter and rehabilitation by the government. Mentally ill persons were not held criminally responsible for their acts. Criminal Law, 1979, Arts. 14 and 15.

as lazy, undisciplined persons whose personal hygiene leaves much to be desired[95] to the remarks of criminologists that women engaged in prostitution because they lacked a sense of shame, had an unrestrained appetite for luxury, and were unable to control their sexual desires,[96] one observes throughout the Chinese literature on crime a strong sense of moral outrage. The criminal is described as a person who has lost, or failed to develop, basic standards of morality, discipline, shame, and concern for others.

At the same time, criminologists and the law assumed that the law-breaker or the criminal did have the potential to be good, and that the social, cultural, and economic milieu of the People's Republic did, despite certain shortcomings, provide the context in which individuals could fairly be expected to develop a healthy sense of morality and self-discipline. The stage was thus set for the punishment by execution of those whose acts were so evil as to signal their complete and utter alienation from human society and for the education and reform of those who, although having taken a wrong turn in life, were considered capable of responding positively to the concentrated efforts of state and society to bring them back into the fold and give them a new life by including them in collective work and study.

---

95. "In recent years, theft has been spreading daily in the cities and the rural areas throughout the country. In some places, especially in urban areas, marketplaces, and along transportation lines, these activities have been rampant, and theft is all the vogue. It is getting worse and worse, and the breadth of the area affected, the numbers of people participating in theft, the cunning of their methods, and the losses caused are shocking. Some victims are fearful of being made targets of revenge and bringing murder on their own heads, so that although robbed, they dare not speak out. When the masses talk about theft, their faces lose color. It is impossible to defend effectively against it. It has already reached the point where 'each fears for himself' and nobody can bear it anymore. Some workers are afraid that their homes will be robbed when they are at work, and afraid of being pick-pocketed when they go out the door. They are nervous and can't put their hearts into their work. In some cases one person is victimized and his whole family suffers. With the family in economic difficulty, he may sell off everything he owns, and even his wife and children may leave him. Some people are left with nothing to live on after being robbed, and are forced into prostitution." Ouyang Tao, ed. *Daoqiezui, guanqiezui*, 27.

96. Zhang Shu, "Shilun maiyin xinli jiegou de tezheng—dui 188 ming maiyin funu de diaocha," 15-16; Zhang Shaoquan and Deng Juncai, "Dangqian maiyin piaochang huodong de tedian ji qi duice," 8; Wang Duoyou, "Dui fan maiyin zuicuo nu laojiao renyuan de diaocha poxi," 21-22. However, Cao Yi, in an investigation of prostitutes in Guangzhou, concludes that only very exceptionally do women engage in prostitution for pleasure. See Cao Yi, "Guangzhou shi maiyin funu qingkuang poxi ," 45.

6

PUNISHMENT: EXECUTION AND LABOR REFORM

The struggle of the proletariat and the revolutionary people to change the world comprises the fulfilment of the following tasks: to change the objective world and, at the same time, to change their own subjective world . . . the objective world that is to be changed also includes the opponents of change, who, in order to be changed, must go through a stage of compulsion before they can enter the stage of voluntary, conscious change.

Mao Zedong, "On Practice," 81.

. . . execution is one of the indispensable means of education . . .

Deng Xiaoping, "Talk at a Meeting of the Standing Committee of
the Political Bureau of the Central Committee," 137.

Increasing crime rates in the context of economic reform and opening to the outside posed new problems for the punitive stage of the criminal procedure. According to law, those individuals whose offenses were considered minor might be fined, given suspended sentences, or sentenced to a term of "control," during which they would remain at their places of work and residence to be supervised and reformed by the masses. But the increasing number of serious criminal offenders faced more severe punishment: imprisonment in labor reform camps or immediate execution.

Note: An earlier version of this chapter was published in *China Information: A Quarterly Journal on Contemporary China Studies*, Leiden, Vol. IX, Nos. 2/3, Winter 1994-1995, pp. 40-71.

Execution and labor reform were both regarded as instruments with which to reform Chinese society. The threat of execution and the negative example of the condemned criminal were meant to exercise a deterrent effect on possible future criminals. Labor reform, in addition to having a deterrent effect on those who stood in danger of falling into patterns of criminal behavior, was also meant to transform each individual criminal offender, remolding him or her through the experience of disciplined study and group labor under a strict, yet humane and caring prison milieu. But while they were intended to perform in ways beneficial to the larger task of the reform of Chinese society, the practice of both execution and labor reform inevitably were accompanied by embarrassments, difficulties and contradictions which were linked to the process of economic reform and opening to the outside world.

EXECUTION

As reflected in the comments of Deng Xiaoping quoted at the beginning of this chapter, one of the goals of execution was to "educate" others. The death penalty was intended not only to punish the offender, but to educate the masses. Thus the choice of which offenders to execute, the mode of their execution, and the presentation of their execution to the public were far more significant than the simple fact of execution itself. The use of the death penalty for particular offenses, the procedure for the approval of death sentences, the announcement of sentence, the public display of the criminal prior to execution, the carrying out of execution, the disposition of the body of the criminal, and the disposition of any written documents or objects that he/she may have left behind were therefore all of matters of the utmost importance.

Announcement of sentence and the public display of the condemned criminal were meant to have an educational effect on the populace at large and on potential criminal offenders in particular. To achieve the desired effect it was not necessary to publicly announce and report each and every capital sentence. Cases for public display were chosen on the grounds of their potential social impact. In chosen cases, the accused might be sentenced at a mass sentencing rally held in a venue of appropriate size (such as a sports stadium), rather than in the smaller confines of a court-room.

In many cities, particularly during the early 1980s, it was common for condemned criminals, sometimes bearing signs announcing their name, crime, and sentence, to be paraded through the streets on flat-bed trucks. This practice of publicly parading the condemned appears to have been the subject of some disagreement between Party and criminal justice authorities at the Party center in Beijing and local party and criminal justice organs. In documents issued in 1984, in 1986, and in 1988, the Communist Party Central Committee's Propaganda bureau, the SPC, the SPP, the Ministry of Justice and the Ministry of Public Security all ordered an end to public parading of condemned prisoners.[1] Such displays, these documents stated, were uncivilized, had a negative social effect inside and outside of China, and were in violation of the Criminal Procedure Law. Nonetheless, the public display of criminals continued. We may conclude that at least some local Party and criminal justice officials were convinced that such displays were an effective means of propaganda.

According to law, executions were not to take place in the public view.[2] Descriptions of executions indicate that the condemned would kneel down and be shot, either through the heart with a semi-automatic rifle, or in the back of the head with a pistol or an ordinary rifle.[3] During the 1980s, executions, although not supposed to be public, were at times held near busy areas or transportation routes, where they could be seen. Photographs and videotapes of executions were made by personnel of the courts and other criminal justice organs, and even, on occasion, by reporters. Publication of photographs of an execution in Guangxi province in *Time* magazine and other foreign media prompted the Propaganda Bureau of the Central Committee of the CCP, along with the SPP, the SPC and the ministries of Public Security and of Justice to call for more strict control over photography of executions. Further regulations concerning the choice of places to carry out executions and the control and display of photographs of executions were issued in 1990.[4] According to the new regulations, only court photographers would be permitted to attend executions. If any other criminal justice units or, in exceptional cases, news media units, should require photographs of an execution, they would be required to borrow them from the court, which would also have to approve any news stories in which such materials were used.

---

1. "Zuigao renmin fayuan, zuigao renmin jianchayuan, gonganbu, sifabu guanyu zhixing sixing yanjin youjie shizhong de tongzhi"; "Zuigao renmin fayuan, zuigao renmin jianchayuan, gonganbu guanyu jianjue zhizhi jiang yijue fan, weijuefan youjie shizhong de tongzhi."
2. Criminal Law, 1979, Article 155. In 1979, however, there was at least one instance in which an execution was televised. Hood, *The Death Penalty*, 133.
3. Huang Tiemao, "Zhixing sixing sheji zuijia buwei de shangque," 22. While reporting that some executions are carried out by shooting the offender through the heart with a semi-automatic rifle, while in others, the shot is administered to the back of the head by a pistol or an ordinary rifle, Huang made it clear that he favored the latter on grounds that the shot is easier to make accurately, it can usually be accomplished with only one bullet, death comes so quickly that there is no worry that someone might steal the corpse and revive it, and that it leaves the vital organs intact for transplant operations. He recommended that a law be passed stipulating that all executions be carried out with a shot in the back of the head.
4. "Zhonggong zhongyang xuanchuanbu, zuigao renmin fayuan, zuigao renmin jianchayuan, gonganbu, sifabu guanyu yanfang fandong baokan liyong wo chujue fanren jinxing zaoyao wumie de tongzhi"; "Gonganbu, zuigao renmin fayuan, zuigao renmin jianchayuan guanyu yange kongzhi zai sixing zhixing xianchang jinxing paishe he caifang de tongzhi."

Another sensitive issue was that of the disposition of the bodies of criminal offenders. In 1981, the authorities noted that although there was an urgent need for bodies for dissection and for the supply of organs for organ transplants, the use of bodies for dissection and medical purposes was regarded with repugnance not only on the part of the family of the offender, but also in Chinese society in general. It was thus necessary to proceed with caution in the use of the bodies of executed criminals. The policy of 1981 was to follow regulations established in the 1950s that allowed the medical establishment to use the bodies of persons who had no family to claim them. Otherwise, the permission of the family of the deceased was to be obtained before his/her body could be dissected.[5] In 1984, provisional regulations regarding the use of corpses or organs of executed criminals was promulgated. These regulations required medical personnel to arrive at the execution grounds in unmarked vehicles and forbid the use of bodies or organs of ethnic minority people in Han majority areas.[6] The harvesting of organs from the bodies of executed offenders reportedly took place at the rate of 2,000 to 3,000 cases per year in the late 1980s-early 1990s.[7]

Although carried out at lower levels, all executions had to be reported to the Supreme People's Court in Beijing.[8] Regulations concerning the reporting of executions were laid forth in 1979. The courts were required to forward the relevant case files, as well as photographs of the condemned taken immediately before and after the execution.[9] In 1984, the SPC re-iterated these regulations, noting that due to the substantial increase in executions in connection with the Strike Hard campaign, courts had been submitting incomplete reports.[10]

Public announcement of selected executions was made in large posters which included the name and other personal information of the condemned, a short description of his/her crime, and an announcement of the sentence. A large red check indicated that the sentence had already been carried out. According to documents issued in the 1980s, cases to be announced were to be carefully chosen for their "educational significance." The posters were not supposed to be displayed in public places in cities or towns open to foreign tourists, advisors, or students.

---

5. "Sifabu guanyu panchu sixing fanren de shiti liyong wenti de fuhan."
6. "Zuigao renmin fayuan, zuigao renmin jianchayuan, gonganbu, sifabu, weishengbu, minzhengbu guanyu liyong sixing zuifan shiti huo shiti qiguan de zanxing guiding."
7. Hood, *The Death Penalty*, 136.
8. According to the Criminal Procedure Law, 1979, Art. 155, the people's court would notify the family of an offender after his/her execution had been carried out.
9. "Zuigao renmin fayuan guanyu baosong sixing fuhe anjian de fanxiang guiding de tongzhi."
10. "Zuigao renmin fayuan guanyu tongyi baosong sixing beian cailiao de tongzhi."

In such areas, execution announcements were supposed to be posted only behind the walls of work units, where foreigners would not see them.[11]

While certain cases were chosen for propaganda use, care was also taken to prevent undesirable images of the condemned and his or her acts from circulating in Chinese society. If the condemned were to leave behind a will or other written material of a "slanderous nature," containing "reactionary language," claiming that he/she was wronged, or revealing concrete details of his/her case, such material was to be confiscated by the authorities and not turned over to the family of the offender. It was also strictly prohibited for family or others to "cause trouble by holding a funeral for a criminal who has been executed."[12]

Over the course of the 1980s and into the early 1990s, the Chinese authorities seem to have turned more and more toward the death penalty in response to rising crime rates. In the Criminal Law, greater use of capital punishment is reflected in an increase in the number of offenses punishable by execution. As Bao Suixian points out in an unusually thoughtful article on the death penalty, the Criminal Law, as promulgated in 1979, provided the death penalty for twenty-eight offenses—sixteen of which were counter-revolutionary offenses. From 1981 though 1991, the government issued seven regulations and decisions providing the death penalty for fifty-two more offenses including violent crimes such as rape and robbery, serious cases of the illegal felling of trees, five different narcotics offenses and certain serious economic crimes. This increase in the number of capital offenses reflects a belief that the only really effective way of addressing crime is to threaten potential criminals with death.[13]

A similar pattern of change may be observed in the development of procedural law regarding the review of capital sentences. In 1979, provisions were made to give the Supreme People's Court the final decision in all capital cases. Article 43 of the Criminal Procedure Law required that all death sentences be reviewed by the Supreme People's Court before being carried out. This provision seems to indicate a concern with accuracy and a belief that accuracy could only be guaranteed through a process of review at the highest level. But if this conviction really did exist, it was soon over-ridden in the interest of attaining and maintaining a high degree of efficiency. The stipulation in the Criminal Procedure that death sentences were to be reviewed and approved by the SPC was waived, first for one year in 1981, then for the period 1981 through 1983, and finally eliminated altogether. The changes were justified by the need to increase judicial efficiency

---

11. "Sifabu fu kaifang chengshi nengfou zhangtie xingshi panjue bugao de qingshi." These regulations were clearly violated. Even in Beijing, it was not uncommon to see execution posters displayed in places visible to foreigners.
12. "Zuigao renmin fayuan, zuigao renmin jianchayuan, gonganbu, sifabu, guanyu zhengque chuli sixing fanzui yishu yiwu deng wenti de tongzhi."
13. Bao Suixian, "Dui Zhongguo sixing wenti de shenceng sikao," 169-170.

in the face of the crime wave of the early 1980s. According to the Legal System Work Committee of the Standing Committee of the National People's Congress, the number of capital cases coming up for adjudication in the early 1980s was so great that the SPC did not have enough personnel to review all of them in a timely manner. Delay in the review and approval of capital cases would weaken the didactic value of executions and they would thus fail to "deflate the arrogance" of criminal offenders.[14]

Under the new rules, the SPC granted the power to review and approve death sentences, first in cases of murder, arson, robbery, and rape, and then in all save cases of counter-revolution and serious economic crime, to the higher (provincial) people's courts. The transfer of review and approval of death sentences to the provincial level must certainly have increased the efficiency of the criminal justice system, but in doing so, it compromised the concern with care and accuracy. Since provincial courts were the courts of appeal for capital cases originally heard at the middle court level, the second (appeals) hearing of a capital case was often combined with the review of the death sentence. Since second hearing and review of capital sentence are two clearly separate parts of the criminal procedure, the combination of the two by higher people's courts constituted a violation of the Criminal Procedure Law.[15]

If its reporting system has worked with a reasonable degree of efficiency, the Supreme People's Court must have, somewhere in its files, an accurate record of the number of people executed in the People's Republic since 1979. Without access to that record, we can only speculate about the number of executions that may have been carried out during the first decade of reform. Anecdotal evidence, the increase in the number of offenses punishable by the death penalty, and the sketchy figures derived from the incomplete reports on executions available suggest that the use of the death penalty increased as economic reform and opening to the outside world progressed. Andrew Scobell estimates that between 1978 and 1987, "at least 10,000 and perhaps as many as 20,000 people were executed in China."[16] This would suggest between one thousand and two thousand executions per year. Another estimated figure—five thousand to twenty thousand executions from 1983 through 1987—would indicate somewhere between one thousand and five thousand executions per year.[17] According to Amnesty International, the figure for this same period (1983-1987) could be as great as thirty thousand—that is, six

14. Quanguo renda changweihui fazhi gongzuo weiyuanhui xingfashi, *Lun "Zhonghua renmin gongheguo xingfa" de buchong xiugai*, 45-46.

15. *Ibid.*, 48.

16. Scobell "The Death Penalty under Socialism, 1917-1990," 205-207.

17. "By Laws or by Cadres," *The Economist* February 6, 1988, 34.

thousand per year.[18] Two Chinese informants interviewed in 1992 estimated that China executed about eight thousand people per year in the late 1980s and around ten thousand in 1991.[19] These figures contrast with Roger Hood's much more conservative estimate of one thousand executions per year for the six year period 1989-1994.[20]

While the available data do not allow us to make any firm statement concerning the number of people executed in China during the 1980s, the various incomplete estimates that we do have, along with the increase in the number of capital offenses defined in law indicate that the leaders of the People's Republic were convinced that capital punishment was an essential part of the state's response to crime and that there was a tendency over the course of the decade to address new problems by increasing the use of the death penalty. As Stephen Davis noted in 1987, this tendency to increase the use of the death penalty stands in contradiction to the letter as well as to the spirit of the criminal and criminal procedure codes of 1979.[21] The contradiction can best be understood as a manifestation of debate within the Chinese legal community and the Chinese leadership itself—the debate between those who, as Jiang Hua so forcefully put it, believed that the criminal justice system should reduce arrests and reduce capital punishment, and those who were convinced that the only way to bring order out of chaos was to "resolutely kill off" the troublemakers.

LABOR REFORM

While those judged to be incorrigible were executed, most criminal offenders were sentenced to labor reform, either for life or for a fixed number of years. Estimates of the number of prisoners in labor reform vary considerably. Jean-luc Domenach estimates 1.5 to 3.2 million prisoners in labor reform camps in the mid-1980s, with an additional one million former prisoners retained for labor at the

---

18. Amnesty International, *When the State Kills . . . the Death Penalty: A Human Rights Issue* (New York: Amnesty International Publications, 1989, 122-123, cited in Scobell, "The Death Penalty in Post-Mao China," 514.

19. Interview files 9 and 6d. Both informants arrived at their estimates through extrapolation from incomplete provincial statistics. While these estimated figures certainly cannot be taken as authoritative, it is interesting that Chinese involved in the criminal justice system should have come up with numbers substantially greater than some of those put out by foreign scholars and human rights organizations.

20. Hood, *The Death Penalty*, 73. Hood points out that according to this conservative estimate, China would have carried out 0.08 executions per 100,000 population per year, which would put the Chinese execution rate considerably short of the Iranian rate of 0.95 executions per 100,000 of population during the same period.

21. Davis, "The Death Penalty and Legal Reform in China," 319.

camps.[22] James Seymour and Richard Anderson put the total number of labor reform and labor re-education prisoners at approximately 1,464,325 in January 1995.[23] In carceral facilities including farms, mines, and factories located all over China, these prisoners were supposed to undergo reform through labor and come out better men and women, skilled, disciplined, and ready to be absorbed as normal members of society. The Chinese government took pride in the claim that its prisoners were useful to society, that they were successfully reformed through their useful labor, and that care was taken to settle them back into society when they completed their terms.[24] Accounts by former political prisoners and by Western human rights groups contested this image as they described labor reform camps as being characterized by unsafe and unsanitary working and living conditions, arbitrary brutality, and the naked pursuit of profit.[25]

A closer look at the theory and the practice of labor reform in the 1980s reveals neither a successful experiment in the humane treatment and reform of criminals nor a brutal economic powerhouse; labor reform, like the larger apparatus of criminal justice, appears to have been an institution combining idealistic belief and practical interests, an institution designed for the socialist dictatorship of the 1950s, unprepared and struggling to adapt to the new conditions of the marketized economy and weakened Communist ideology of the 1980s. We can get a sense of the severity of these challenges when we observe developments in the theory and in the practice of labor reform in the 1980s.

The institution of labor reform rested on certain beliefs concerning the relation of thought to behavior. The individual's subjective consciousness—his/her thoughts, beliefs, world-view, habits, and emotions—was regarded as being the root of behavior. Criminal behavior was thus understood to have its roots in criminal thought. Inasmuch as the individual was inherently capable of improvement through reform of his/her subjective world, socially undesirable behavior could be reduced, and eventually eliminated, through the systematic application of programs of thought reform.

The concepts of human nature expounded by Mencius and Confucius, and manifest in the Qing legal system may have pre-disposed the Chinese rulers of the mid- to late twentieth century to be receptive to the idea that criminal behavior has its roots in the criminal's subjective consciousness and that it can be eliminated

---

22. Domenach, *Chine: L'archipel oublie*, 489.

23. Seymour and Anderson, *New Ghosts Old Ghosts*, 206. For an overview and discussion of various estimates as to the population of the labor reform system, see *ibid.*, 18-28, 181-184, 196-198, 201-207, and 218-221.

24. For a discussion of the use of labor reform as a practical demonstration of China's enlightened social policies to the world, see Wei Bomin and Ren Licheng, "Xuanchuan woguo laogai zhengce de chuchuang."

25. For example, see Amnesty International, *China: Torture and Ill-Treatment of Prisoners*; Asia Watch, *Prison Labor in China*; Wu, *Laogai*.

through the process of thought reform. However, the theoretical bases of reform through labor can be traced more directly to the ideas of Marx and Engels regarding class struggle, to the theory and practice of labor reform in the former Soviet Union, and to Mao Zedong's understanding of the ideological dimensions of class struggle.

Labor reform in the 1980s found its theoretical justification in the concepts of socialist revolution and the historical task of the proletariat as they were understood and propounded by Mao Zedong in the 1930s and 1940s. In this view, the proletariat, through revolutionary practice, was to transform both the material and the spiritual worlds of mankind in order to advance the to the historical stages of socialism and, finally, communism.

Within the context of this national project of human transformation, the task of labor reform was to eliminate the ideology of the "exploiting class" (their morals, their ideas, their habits, their world-view, their culture) and replace it with proletarian revolutionary ideology. While this transformation might be undertaken voluntarily by the majority of the population, there were bound to be some who resisted, clinging stubbornly to the reactionary thoughts and habits of the past. In the words of Chairman Mao—words that were still quoted in the 1980s: "the objective world which is to be changed [by the proletariat] also includes the opponents of change, who, in order to be changed, must go through a stage of compulsion before they can enter the stage of voluntary, conscious change."[26] Prisoners and their thoughts were the objects of coercive reform.

It was assumed forced participation in collective labor was the fundamental technique by which the authorities could gain access to and reform the subjective world of the prisoner. In texts on labor reform published in the 1980s, the efficacy of collective labor was explained in terms of Marxist theory of cognition, according to which the individual's subjective consciousness is said to be a product of his or her material existence. In an article entitled "Tentative Discussion of the Basis of the Fundamental Theory of Labor Reform," Wang Tai explained the transformative power of collective labor as follows:

> . . . when organizing this type of productive labor, the labor reform institution has instituted conscious choices and controls in order to adapt it to the special needs of the reform of prisoners. It consciously brings into play the reformative aspects (those aspects which bear on the thought and the consciousness of the laborer) thus greatly strengthening the capacity of this productive labor to reform the human being. Under these circumstances the prisoner, when obliged to participate in productive labor, is subjected to the restrictions of its various elements (for example, work quotas, work evaluation, quality control,

---

26. Mao, "On Practice," 81.

144

the organization and coordination of labor, etc.) causing him *constantly to be aware of his own existence and constantly producing the conscious knowledge of adapting to this existence.* This leads gradually to qualitative change and hence to realization of the goal of reform."[27]

All collective labor, whether undertaken freely or under coercion, was regarded as having the salutary effect of transforming the individual's subjective consciousness. There was, however, an essential difference between the collective labor of free men and women in society and that of prisoners undergoing labor reform. The primary goal of the former was material production; the primary goal of the latter was held to be a form of spiritual production—the reform of the prisoner's subjective consciousness. In labor reform, material production was to be subordinated to the goal of thought reform; reform was to be based on participation in productive, collective labor, supplemented by the inculcation of political and moral norms through study sessions. This relationship was summed up in the slogan "reform first, production second."[28]

The theoretical explanation of the transformative power of collective labor in the 1980s was substantially the same as that formulated by Chinese labor reform theorists in the 1950s.[29] But in the intervening years, there had been a significant change in the type of prisoner being subjected to reform. In the 1950s, people who had been labeled as counter-revolutionaries made up 90% of the population of the labor reform camps. In the 1980s, prisoners found guilty of counter-revolutionary offenses seem to have accounted for 10% or less of the total.[30] Rather than being political offenders, the prisoners of the 1980s were young working-class men (and some women) found guilty of common criminal offenses—theft, assault and battery, swindling, rape, hooliganism and so on. According to the labor reform theory of the 1980s, the typical working class offender had not been properly socialized in the family or in school or through participation in productive labor. The criminal was said to be lazy, apt to avoid work, to be afflicted with the desire to get something for nothing, to be illiterate, unskilled, immoral and undisciplined.[31] It was those character flaws, and also the prisoner's lack of job skills, which labor reform now had to correct.

27. Wang Tai, "Shilun laodong gaizao de jiben lilun yiju," 248. Emphasis in original.
28. *ibid.*, 251.
29. For a discussion of the development of labor reform theory from the 1950s to the 1980s, see Dutton, *Policing and Punishment in China*, 295-301.
30. Wu, *Laogai*, 19. The figure may be less than 10%. According to Seymour and Anderson, "Only a tiny percentage of post-Mao-era laogai prisoners have been sentenced for political reasons." Seymour and Anderson, *New Ghosts Old Ghosts*, 181.
31. Shi Po, "Qingshaonian fanzui yu jiating jiaoyu" (Youth Crime and Family Education), *Beijing fazhibao* (Beijing legal system news) October 6, 1990, 2.; Liu Yunxiang, "Daoqie leiguanfan de sixiang xingge tedian he gaizao duice," 38.

In addition to collective labor, the reform of the prisoner was to be accomplished through education. As commonly understood, and as seen, for instance, in the classic account of the "thought reform" of the last emperor Aisin-Gioro Pu-yi, and in the accounts of foreign prisoners subjected to thought reform in the 1950s, the "educational" aspect of reform was primarily political.[32] Education was said to be a matter first of getting the offender to confess and to recognize the error of his/her ways, to accept the justice of the sentence which the state had imposed upon him/her, and to resolve to undergo reform and become a new, useful person. Second, education was to inculcate the political line of the Chinese Communist Party, to teach the Communist world-view, norms, ethics and morality. As a part of the educational process, prisoners were supposed to keep tabs on and report on each others' thoughts and behavior, to study political philosophy and current events, and to hold regular meetings for the discussion of political issues and for the purposes of criticism and self-criticism. This was all a part of the legacy of labor reform as "class struggle" played out in the minds of the prisoners.[33]

These "educational" practices, established in the 1950s, continued to play a part in the labor reform of the 1980s. There were, however, other aspects of education that were introduced into labor reform specifically to meet the needs of the new prisoners of the 1980s. These tended to dilute the element of class struggle within the overall theoretical structure of labor reform, although not by any means eliminating it.

One way in which the rhetoric of class struggle was weakened was through the redefinition of labor reform and labor re-education camps as "special schools" in which the predominantly young, working class criminals of the 1980s would be socialized and trained in basic literacy and job skills which would enable them (theoretically) to become useful members of society upon their release.[34] This theoretical shift was not accompanied by rapid and fundamental changes in the organization or staffing of the labor reform camps. Suggested changes such as a full staff of qualified teachers at each labor reform camp were simply not possible in practice. The idea of labor reform camps as "special schools" amounted to a change in the representation of labor reform and its tasks, in which the issue of class struggle, while not eliminated, was overlain by the goals of socializing and training delinquent members of the working class itself.

As the rhetoric of class struggle was played down in the 1980s, relatively more emphasis came to be placed on the third aspect of labor reform—the technique of appealing to the prisoners' feelings (*renqing*). This technique was implied in the commonly used term "education and reform" (*jiaoyu ganhua*). The

---

32. Pu Yi, *From Emperor to Citizen*; Lifton, *Thought Reform and the Psychology of Totalism*.

33. Wu, *Laogai*, 27-33.

34. The "scholasticization" of labor reform is discussed in Domenach, *Chine: l'archipel oublié*, 361-63, 400.

first element of the word *ganhua* means to feel, to sense, to affect, to move or touch a person emotionally. It also means to feel obligated or obliged to someone. *Hua*, the second element of the word, means to transform. Thus, to *ganhua* is not simply to reform a person in the mechanical sense implied by the English word, but to do so through an appeal to the feelings, by moving the other, inspiring in him or her a sense of obligation which, in turn, will call forth a reciprocation of the feelings and care which have been thus extended.

The importance of "feelings" or "emotions" in labor reform was referred to by Yang Diansheng in his textbook *Labor Reform Law*. Yang noted that part of the responsibility of a labor reform cadre was to:

> arrive at a good combination of education that appeals to the reason with that which appeals to the emotions, using concrete facts to educate prisoners. For instance, organize the prisoners to tour factories and villages, so that they may see with their own eyes the great accomplishments of socialist construction and the huge changes taking place in the motherland; arrange for former prisoners who have gone on to make outstanding contributions to the building of the four modernizations to come to the labor reform unit to discuss their experience and to stand as examples before the prisoners; do a good job of running the prisoners' cafeteria, conscientiously heal them when they fall ill, and so on."[35]

In doing all this for their prisoners, cadres would be able to "move them with emotion" (*dong zhi yi qing*) to accept reform.[36]

The theme of moving prisoners to reform by expressing care for their material and spiritual well-being was also manifest in the laws, regulations and policies established for the guidance of labor reform work. These required that prisoners be given adequate, sanitary food and living conditions. When released, prisoners were to be subject to continuing supervision and indoctrination, but also to be helped to find employment, housing, and spouses.[37] The long-term transformative effects of marriage, for example, were pointed out by Wang Wenyuan, Assistant Chief Procurator of the Supreme People's Procuratorate. In comments published in 1993, Wang specifically called on local authorities to help former prisoners to get married in order to reduce crime.[38]

---

35. Yang Diansheng, *Laodong gaizao faxue*, 192.

36. *ibid.* 31.

37. *ibid.*, 31-32, 231.

38. "Yibu juyou Zhongguo tese de chongxin fanzui yanjiu de lilun zhuanzhu," 8. According to another report, cadres in a county in Zhejiang province made a point of arranging marriages for released convicts, because they observed that those with families to care for were less likely to commit new crimes. See: Zhejiang sheng sifating laogaiju, "Guanyu xingman shifang renyuan gaizao zhiliang de

The transformative power of appeal to the emotions was also a prominent theme in propaganda describing labor reform. In one such account entitled *Great Prisons of Western China*, Jia Lufeng and Feng Shou repeatedly contrast images of youth, innocence and warm-heartedness with those of lost youth, evil, and coldness. In their description, the labor reform cadres are fresh-faced boys, workers and students who had just been thrown into uniform a few days before the arrival of the first batch of criminals at their newly established labor reform unit in Xinjiang in 1983. The criminals, by contrast, are slightly older, most of them bearing tattoos acquired during earlier sentences in youth reformatories. They are described as being physically clean, but with the filth of their souls evident in their behavior and in their virtually uncontrollable appetites for food, tobacco and sex.[39] The cadres are portrayed as doing their best for the prisoners, giving them better food than they get themselves, spending their own money to buy socks, canned food, cigarettes, quilts and other supplies for the prisoners, giving them special meals on holidays, and making generous arrangements for spousal visitation, all in the hope of moving the prisoners with kindness.[40]

In one such scenario, a prisoner was allowed to return, unaccompanied, to Beijing to visit his dying father:

> The furlough seemed to be over in no-time. The local public security office issued Wang Jianhua an extension. He knew that it was to allow him to take care of his father. He understood the government's good intentions. It was a decision so rich in compassion! What else could it do but to strengthen his remorse over his past behavior? He was moved by the kindness of the government, but should he stay or not? In three days it would be the fifteenth day of the eighth lunar month. He could stay for the Mid-Autumn Festival and then go. Father had only a few days to live, and if his son was not by his side at his last Mid-autumn Festival, what a sad occasion it would be! Just as he was hesitating, his father coughed violently. Then, in a low, hoarse voice he said, "Go, don't overstay your furlough. I saw you. Now I can die in peace."[41]

Needless to say, Wang Jianhua returned to the labor reform camp in time and went on to become a model prisoner.

The idea that reform could be brought about through appeal to the prisoner's emotions was not an innovation of the Deng era. Beginning in the 1950s, regulations concerning labor reform and Mao Zedong's pronouncements on the

---

diaocha baogao," 373.
39. Jia Lufeng and Feng Shou, *Zhongguo xibu dajianyu*, 39-41.
40. *ibid.*, 44-45, 55, 60-61, 89-108.
41. *ibid.*, 130.

subject demanded that prisoners "be treated as human beings," banning torture, beatings and ill-treatment.[42] What was different in the 1980s was that theoreticians placed more emphasis on the resolution of prisoners' practical problems and the fulfillment of their material needs as instruments of reform. It was thought that:

> . . . in the process of carrying out educational work on prisoners, we must uphold the principle of combining the resolution of ideological problems with the resolution of practical problems. This demands that in doing thought work on prisoners, we cannot abstain from saying something about important truths, nor can we simply talk about important truths and fail to resolve practical problems and practical difficulties. *One of the notable characteristics of the young prisoners of the 1980s is that they place great emphasis on "material benefits."* Included in this is that when prisoners have practical problems which they hope that the state will resolve, some of them tell the cadres straight-forwardly: "You don't need to talk all that much, I understand everything that you say. You resolve my practical problems, and I'll be sure to do my best." In our own practical work, when we've done a practical thing for a prisoner, resolved some concrete problem, although we haven't talked a lot about deep truths, it generally moves the prisoner to tears.[43]

RESISTANCE TO REFORM

Successful reform of the hearts and minds of prisoners required that the theory of labor reform be carried out rigorously in practice and in a highly controlled environment. Both the long-term and the short-term success of reform depend on the creation and the maintenance of a milieu which eliminates any information or stimuli that might undermine the principles which the reform process is meant to inculcate.[44]

In practice, this proved to be virtually impossible in the 1980s. Even in the late 1950s and early 1960s, the lessons which prisoners learned in labor reform could be quite different from those intended. In theory, labor reform was to eliminate selfish individualism and replace it with a collective consciousness, love of the Party and the motherland, and obedience to authority. In some cases, such as that of Aisin-Gioro Pu-yi, this may well have occurred. On the other hand, descriptions of labor reform as experienced by two political prisoners in the 1950s and 1960s (Bao Ruowang and Harry Wu) reveal a process in which prisoners

---

42. Li Long.,"Mao Zedong tongzhi guanyu laodong gaizao zuifan de lilun he shijian," 5.

43. Tu Fazhong, "Tantan dui zuifan jinxing zhengzhi sixiang gongzuo de yuanze," 46-7. Emphasis added.

44. Lifton, *Thought Reform and the Psychology of Totalism*, 420-21.

learned to manipulate the system, to fight, to scavenge for grain in rats nests and horse manure, and to think first and foremost of their own self-interest, all in order to survive in the dog-eat-dog world of the camps.[45] Still, in the 1950s and 1960s, the labor camp milieu and the political, cultural and economic milieu of Chinese society outside the camps were relatively well-controlled. In the 1980s, fundamental changes took place. The theory of labor reform clashed with the social realities of a China undergoing economic reform and opening to the outside world. Openly expressed resistance on the part of prisoners emerged as a more significant challenge to the labor reform system.

Resistance was expressed, in the first instance, in the form of refusal to confess one's crimes or to acknowledge the wrongness of one's actions. Confession, a heart-felt expression of regret, and an equally heart-felt acceptance of the justice of one's punishment were regarded as being the first steps on the road to reform. Throughout the criminal process, both legal and extra-legal pressure were routinely brought to bear in order to force the prisoner to confess and to express contrition.[46] Despite these efforts, the labor reform cadres of the 1980s found that significant numbers of prisoners refused to confess or to accept the justice of their punishment—in many cases, it seemed that their only regret was that they had been caught. Surveys carried out by the Ministry of Justice in labor reform units in Guangdong, Jiangsu and Yunnan in the late 1980s indicated that around half the prisoners surveyed openly expressed denial of guilt and/or refusal to accept their sentences.[47] A study on woman prisoners in Jiangsu in 1985-86 showed that almost 70% felt that they had been unjustly sentenced. Even more (88%) did not regard their behavior (overwhelmingly some form of sex crime—either prostitution or "hooligan promiscuity") as criminal.[48]

Some cadres attributed the increased rates of refusal to confess and/or to accept the justice of one's punishment to problems in the criminal process itself. Under the loosely drafted Criminal Law, the courts could (and did) impose a very broad range of punishment for any given offense. For many offenses, the range of punishment extended from "control" (supervision by the masses while remaining at one's place of employment) to death. In each case, the sentence was determined according to an evaluation of the "circumstances" of the crime. Such evaluations could be highly subjective. Moreover, evaluation of the circumstances of a case were influenced by the political atmosphere prevailing at the time when the

45. Wu, *Bitter Winds*; Bao and Chelminski, *Prisoner of Mao*.
46. Liu Siqi, "Xingxun bigong lujin buzhi de yuanyin," 3.
47. Sifabu yanjiusuo "zuifan xin qingkuang yanjiu" ketizu, "Xin de lishi shiqi zaiya zuifan de xin qingkuang, xin tedian," 4.
48. Zhao Rongguo, "'Yanda' tougai de nu shaonianfan zhong chuxian de xin qingkuang," 215. See also Chen Yu, Tang Guofang, Xu Shiying and Chen Xiuping, "Yanda hou xinshou nufan de qingkuang he tedian," 205-6; Da Dan, "Dui 203 ming maiyin renyuan bijiao fenxi," 46.

offender was sentenced. During campaigns against crime, specific offenses would be targeted. At such times, behavior that would have been (or in some cases already had been) dealt with by light criminal sanctions or administrative measures could receive an unusually harsh sentence. Prisoners were aware of the fickle nature of the justice system. Those who had been unlucky enough to be sentenced during a campaign were unlikely to accept the justice of their sentence, particularly after comparing notes with fellow prisoners.[49]

Prisoners also expressed resistance to reform in open confrontations with labor reform cadres. An account of such a confrontation describes how a group of prisoners pretended to brawl among themselves and then purposely shoved and pummeled the young cadre who came to intervene:

When the young cadre entered the cell, "Magnet" (a prison bully) gave his buddies a look, and seven or eight of them began fighting with each other. The young cadre hurriedly intervened. "No fighting!" "I report to the government, he swore at me," one said, striking a cell-mate a slap on the ear. "Mother's-head, I'll whip your father," the other replied, striking a blow on the first man's chest. The bunch of them fought together, purposely catching the young cadre in the middle. They shoved him back and forth, shouting "Excuse me," but landing their fists most impolitely on his body. The young cadre got impatient, pulled out his electric baton, and shouted: "Behave yourselves! Stand still!" "Little comrade, don't mess around with that thing, be careful or you'll shock yourself," "Magnet" cautioned him in an oily, teasing voice. The young cadre suddenly lost his temper. "You hooligan!" He glared at the evil visage before him, thinking of all the young women this hooligan had victimized. He lifted his hand, and brought it down with a ringing slap, leaving five finger-marks on that ugly face. "He hit somebody, the cadre hit somebody!" All of the prisoners shouted together. The unlucky young cadre! He got chewed out and had to make two self-criticisms in front of the entire squadron.[50]

This account, drawn from a work of reportage literature, may be fictionalized. However, articles published in labor reform journals and legal interpretations regarding labor reform combine to give us a picture of a growing minority of prisoners disobeying orders, refusing to work, picking quarrels with and

---

49. Sifabu yanjiusuo yunei anjian yanjiu ketizu, "Jin shinianlai quanguo yunei anjian de tedian ji jinhou de duice yanjiu," 12; Xing Guozheng, "Xinjiang jianguan gaizao zuifan gongzuo zhong 'sanlu' piangao de yuanyin poxi," 23-24; Ding Haihai, "Cong yiqi teda de yunei baozha anjian yinchulai de fansi," 57; Ma Shucai, Yan Xiujun, "Qianxi guanjiao ganbu sixiang zhuangkuang," 67.
50. Jia Lusheng and Feng Shou, *Zhongguo xibu dajianyu*, 42-43.

manipulating cadres,[51] tattooing (a prohibited activity and thus considered a form of resistance), circulating pornography, engaging in homosexual behavior, and writing songs and poems expressing mutual solidarity and rejection of social norms.[52]

In addition to open conflict with cadres, some prisoners expressed resistance to reform by committing acts of self-injury or self-mutilation. On a psychological level, self-injury and self-mutilation may imply self-hatred and self-punishment. But at the same time, such acts had the effect of forcing cadres and the labor reform system as a whole to show a greater degree of care for the prisoner's physical needs than they ordinarily would. In this sense, it was understood clearly as a means of resistance. The function of self-injury and self-mutilation in labor reform may be comparable to that of the hunger strike in Western prisons. While political prisoners in China have used the method of hunger strike, it has achieved mixed results. More often than not, the response of the authorities has been to force-feed the prisoner through a rubber tube inserted into the nose and down the throat.[53] The hunger strike was rarely mentioned in the labor reform press or in legal interpretations concerning labor reform in the 1980s and early 1990s. Self-injury and self-mutilation, both real and feigned, however, were mentioned regularly. The prisoner who maimed or injured himself would have to be taken to the hospital for treatment. There, he would get rest, better sleeping conditions, and better food. If his injury was serious enough, the labor reform system might be unwilling or unable to treat it and could release him on medical furlough.

The techniques of self-injury and self-mutilation seem to have been limited only by the imagination and the daring of the prisoners. A common technique was to swallow some harmful object, or to pretend to have done so. A description of prisoners transferred to Xinjiang in 1983 contains the following passage:

> Aside from roundworms, a lot of them had steel wire, nails, small spoons, empty tooth-paste tubes, and pieces of glass in their stomachs. They'd swallow this "food" into their bellies like meat, just to give themselves pain. When they were in pain, they wouldn't have to dig ditches, open wasteland, or make adobe bricks. They could lie in bed, knitting their brows and moaning, and they'd get a bowl of noodles or some fried eggs. Look at that

---

51. Chen Yu, Tang Guofang, Xu Shiying and Chen Xiuping, "Yanda hou xinshou nufan de qingkuang he tedian," 204-5.

52. Ding Haihai, "Cong yiqi teda de yunei baozha anjian yinqi de fansi," 57. Homosexuality in the labor reform system is referred to in Jia Lusheng and Feng Shou, *Zhongguo xibu dajianyu*, 40. According to an article on sex crimes in the labor reform system, some of the stronger prisoners asserted their authority by seducing, purchasing, or raping other men. See Zhu Yongling, "Laogai changsuo xing fanzui de biaoxian xingshi ji yufang," 25.

53. For example, see Black and Munro, *Black Hands of Beijing*, 287, 302, 326-28; Wu, *Bitter Winds*, 184.

fellow over there. He's had two operations, and they didn't find a thing in his stomach! He's afraid of pain, so he doesn't dare to swallow glass. He'd just hold his belly and roll around in the sand, rolling so he worked up a sweat, and the doctor believed he really had swallowed something and cut his stomach open in a hurry to see what was there. They use anesthetic during the operation, so it doesn't hurt. After one operation, you can rest for at least half a year.[54]

Perhaps the most extreme form of self-injury reported in the available sources is the act of swallowing caustic soda. According to a document issued by the Ministry of Public Security and the Ministry of Justice there was, for several years in the late 1980s, something of a trend of swallowing caustic soda among prisoners in labor reform and labor reeducation units in the city of Shenyang.[55] Eleven prisoners tried this in 1985, twenty-seven in 1986, and seventy-nine in 1987. The caustic soda burned the throat and esophagus so that eating was impossible. These prisoners had to be fitted with stomach tubes in order to keep them alive and released on medical furlough. Because these prisoners on medical furlough were not effectively supervised,[56] they began turning up in Guangzhou, Wuxi, Shanghai and other major cities in such numbers that they were labeled collectively as "the tube gang" (guanzibang). There, they committed offenses ranging from pick-pocketing and purse-snatching to robbery and rape.

Local police found members of the "tube gang" difficult to deal with. There were no regulations regarding the handling of offenders who had maimed themselves and were in need of medical attention. When arrested, these men would intimidate the police by swallowing more caustic soda, or by pulling out their stomach tubes and claiming to have cancer or threatening to commit suicide. Labor reform and labor reeducation units refused to accept them as new prisoners and hospitals refused to accept them as patients. In the absence of regulations, public security offices dealt with the problem in the easiest way available to them, releasing members of the "tube gang" in custody of a guarantor, which meant that they went back on the street.

Resistance to reform was also expressed in the commission of new criminal offenses inside the labor reform camps. According to research carried out by the Ministry of Justice and other organs, the overall rate of crime inside the labor reform system decreased during the 1980s. However, during the same period, the rate of violent resistance to reform (such as violent attacks on cadres or group

---

54. Jia Lufeng and Feng Shou, *Zhongguo xibu dajianyu*, 39.

55. "Gonganbu, sifabu guanyu jianjue yifa chengchu yi zican shouduan taobi chengchu de fanzui fenzi de tongzhi." The following is based on this document.

56. On problems with the medical furlough system, see Jin Jixiang and Liu Zhengxiang, "Dui dangqian baowai jiuyi zhong jige wenti de fenxi he jianyi," 19.

escapes), although decreasing during the anti-crime campaign of 1983-84, began to increase again within two to three years.[57] In one case, a prisoner in a labor camp in Shandong succeeded in making a bomb with which he entered a conference room where the cadres of his labor reform unit were holding a meeting. The prisoner demanded to talk to the leader of the reform unit, and while the affair was being "handled" (the account does not say how), he set off the bomb, killing himself and injuring thirty-four cadres.[58] In another case, two prisoners in Henan killed a cadre, stole his uniform, and escaped in a stolen paddy-wagon.[59]

All the various manifestations of resistance to reform—refusal to confess, violence, self-injury, tattooing, homosexuality and the rest—were regarded by the authorities as being parts of a labor-camp sub-culture of resistance. As one observer described it: "in practice, the criminal sub-culture has always struggled against the mainstream culture of the prison, competing for territory, its role no less than that of the mainstream prison culture."[60] In the 1950s and 1960s, this "criminal sub-culture" could be effectively repressed. But in the 1980s, the intellectual, the social, and the economic atmosphere outside the camps was increasingly in contradiction to the official ideology of socialism, collective solidarity, collective labor, discipline and communist ideals which the labor reform system was expected to instil. Even more seriously, the market economy and its values entered the world of the labor camps themselves.

THE ECONOMIC VULNERABILITY OF LABOR REFORM

From the beginning, money had been an important consideration for the labor reform system. One of the reasons for establishing the system in the early 1950s had been to reduce the financial burden that a massive influx of political prisoners had imposed on the decrepit prison system that the PRC had inherited from the Nationalist regime.[61] Afterwards, prison labor was used to open remote border areas and in mining, agriculture, and industry.[62] As Jean-luc Domenach has pointed out, the official Chinese press periodically published reports on the labor reform system's economic contributions to the state—claims that are echoed in the

57. Li Qi and Dai Yanling, "Jiushi niandai de Zhongguo laogai gongzuo," 47; Li Yuqian, "Dangqian yunei fanzui huodong xin dongxiang ji qi duice," 139-40; Sifabu yanjiusuo yunei anjian yanjiu ketizu, "Jin shinianlai quanguo yunei anjian de tedian ji jinhou de duice yanjiu," 15.
58. Ding Haihai, "Cong yiqi teda de yunei baozha anjian yinqi de fansi," 56.
59. "Sifabu, guanyu jin yibu jiaqiang anquan fangfan gongzuo de jinji tongzhi."
60. Ding Haihai, "Cong yiqi teda de yunei baozha anjian yinchu de fansi," 57.
61. Yang Diansheng, *Laodong gaizao faxue*, 58.
62. Wu, *Laogai*, 33-40.

accounts of former prisoners such as Bao Ruowang, who stated that "China surely must be the only country in the world whose prisons turn a profit."[63]

Discussion of the labor reform system in its own internally published journals contradicts the picture of profitability conveyed by the openly published press. Rather than serving as an economic prop for the regime, the labor reform system of the 1980s and early 1990s appears to have been a huge, but ramshackle operation, partially dependent on state subsidies, struggling to adjust to the new economic pressures of the reform era, and with the accomplishment of its basic tasks (guarding and reforming prisoners) compromised by the unaccustomed pressures of the marketplace.

In an article published in 1990, the "Labor Reform Economic System Study Group" under the Ministry of Justice Research Institute traced the development of the labor reform economy from the 1950s through 1990. Their account of the 1950s through the 1970s is very general. There is little of interest to be noted here, except that during this period of time, the labor reform system was estimated to have had its arable land reduced by 60% while its fixed capital (*guding zichan*) suffer a loss of over two billion yuan.[64]

The Study Group declared categorically that as of 1990, the labor reform system still had not entirely recovered from these losses. Nonetheless, by the late 1970s, the system had recovered sufficiently to reach record gross annual product of approximately 3.1 billion yuan in 1978 and 1979, turning over approximately 400 to 500 million yuan in profits to the state. This success was followed by two years of failure. The gross product for 1981-82 was approximately 2.5 billion yuan, and in 1982 the system made a loss of over twenty million yuan.[65]

The Study Group found the causes of this economic decline in the labor reform system's inability to compete in the market economy and in certain changes in the structure of the Chinese state bureaucracy that made it impossible for the labor reform system to tap important sources of state revenue. As a result of these changes:

> The labor reform economy came to be regarded as 'local enterprise' [and] could not establish an account (*lihu*) with the central planning and economic management departments. All basic construction investment, renewal and

---

63. Domenach, *Chine: l'archipel oublié*, 411; Bao Ruowang, *Prisoner of Mao*, 12. See also Harry Wu's analysis of the profitability of labor reform in *Laogai*, 41-49. While not directly addressing Wu's figures, Domenach argues that claims of the profitability of labor reform are made on the basis of unreliable statistical information and without taking into full account the costs of running the labor reform system. See *Chine*, 413-14.

64. Sifabu yanjiusuo "laogai jingji tizhi yanjiu" ketizu. "Zailun laogai jingji tizhi de gaige," 2. The following two paragraphs draw on this article.

65. *ibid.*, 3.

restructuring funds (*gengxin gaizao zijin*) and materials allocated by plan (*tongpei wuzi*) had to be resolved by the localities. Because the labor reform economy also didn't have official accounts at the local level, in addition to which the local economic base is unbalanced, the labor reform economy in most areas sank into extreme difficulties.[66]

This economic difficulty was only partially resolved in the period between 1983 and 1990. In 1983 the labor reform economy underwent a basic re-structuring. Prior to 1983, all income from production was turned over to the state, and the state allocated funds to cover all expenses associated with the operation of the labor reform system. After 1983, finances were contracted to the individual labor reform unit. Units were no longer required to turn their income over to the state, but the state no longer provided for the operation of the labor reform camps in its budget. Labor reform units were forced to pay their own way.[67] Coinciding with these administrative changes was the Strike Hard campaign which began in August 1983 and soon led to a doubling of the population of the labor reform camps.[68]

Contrary to what might be expected, this sudden influx of inmates did not mean that the regime was immediately enriched in terms of its ability to exploit prison labor. To be exploited, labor needs to be combined with the means of production—fields, mines, factories, and tools. Prison labor also requires sufficient prison buildings, dormitories, guards, guard-rooms, and security equipment. Faced with a sudden increase in the number of prisoners, the labor reform system lacked these vital resources. The central government responded with subsidies, and local governments followed suit.[69]

According to Ministry of Justice documents, labor reform units taking in large numbers of prisoners in 1983-84 were temporarily subsidized at the rate of four hundred yuan for each new prisoner sentenced to labor reform and one-hundred and fifty yuan for each new prisoner sentenced to labor re-education. In addition, Beijing, Tianjin, Shanghai, Guangdong and Fujian were ordered to subsidize (at the rate of 1,200 yuan per head) the expenses of settling prisoners transferred from their jurisdictions to Xinjiang in 1984. These subsidies were extended in 1985 on the grounds that the labor reform system was still under serious financial strain from having to handle large numbers of prisoners who had not yet been brought

---

66. *ibid.*
67. Pan Zhenhua, "Lun laogai danwei yao zuohao jingji wenzhang," 34-5. This reform coincided with the transfer of the labor reform system from the Ministry of Public Security to the Ministry of Justice.
68. Sifabu yanjiusuo, "Zailun laogai jingji tizhi de gaige," 3. The phrase "doubling" should be taken as an approximation.
69. *Ibid.*

into productive labor.[70] From 1984 through 1990, central and local governments also loaned the labor reform system approximately three to four billion yuan.[71]

Despite these subsidies, the overall level of subsidization is said to have decreased in the 1980s. According to one source, central and local subsidies only covered 15% of the expenses of running the labor reform system after 1983. The rest had to be made up within the system itself.[72] These figures indicate that the labor reform system was largely self-supporting; but it does not follow that the labor reform system had successfully resolved practical issues such as backward plant and equipment, or that it no longer suffered from financial difficulties. It is true that as a whole, labor reform was a big business. In 1993, the system was reported to have 10.5 billion yuan in fixed assets (*guding zichan yuanzhi*) and over 4 billion yuan in cash flow (*liudong zijin*).[73] Even so, the labor reform system comprised only a very small part of the national economy. Seymour and Anderson suggest that the labor reform system experienced declining profitability throughout the 1980s and that its national output in 1988 accounted for only 0.2% of China's total industrial and agricultural output.[74]

In considering the economic performance of labor reform, we must also be aware of differences within the labor reform system itself. The state of individual labor reform farms and industries seems to have varied, reflecting regional variations in the Chinese economy. Certain sectors of the labor reform system not only supported themselves, but also made a substantial profit, part of it in foreign currency. The decision to set labor reform units on an aggressive export drive was reportedly made by the Party Central Committee; it was this decision that paved the way for the rapid development of coastal labor reform units in the mid- to late 1980s.[75] In the late 1980s and early 1990s, labor reform units exported a wide variety of goods—from Christmas tree lights to tools to wine—and entered into business deals with major foreign corporations.[76] By 1988, for example, labor reform units in Liaoning had exported products worth 2.4 billion yuan to thirty different countries, earning over forty-nine million American dollars. Of thirty

---

70. "Caizhengbu, sifabu guanyu xinzeng fanren he laojiao renyuan jingfei wenti de buchong tongzhi"; "Sifabu, laogaiju, laojiaoju guanyu xinzeng fanren, laojiao renyuan jingfei wenti de tongzhi."

71. Sifabu jingji yanjiusuo, "Zailun laogai jingji tizhi de gaige," 3.

72. Li Qi and Dai Yanling, "Jiushi niandai de Zhongguo laogai gongzuo," 46.

73. Wang Zengfeng, "Jiefang sixiang, zhuazhu jiyu, jiakuai fazhan disan chanye," 10.

74. Seymour and Anderson, *New Ghosts Old Ghosts*, 209.

75. "Wosheng laogai laojiao qiye jianchi gaige kaifang," 1.

76. The labor reform system's export drive and its relations with multi-national corporations have been documented in Wu, *Laogai* and in Human Rights Watch/Asia, "New Evidence of Chinese Forced-Labor Imports to the U.S."

agricultural and industrial labor reform units in Liaoning, half had engaged in production for export.[77]

While noting the success of some units, particularly in the coastal regions, Chinese observers of the labor reform economy did not find its overall performance to have been one of the economic success stories of the 1980s. The system as a whole, despite great improvements, saw profits fall every year of the Seventh Five-year Plan save 1988.[78] According to the Study Group's article cited above, "From the 1980s through 1989, aside from the six or seven coastal provinces and cities and Yunnan, which made a profit, the majority of provinces, cities and districts could not but depend on special financial allocations (*caizheng zhuanxiang bokuan*) and subsidies to cover losses (*kuisun butie*) to survive. Many provinces and cities even suffered the heavy burden of years of losses."[79]

These money-losing units in the central and western parts of the country, many of them agricultural, acted as a drag on the labor reform economy as a whole.[80] For example, in the early 1990s one third of the labor reform units in Jiangsu Province were agricultural. They held more than half of Jiangsu's prisoners, over 50% of the provincial labor reform system's cadres and guards and over 80% of its workers. Nonetheless, production was low. In 1992—a good year—the total value of these agricultural labor reform units only amounted to 17% of the value produced by the provincial labor reform system as a whole.[81]

The fiscal weakness of the labor reform system had a direct impact on the administration of labor reform. In June 1990 the national labor reform system's financial problems were such that cadres and guards in 20 provinces were owed back-pay, some as far back as eighteen months. In some cases, cadres were forced to use their own funds to cover expenses incurred in pursuing escaped prisoners.[82] In 1993, after what was alleged to have been a particularly bad year (attributed to the floods of 1992 and to increases in the number of prisoners and in expenses), an author writing in *Studies in Crime and Reform* warned that: "If we can't make a timely adjustment of the economic structure, strengthen the technical reform of our enterprises, and push forward with technological improvements, we will face the serious consequences of being gradually squeezed out of the market."[83] Another cautioned that the labor reform economy, with its over-dependence on a

---

77. "Wosheng laogai laojiao qiye jianchi gaige kaifang, gan dao guoji shichang shang qu zhanju yixi zhi di," 1.
78. Ma Weiguo, "Guanmao zong xieding jiang dui laogai jingji chansheng de yingxiang tanxi," 27.
79. Sifabu yanjiusuo "zuifan xin qingkuang yanjiu" ketizu, "Xin de lishi shiqi zaiya zuifan de xin qingkuang, xin tedian," 3.
80. Ma Weiguo, "Guanmao zong xieding jiang dui laogai jingji chansheng de yingxiang tanxi," 27; Li Qi and Dai Yanling, "Jiushi niandai de Zhongguo laogai gongzuo," 48.
81. Pan Zhenhua, "Lun laogai danwei yao zuohao jingji wenzhang," 36.
82. Li Qi and Dai Yanling, "Jiushi niandai de Zhongguo laogai gongzuo," 46.
83. Wang Zengfeng, "Jiefang sixiang, Zhuazhu jiyu, jiakuai fazhan disan chanye," 10.

relatively small industrial sector producing industrial and electronics products (cars, factory machinery, gauges, televisions etc.) was very fragile and would be seriously hurt by China's expected entry into the General Agreement on Trade and Tariffs.[84]

The economic weakness of the labor reform system meant that as the 1980s advanced, cadres and their prisoners came under pressure to increase production and profits. This pressure was institutionalized in the form of the "dual responsibility contract system" which tied cadres' income to their fulfillment of production quotas and the quality of the reform of their prisoners.[85] This system, in turn, was seen as having a negative effect on the discipline and morale of both cadres and prisoners, and to undermine the means which the system was accustomed to rely on for both control and reform of prisoners.

In practice, the dual responsibility system appears to have resulted in a greater emphasis on production than on reform. Articles in labor reform journals repeatedly mention the one-sided emphasis on production as being detrimental to reform. The pursuit of profit was seen as leading cadres to ignore political and moral instruction in favor of using their prisoners in production. The result of this concern with production, as one author put it, was that "our labor reform institutions, the implement of the state's dictatorship, have to use the greater part of their energies in making ends meet and putting food on the table, leaving only a small part of their energy to the task of reforming the criminals of the late 1980s and early 1990s."[86]

The emphasis on production and profit also undermined security. Many escapes were found to have occurred when cadres took their prisoners out on work details without a sufficient number of guards.[87] Other reports cited instances of labor reform units using the medical furlough system to get rid of burdensome, non-producing prisoners as an example of the corrosive effect of the pursuit of profit on labor reform work.[88] There were also a number of incidents in which labor reform and labor reeducation cadres took prisoners with them on business trips on behalf of the labor reform or reeducation unit. In some cases the cadres took such prisoners in as house-guests, or stayed as guests with a prisoner's family, thus blurring the distinction between the prisoner, a target of the "dictatorship of the proletariat," and the cadre responsible for carrying out that

---

84. Ma Weiguo, "Guanmao zong xieding jiang dui laogai jingji chansheng de yingxiang tanxi," 27.
85. Yang Diansheng, *Laodong gaizao faxue*, 212; Wu, *Laogai*, 35-36. In practice, "quality of reform" tended to be interpreted in terms of minimal number of escapes and minimal number of unnatural deaths. See Zhang Zhong and Li Xiaobo, "Dui laogai laojiao ganjing tanwu, shouhui, weiji anjian de poxi ji duice," 22.
86. Ding Haihai, "Cong yiqi teda de yunei baozha anjian yinqi de fansi," 57.
87. Zhang Xianqin, "Dui Sichuansheng tuotao fanzui anjian qingkuang de fenxi," 43.
88. Qin Jixiang and Liu Zhengxiang, "Dui dangqian baowai jiuyi zhong jige wenti de fenxi he jianyi," 19.

dictatorship. There were also instances in which cadres sent prisoners on business unaccompanied. Some were never seen again. Similarly, some labor reeducation units in Anhui and Henan provinces released prisoners and allowed them to work as private entrepreneurs on the condition that they pay the labor reeducation unit sixty to seventy yuan a month.[89]

In addition to the deterioration of security caused by cadre's attempts to use their prisoners in the most profitable way possible, economic pressure influenced security and reform by its effects on the strength and morale of cadres. Under-staffing—an average of five to six cadres per hundred prisoners, with only three per hundred in some units—meant that many provisions concerning supervision, separation of different types of prisoner, and thought reform work existed only on paper.[90] The low pay and low social status of labor reform work contributed to morale problems and corruption among cadres. It was also reported to have led to loss of personnel in the 1980s. This problem was expected to continue in the 1990s as underpaid labor reform cadres left their jobs in favor of more lucrative and less dangerous work.[91]

Low morale among cadres, emphasis on production to the detriment of the goal of reform, and inattention to guarding and discipline were represented in the labor reform journals and documents as one aspect of the corrosive effects of the market economy. Underlying these debilitating changes in the incentive structure and in the administration of labor reform, observers of the labor reform system pointed to changes on the deeper level of human relationships and of institutional relationships, both within the labor reform system itself and in society at large.

THE PROBLEM OF RELATIONSHIPS

A sense that the years of economic reform had brought a change for the worse in the human relations upon which the practice of labor reform was based appears as the theme of the Ministry of Justice's report regarding "The New Situation and New Characteristics of Criminals in Custody In the New Historical Era," published in 1990 in *Studies in Crime and Reform*. In describing the apparently increased sense of solidarity among prisoners, the Ministry found that:

---

89. "Sifabu guanyu yanjin lanyong fanren he laojiao renyuan waichu gao shengchan jingying de tongbao."
90. Sifabu yanjiusuo yunei anjian yanjiu ketizu, "Jin shinianlai quanguo yunei anjian de tedian ji jinhou de duice yanjiu," 16; Xing Guozheng, "Xinjiang jianguan gaizao zuifan gongzuo zhong 'sanlu' piangao de yuanyin poxi," 23-24.
91. Ma Shucai and Yan Xiujun, "Qianxi guanjiao ganbu sixiang zhuangkuang," 67; Li Qi and Dai Yanling, "Jiushi niandai de Zhongguo laogai gongzuo," 48; Zhang Zhong and Li Xiaobo, "Dui laogai laojiao ganjing tanwu, shouhui, weiji anjian de poxi ji duice," 21-23.

In the past, prisoners looked on mutual supervision and reporting other prisoners' illegal or criminal behavior as a way of establishing merit and atoning for their crimes, and as a manifestation of their willingness to draw close to the government and show enthusiasm for reform. Nowadays prisoners believe in caring for themselves, covering up for each other and cultivating good relationships with each other. Many prisoners believe that "the more friends, the more opportunities," and that the more "brothers" there are in prison, the better they can help supply each other's needs, share each others cares and burdens, and that after leaving prison, they will have more friends to help them find a way of making a living. Among the prisoners there have developed both the psychological state and the self-aggrandizing behavior of relying on connections, loyalty to friends, and of praising fellow-prisoners' good behavior but not reporting their transgressions, so that even when criminal behavior occurs among the prisoners, nobody reports it. In a number of serious cases occurring in the system in recent years, others in the offender's mutual supervision group, even the head of the group, and the prisoners responsible for control of the offender have known the details ahead of time, but pretended not to know, and did not report it to the government's cadres.[92]

The willingness of prisoners to cooperate with each other, thus undermining the labor reform system's ability to "use prisoners to control prisoners" was found by the Ministry and by other writers on labor reform to be accompanied by a weakening of the authoritative role of cadres vis-a-vis the prisoner. This was ideally a relationship in which the cadre, representing and carrying out the "dictatorship" of the state, both punished and reformed the prisoner. Incidents like those described in the discussion of resistance to reform and of crime inside the labor reform system did not fit the ideal. Neither did instances of cadres using prisoners to do business outside the prison walls or the presence in areas like Shanghai of prisoners whose families were wealthy enough to keep them supplied with food and spending money.[93] One commentator even questioned the use of production contracts between cadre and prisoner within the labor reform system, because it gave the two, at least symbolically, an equal status.[94]

---

92. Sifabu yanjiusuo 'zuifan xin qingkuang yanjiu' ketizu, "Xin de lishi shiqi zaiya zuifan de xin qingkuang, xin tedian," 4. See also Guangdong sheng laogaiju, "Xin shiqi dui zuifan de zai renshi ji gaizao duice," 28-9. Like the Ministry of Justice research, this report finds a decrease in the effectiveness of mutual surveillance by prisoners and an increase in prisoners' exchanging gifts and food—two methods by which social networks are built and maintained.
93. Sifabu yanjiusuo, "Zaifan xin qingkuang," 3.
94. Xie Bing and Liu Zhenghui, "Tan gaige zhong de laogai gongzuo," 15.

161

The Ministry of Justice lamented this change, observing that "Nowadays, some prisoners consciously or unconsciously place themselves on an equal footing with the cadres. . . . Some make an emotional investment in cadres, giving them money and gifts. . . . there have been some cadres whose consciousness of [their role in carrying out] dictatorship has been dampened, and the boundaries between [them and] the prisoners have been obscured."[95] Other sources accused cadres of fraternizing with criminals or of being too soft on them due to feelings of sympathy that had a basis in their common working-class background.[96]

These changes in human relationships *within* the walls and fences of the labor reform system were accompanied, the Ministry of Justice and others observed, by changes in the relationship between the prisoner and society *outside* the camps. The Ministry of Justice report cited above, for example, found that rather than draw a clear line between themselves and a family member who had been imprisoned, an increasing number of family members used connections or money to attempt to get the prisoner's sentence reduced or to have him released on medical furlough. Others continued to support the prisoner with liberal gifts of food and money.

The Ministry also complained of a growing tendency for families to extend support and concealment to escaped prisoners, and to give released prisoners a warm welcome, rather than to ostracize them.[97] At the same time, however, the sources indicated an increasing problem with prejudice against former prisoners in society at large. This is not to say that prejudice against released prisoners was necessarily stronger in the 1980s and 1990s than it had been in past decades. As noted above, there is reason to believe that in some respects, prejudice had weakened. On the other hand, as greater numbers of common criminals were cycled through the labor reform system on relatively short sentences, and as changes in the administrative system increased the ability of public security offices and work units to make such prejudice manifest by refusing to cooperate in the task of re-integrating ex-convicts into society by giving them household registra-

95. Sifabu yanjiusuo 'zuifan xin qingkuang yanjiu' ketizu, "Xin de lishi shiqi zaiya zuifan de xin qingkuang, xin tedian," 4.
96. Investigation carried out by the Guangdong provincial labor reform bureau similarly reported that prisoners regarded themselves as equals to the guards and cadres, refusing to step aside for them if they met them in a corridor, for instance, or otherwise breaking discipline. Guangdong sheng laogaiju, "Xin shiqi dui zuifan de zai renshi ji gaizao duice," 29. For the accusation that cadres take a lenient attitude toward the criminals of the reform era because they are of working class origin, see Bao Gang, "Tantan qianghua laodong gaizo shouduan," 5.
97. Sifabu yanjiusuo 'zuifan xin qingkuang yanjiu' ketizu, "Xin de lishi shiqi zaiya zuifan de xin qingkuang, xin tedian," 4.; Min Cheng, "Xinshou zuifan burenzui xinli fenxi," 42. The research done in Guangdong province, referred to in the two preceding notes, also points to a loss of the sense of difference between citizen and criminal offender, and between prison and society, to the point where: "it seems that committing a crime and going to prison is no longer a thoroughly terrifying thing." Guangdong sheng laogaiju, "Xin shiqi dui zuifan de zai renshi ji gaizao duice," 29.

tion or jobs, prejudice came to be viewed as a problem within the labor reform system.[98] This was, then, a problem involving institutional as well as human, relationships.

Prejudice against the ex-convict began in the labor reform system itself, where it was enshrined in the laws and regulations dealing with the placement of labor reform and labor reeducation prisoners back into society after completion of sentence. The state always retained a number of prisoners for "forced job placement" (liuchang jiuye) at the labor reform camp after completion of their sentences. Such prisoners were given higher pay and more personal freedom than labor reform prisoners, but they continued to be guarded by uniformed cadres and could be forcibly prevented from leaving the vicinity of the labor reform camp.[99] From the mid-1980s onward, however, forced job placement came to be less important and less coercive. Fewer prisoners were subject to retention for labor after completion of their sentences, and restrictions on the personal freedom and freedom of movement of persons "retained for labor" were eased.[100]

When prisoners were returned to society, there were restrictions on where they might live, what sort of job they might have and what level of wages they might be paid. The overall policy in the first half of the 1980s was to return prisoners to the rural areas if at all possible, and to be particularly cautious about returning them to major cities such as Beijing, Shanghai and Tianjin.[101] Prisoners themselves were reported to be aware not only of these regulations, but also of the prejudice which they could be expected to receive from society as a whole. Analyses of the "state of mind" (xinqing) or of the "psychology" (xinli) of the prisoner repeatedly pointed to his or her fear that there was no future to look forward to, and that discrimination is all that one can expect from society after

---

98. The unwillingness of public security offices to give released prisoners a household registration and the evident inability of the labor reform units to assure that this is done may be in part due to the fact that the labor reform system has since 1983, been under the jurisdiction of the Ministry of Justice, whereas local public security offices are under the leadership of the Ministry of Public Security.

99. Wu, Laogai, 108-15.

100. Seymour and Anderson, New Ghosts Old Ghosts, 195-96. According to Seymour and Anderson, the number of prisoners retained for labor in 1988 was under 100,000, that is, about 5% of the number of actual prisoners. Ibid., 197.

101. "Gonganbu, laodong renshibu, nongmuyuyebu, jiaoyubu, shangyebu guanyu fanren xingman shifanghou luohu he anzhi de lianhe tongzhi"; "Sifabu, gonganbu, zuigao renmin jianchayuan, zuigao renmin fayuan guanyu dui fanren xingman he laojiao qiman de renyuan zanting fanghui shehui de jinji tongzhi"; "Sifabu, gonganbu, zuigao renmin jianchayuan, zuigao renmin fayuan guanyu jiang yibufen xingman he jiechu laojiao de zanliu renyuan fanghui shehui de tongzhi"; "Gonganbu guanyu laojiao, laogai gongzuo ganbu gangwei butie he zhuozhang de buchong tongzhi"; "Zuigao renmin jianchayuan, gonganbu, sifabu guanyu qiangzhi liuchang jiuye renyuan shanzi lichang zhuihui tuzhong kefou shiyong jieju he jiya de tongzhi."

release.[102] Both prejudice against prisoners shown in the regulations concerning their release and the expectation of discrimination from the outside world indicate the extremely limited faith which the system and the people actually put in the efficacy of reform through labor.

Lack of confidence in the ability of labor reform to transform criminal offenders into useful and reliable workers was evident in the increasing difficulty of labor reform units in placing released prisoners in regular, full-time jobs with work units. From the point of view of the labor reform units, one of the changes in their work brought about by the economic reforms of the 1980s was that it was no longer an easy task to place released prisoners in work units by simple administrative order. Prior to the economic reforms, if a criminal had a work unit, he could be returned to it. If he did not, a unit could be told to accept him as a worker. If he were a peasant, he could be returned to his work brigade.

When the economic reform program gave production units more fiscal autonomy and a greater degree of control over the management of the work force, they made it much more difficult for the labor reform system to settle released prisoners back into society. In a study of policies regarding the return of prisoners to society, Wang Yanxin and Zhen Jianping explain that before the economic reforms of the 1980s, a labor reform unit needed only to contact the local labor office, which would arrange assignment of released prisoners to local units. With the reforms, they note, came an increasingly complex labor market, which involved not only the labor offices, but also a number of other government organs: those responsible for industry and commerce, taxation, health and sanitation, management of urban beautification and so on.[103] Because labor reform units did not have any connections with these other government organs, they were at a disadvantage in arranging job assignments in the new labor market.[104]

Another problem was that in the labor market of the 1980s and 1990s, a work unit might not necessarily have any quota for new workers. If it did, its increased power to manage the work force meant that it could refuse to hire released prisoners, either out of sheer prejudice or because released prisoners—largely poorly educated and unskilled—were not competitive on the labor market. The

---

102. "Yibu juyou Zhongguo tese de chongxin fanzui yanjiu de lilun zhuanzhu—Zhongguo chongxin fanzui yanjiu zuotanhui fayan zhaiyao," 8; This fear may be more common among women than among male prisoners. Research on women convicted of sex crimes during the anti-crime campaign, for example, found that 70% of them feared prejudice from society and that the families of about half had already, in fact, cut off relationships with them. There was also said to be a higher rate of suicide among women prisoners than among men. Chen Yu, Tang Guofang, Xu Shiying and Chen Xiuping, "Yanda hou xinshou nufan de qingkuang he tedian," 202-3; Da Dan, "Dui 203 ming maiyin renyuan bijiao fenxi," 46-7.

103. Wang Yanxin and Zhen Jianping, "Gaige yu wanshan xingshi renyuan anzhi jiuye zhidu de zonghe sikao," 47.

104. *ibid.*

situation led Wang and Zhen to state bluntly that because of these difficulties, none of China's various policies concerning the return of released prisoners to society worked very well.[105]

The problems faced by prisoners returning to society were demonstrated in follow-up research done by the Tianjin Labor Reform Bureau on prisoners released from labor reform and reeducation in Tianjin from August 1983 through July 1984. Of the released prisoners surveyed, less than one third of those who were urban residents were able to find a full-time job. About half were either self-employed or temporarily employed, and another 19% were unemployed. Of those who had been employed before arrest, only 19% were taken back by their original units. By comparison, 81% of former criminals who had been employed had been taken back by their work units in 1980.[106]

This research also points to the difficulty of arranging follow-up "help and education" (*bangjiao*) for 40% or more of released prisoners, and to the failure of the authorities to bring families actively into the effort to exercise continued supervision and reform of released prisoners. Part of the problem was that a small number of the families of prisoners utterly rejected their criminal offspring. Other families could not afford to support the newly released prisoner. In still more cases, the problem was said to be the same as that which caused the offender to become a criminal in the first place—that he was the product of a dysfunctional family. In such cases, a return to the family was seen as a return to the same environment that was thought to have contributed to the problem of criminality in the first place.[107]

The difficulties associated with the return of prisoners to society might be expected to lead to increased recidivism. In fact, recidivism is described in the literature as being a relatively small (in comparison with the United States and other foreign countries) but growing problem. The research on prisoners released from labor reform in Tianjin, cited above, found a very low rate of recidivism—6.73%.[108] At the same time, prisoners who had "entered the palace" two or three times were said to comprise a growing proportion of the prisoner population.[109]

This anecdotal evidence cannot be backed up with reliable data. As discussed in Chapter Five above, the statistical picture of crime in general is not entirely

105. *ibid.*
106. Tianjinshi laogaiju, "Tianjinshi dui xingman shifang qiman jiejiao renyuan qingkuang de diaocha baogao," 380.
107. *ibid.*
108. The figure includes the commission of both offenses against the administrative Security Administration Punishment Act, which are less serious than criminal offenses, similar to the concept of a misdemeanor in American law, and criminal offenses.
109. For example, see Zhou Qingzheng, Fang Xueguang, and Guo Shengjun, "Yige zhide zhongshi de shehui wenti," 49.

clear. Statistical information for recidivism is even more problematic. Part of the problem is that until 1984 there was no standard legal definition of the term "recidivism." In that year the Ministry of Justice defined recidivism as the commission of a new criminal offense by a person within three years after release from labor reform.[110] In 1987, the Ministry of Justice re-emphasized and further clarified the definition of recidivism to include the commission of a new criminal offense within three years after release from labor reform or, in the case of counterrevolutionary offenders, the commission of a new counterrevolutionary offense at any time after release, or the commission of a common criminal offense within three years of release. In the compilation of statistics on recidivism, the Ministry of Justice directed that new SAPA offenses committed by labor reeducation personnel within three years after release not be included in the recidivism figures, but be tabulated separately.[111]

Standard sources such as the *China Law Yearbook* do not include statistics on recidivism. Various studies refer to national rates of anywhere from six to fifteen percent for the late 1980s and early 1990s.[112] One study carried out by the Ministry of Justice traced over 160,000 labor reeducation and labor reform offenders released between 1982 and 1986 for three years. Adult labor reeducation offenders had a recidivism rate of 1.4% and adult labor reform offenders, 6.59%. The recidivism rate for juvenile labor reeducation and reform offenders was considerably higher—20.54%, but since juvenile offenders accounted for only 2% of the total number of recidivists, the high juvenile rate did not appreciably raise the total rate of recidivism.[113]

As would be expected, recidivism statistics from particular localities, time periods, age groups and labor reform units show considerable fluctuation. Thus, while the country as a whole is said to have seen recidivism *increase* to reach 15% in the late 1980s, the rate of recidivism for prisoners released from China's largest labor reform farm (Shayang in Hubei Province) was reported to have *decreased* from 20.8% in 1986 to 8.7% in 1990.[114] One study pointed to a decrease in recidivism by prisoners released from labor reform, from 10.47% in 1982 to 6.76% in 1984.[115] Another study indicates that over 15% of prisoners released from labor reeducation committed a new offense within three years, and that while

---

110. "Sifabu guanyu kaizhan gaizao zhiliang kaocha gongzuo de tongzhi."
111. Li Zhunren, ed. *Zhongguo chongxin fanzui yanjiu*, 26-27.
112. Zhang Panfu and Deng Zengrong, "Jianchi dui xingshi jiejiao renyuan kaizhan diaocha yanjiu de jianyi," 42; Wu, *Laogai*, 134; Wang Zhongfang, *Zhongguo shehui zhian de zonghe zhili de lilun yu shijian*, 28. The national average recidivism rates for 1995 and 1997 were reported to be 6-8%. See Seymour and Anderson, *New Ghosts Old Ghosts*, 199 and 290, endnote 350.
113. This research is discussed in Li Zhunren, ed. *Zhongguo chongxin fanzui yanjiu*, 409-410.
114. Zhang Jian, "Woguo zui da de laogai nongchang—Hubeisheng shayang nongchang gaikuang," 65.
115. Lin Li, "Woguo de fanzui yu kongzhi," 25.

Shanghai and Liaoning had above-average rates of recidivism for prisoners released from labor re-education (20.92% and 18%), the interior provinces of Shaanxi and Qinghai had below-average rates (5% and 6.5% respectively).[116] Juvenile offenders had higher rates of recidivism than adults, and released prisoners who lacked family support, employment, and "help and education" committed new offenses at higher than average rates.[117]

THE RESULTS OF EXECUTION AND LABOR REFORM

In a criminal justice system whose goals are preventive rather than purely retributive, the ultimate purposes of punishment and reform are to prevent increases in crime and, if possible, to bring about a reduction, or even an elimination, of criminal behavior. We must then ask whether or not execution and labor reform have contributed to the prevention of crime. But as we ask this question, we should be aware that the quality and quantity of the available statistical information on crime patterns in China is not sufficient to allow us to draw more than some tentative conclusions.

At the very least, it would appear that the liberal use of capital punishment was unable to prevent the overall increase of Chinese crime rates from 8.9 per 10,000 of population in 1981 to 20.1 per 10,000 in 1990. The rate of increase was observed to be greater than that of the developed countries of the west and even greater than that of many other developing countries.[118] This would seem to indicate that capital punishment was not an effective deterrent. There is, of course, some disagreement on this issue. Some Chinese legal scholars, pointing to the decrease in crime rates between 1979 and 1986-87 (from 8.9 per 10,000 in 1979 to just above 5 per 10,000 in 1986-87), argue that this was due partly to the use of the death penalty.[119] Others, looking at the increasing crime rates of the late 1980s and observing the simultaneous increase in the number of offenses punishable by execution conclude that the belief that crime can be controlled by executing offenders is an illusion and that in fact, the use of the death penalty has very little bearing on the rise and fall of crime rates.[120] Certainly the bulk of the evidence appears to support the latter conclusion.

---

116. Sifabu laojiaoju, "1984 nian jiejiao renyuan genzong diaocha qingkuang de zonghe baogao," 28-9.

117. Bao Shengqing, "Xingshi jiejiao renyuan chongxin fanzui de tedian yuanyin je duice," 49-50; Sifabu laojiaoju. "1984 nian jiejiao renyuan genzong diaocha qingkuang de zonghe baogao," 29; Tianjinshi laogaiju, "Tianjinshi dui xingman shifang qimanjiejiao renyuan qingkuang de diaocha baogao," 382-3.

118. Wang Zhemin and Huang Jingping, ed. *Jingji fazhan yu fanzui bianhua*, 7.

119. Hood, *The Death Penalty*, 180.

120. Bao Suixian, "Dui Zhongguo sixing wenti de shenceng sikao," 174.

While it seems clear that the death penalty has not been an effective deterrent, the efficacy of the labor reform system is more difficult to assess. China's relatively low recidivism rates appear to indicate that the experience of labor reform does to some extent succeed in reforming prisoners. That is certainly the conclusion the Ministry of Justice reached in its extensive research on recidivism. We can, with some reservations, agree with this conclusion. While labor reform has certainly not brought about the decreasing crime rates hoped for in official Party ideology, it seems to have been as effective, or at least no less effective, than prison regimes in developed countries including the United States.

Here too, though, there are questions (aside from the obvious questions concerning the objectivity of the Ministry of Justice itself). First, it is clear that China's overall crime rates and recidivism rates would be higher if it were not for the distinction between SAPA offenses and criminal offenses. Furthermore, the Ministry of Justice and other Chinese research makes no effort to disentangle the effects of labor reform and reeducation on the one hand and patterns of economic growth on the other hand. It seems likely that recidivism rates would be higher in times of economic slowdown, and conversely, that the low rates of recidivism in the 1980s and early 1990s might well be linked to China's economic growth and to the opportunities for small-scale private enterprise.

7

CRIMINAL JUSTICE AND CHINA'S PURSUIT OF MODERNITY

> ... if we are to make progress in an orderly way, when liveliness clashes with stability and unity, we can never pursue the former at the expense of the latter. The experience of the Cultural Revolution has already proved that chaos leads only to retrogression, not to progress, and that there must be good order if we are to move forward."
>
> Deng Xiaoping, "The Present Situation and the Tasks Before Us," 237.

Deng Xiaoping and the Chinese Communist leadership clearly believed that any form of deviant behavior, common crime as well as political offenses, would undermine social stability and unity in China and thus impede the process of modernization. Beginning with the criminal and criminal procedure codes of 1979, Chinese leaders attempted to construct and implement a criminal justice system that would attack crime through a combination of preventive and punitive techniques and thus guarantee the social basis considered essential to the achievement of national modernization. The rhetoric surrounding the construction of the criminal justice system and the practice of criminal justice reflected the conviction that in China, unlike the West, material and spiritual modernization would proceed hand in hand and that China would thus achieve the transformation from traditional to modern productive technology without experiencing the high crime rates that Chinese observers found to be characteristic of the modernized capitalist West.

China's experience of modernization in the 1980s proved otherwise. Contrary to all hopes and convictions, China's pursuit of modernity in the Deng era was accompanied by increased crime rates China, it seemed, was undergoing a process of modernization disturbingly similar to that experienced by the West. Recognition of this problem demanded that Chinese theorists re-think the problem of the relationship of crime to modernization. Could it be that socialist China was following a universal pattern of development? In this chapter we will consider how some Chinese criminologists approached this problem. We will then go on to consider from a broader perspective the relationship of crime rates and changes in the criminal justice system to the process of modernization, understood as industrialization, urbanization, and the application of the scientific method to the resolution of the problems of society and of government.

ADDRESSING THE PROBLEM OF CRIME AND MODERNIZATION

From the establishment of the People's Republic in 1949 through the early 1990s, mainland Chinese scholars' understanding of the relationship between modernization and crime rates progressed through three stages.[1] For the first thirty years of the People's Republic, criminological theory held to a simple dogma: in capitalist societies, modernizing economic growth is accompanied by increased crime rates; in socialist societies, modernization is accompanied by decreasing crime rates and eventually by the disappearance of crime. Then, in the years between 1978 and 1983, China's relatively high crime rates were explained away as an aberrant phenomenon brought on by the destructive influence of Lin Biao and the Gang of Four. In this way, criminologists could both account for the crime wave of the early 1980s and at the same time reassert the conviction that a return to normal socialist policies would result in a return to low and falling crime rates. Subsequently, some scholars interpreted the apparent success of the Strike Hard Campaign and of comprehensive management as evidence of China's ability to achieve decreasing, or at the very least, stable crime rates in the context of modernization. As long as the Chinese paid close attention to both the preventive and the punitive aspects of the struggle against crime, success was assured. Thus the Chinese delegate to the 1985 United Nations conference on crime and crime prevention stated the officially approved position when he argued that although a capitalist system would be unable to respond effectively to the problem of crime, in a socialist country, firm preventive and punitive measures, taken together, could control and eventually eliminate crime. Under socialism, it was simply a matter of the state being "tough with both hands."[2]

---

1. Wang Zhemin and Huang Jingping, *Jingji fazhan yu fanzui bianhua*, 5. The following description of the development of the mainland Chinese understanding of the relationship between crime rates and modernization summarizes Wang and Huang's description on pages 5-6.

2. "Yibu juyou Zhongguo tese de chongxin fanzui yanjiu de lilun zhuanzhu," 8.

As the apparent success of the Strike Hard campaign gave way to rising crime rates in the mid- to late 1980s, Chinese criminologists began to suggest that there might be a relationship between modernization and crime—a relationship so fundamental that even socialist China could not entirely avoid the problem of rising crime rates in the context of modernization.[3] In addressing the problem of increasing crime rates in the 1980s, these scholars began to place China's experience in a comparative historical context. The historical experience of the early modern West, they observed, was one in which crime rates had increased in the context of urbanization and industrialization, The socialist states of Eastern Europe and the developing countries of Asia and Africa had likewise experienced increased crime rates along with modernization.

This being the case, modernization appeared to be a stage of historical development that transcended the differences between economic systems or cultures. As a stage of development, modernization had its own laws to which any modernizing nation was bound to submit. One of these laws appeared to be that as a country's productive forces and economy modernize and as it undergoes urbanization, higher crime rates will inevitably follow. China's increased crime rates of the 1980s could then be ascribed to the process of modernization itself, while the rapidity of the increase in crime could be accounted for by the forced-march nature of China's drive to achieve modernization. China, after all, was attempting to accomplish in twenty years the socio-economic transformation that Europe had undergone over the course of the nineteenth century, and it must lift out of poverty a population forty times that of nineteenth-century Europe.[4]

If China in the 1980s was going through the same historical process of modernization that the West had undergone in the nineteenth century, then it was natural, even inevitable, that China should experience similar increases in crime. But what precisely was the link between modernization and rising crime rates in China? One possible explanation was that the social and cultural changes brought on by modernization had proceeded so rapidly that institutions such as the educational system, the family, and the Party and state apparatus of social management had been unable to keep pace. Criminologist Nan Shan, for example, drew on Alvin Toffler's *Megatrends* (in Chinese translation) when he explained the increasing crime rates of the 1980s and early 1990s as attributable, at least in part, to "information overload." "In a rapidly developing society," Nan argued, "all sorts of information are jumbled up together in masses of inter-related elements. It is impossible to completely process this raw information solely on the basis of inference and intuition, and then on that basis to make correct decisions. If correct

---

3. Wang Zhemin and Huang Jingping, *Jingji fazhan yu fanzui bianhua*, 14.
4. Xiao Jianming, "Lun jingji fazhan yu fanzui wenti," 15.

decisions are not made, people's behavioral systems, in the process of their operation, will depart from the goals predetermined by society . . ."[5]

Nan Shan and others argued that this flood of information had such a detrimental effect on the thinking of the Chinese people that some were unable to discriminate and choose properly between right and wrong behavior. Furthermore, the effects of this "information overload" were exacerbated by fundamental changes in the structure of the Chinese economy and Chinese society. As another scholar, Xiao Jianming, described the situation:

Following economic reform and the growth of the commodity economy, profit relationships, mediated by cash, became one of the leading elements of social life. Traditional values and moral concepts were challenged. The functions of factory, mine, enterprise, government and educational units became increasingly dispersed (developing toward professionalism), while their social function atrophied. Political indoctrination and the authoritative nature of administrative orders, which had provided cohesiveness between work units, declined significantly. In both horizontal and in vertical terms, gaps appeared between work units, and, as a result, left huge empty social spaces. Consequently, the public security organs became isolated. This change in the internal structure of the social prevention system has inevitably resulted in a tremendous decline in the effectiveness of the social control of crime."[6]

In the view of Xiao and others (a view that seems to purposely leave to one side the problem of the Cultural Revolution), the stability of Chinese society under the People's Republic from 1949 through 1979 had been preserved by a mutually reinforcing combination of traditional Chinese morality, Communist Party ideology, and the Communist Party's organization and occupation of social space and time. Now, in the reform era of the 1980s, these anchors of stability had been swept away by the forces of modernization, while no similar moral principles or institutions had effectively taken their place.

---

5. Nan Shan, "Xinkeji geming tiaojian xia de fanzui wenti," 14.
6. Deng Qun, "Shilun jingji fazhan yu fanzui zengzhang de guanxi,""6. See also Nan Shan, "Xinkeji geming tiaojianxia de fanzui wenti," 14; Li Meijin, "Shixi Zhongguo muqian de jingji fazhan dui shehui fanzui wenti de yingxiang," 34-5; Xiang Xuezhi, "Zhengque renshi shehui zhuyi chuji jieduan fanzui wenti," 12.

A similar analysis of the changes undergone by Chinese society in the 1980s and the significance of those changes for the control of deviance may be found in the results of a survey of 371 district and township level Party secretaries carried out in Sichuan province in 1988.

Eighty-eight percent of those surveyed indicated that "rural social management work" was more difficult than it had been before the economic reforms. The author of this study of cadre attitudes concluded that rapid social and economic change had left rural cadres with very limited resources in their struggle to maintain social stability. Although the cadres considered law to be the main instrument of social control, they thought that dependence on law alone would not be sufficient for the effective maintenance of social stability. Outstanding rural social problems, including clan feuds, disputes over water rights and an increasing crime rate could not be adequately addressed by reliance on the law alone.

Ideally, a rural cadre should "rely on many means other than law but still reasonable and legal, such as morality, administrative power, economic means, mediation, carrying out of patient ideological and political work and so on."[7] These were the instruments of "social management" that could serve to supplement to the law, and these were the instruments that had been the mainstay of the Party secretaries' management of rural society in the past. But it was precisely these extra-legal instruments of social management that had been undermined and lost their efficacy as a result of economic reform. In practice, the Party secretaries were increasingly thrown back onto an almost complete reliance on the coercive techniques of administrative fiat in combination with a legal system regarded by all as incomplete and in itself insufficient to produce and maintain social order.

In the analysis of Chinese criminologists in the late 1980s, then, the causes of China's increased crime rates were partly to be found in the inability of the legal system to keep pace with social and economic change and partly in the decay of the traditional Chinese and Communist Party techniques that had maintained social order in the past. At the same time, increased crime rates were understood to be linked also to the morally questionable aspects of modernization itself. Criminologists argued that the Chinese leadership of the 1980s, recognizing that China remained a backward nation, had consciously allowed a limited degree of capitalism to exist in socialist China as a means of achieving modernization, and that this decision itself was part of the problem.

Taking their cue from Marx's analysis of the revolutionary accomplishments of the bourgeoisie in overthrowing feudalism and laying the economic foundations of socialism by bringing large-scale industrial production into being, Chinese scholars argued that only by allowing a degree of capitalism could China attract sufficient investment capital, build up its industrial infrastructure, destroy the

---

7. Wang Ge, "Dangqian nongcun shehui wenti yu shehui guanli wenti jianxi," 30.

agricultural-handicraft-small-producer economy, overcome the conservatism and backward, feudal attitudes of the small-producer, and thus lay the foundation for the large-scale industrial economy that in turn was a necessary condition for the attainment of full-scale socialism and, eventually, communism. But one of the prices to be paid for this temporary allowance of the capitalist mode of production in China was, unfortunately, an increase in crime.

In the view of scholars who argued this position, China had made a bargain with history—a temporary increase in crime and other problems due to capitalism in return for an eventual eternity of communist utopia. The bargain might seem immoral—who, after all, would be willing to allow increases in crime, and therefore increases in human suffering? But as one scholar put it:

> Historical progress has never relied primarily on morality for its maintenance or its motive force. Therefore, while we clearly know that private ownership is the seed-bed of crime, we cannot but allow it to exist within a limited scope as a supplement to the socialist system. We clearly know that the hiring of labor inevitably brings with it the rebirth of exploitation, and that the poison of exploitation will inevitably spread throughout society, but we are forced to accept temporarily a certain degree of exploitation of hired labor.[8]

In this way, the existence, and even the growth, of crime under socialism could be explained as a temporary phenomenon attributable to the unfortunate but historically necessary employment of the capitalist mode of production as a tool in socialist China's pursuit of modernity. The increased crime rates of the 1980s and 1990s were thus an undesirable side-effect of modernization. But in order to distinguish socialist China from the capitalist West, it was also necessary to show how, in the long run, China would transcend this vexing stage of historical development and resolve the crime problem that came along with it.

In order to demonstrate the long-term superiority of the Chinese socialist path to modernity, criminologists looked to the possibilities inherent in the socialist system once China had undergone the initial, unsettling stages of modernization. Their position was that despite the short-term increases of crime associated with the employment of the capitalist mode of production during the traumatic transition to modernity, continued economic growth, in combination with the equitable distribution of wealth would make it possible to eliminate crime in the long-term. Xiao Jianming, for example, looked forward to the day when the capitalist sector of China's economy, having fulfilled its historical task, would give way to a more purely socialist system. Unlike the capitalist countries, China, under the leadership of the Communist Party, would use its resources to build not only a modern

---

8. Xiao Jianming, "Lun jingji fazhan yu fanzui wenti," 15.

'material civilization, but also a modern spiritual civilization. Human thought and behavior, as well as production, would be "modernized." The educational and the moral level of the Chinese people would be "raised" and their inter-personal relations "perfected" in unspecified ways.[9] Others argued that China's ability to eliminate crime was based not only on the socialist system, but also on the "facts" of China's "long and brilliant history" and the "unique ideological and cultural system" of "the Chinese race, with the Han nationality as its principle part." As equitable distribution of wealth removed the material causes of crime, these superior Chinese cultural assets would combine with "Communist moral education" to weaken the ideological roots of crime.[10] In short, China, having attained material and moral perfection, would become the ideal modern society.

CHINA'S EXPERIENCE IN HISTORICAL PERSPECTIVE

The question of how crime rates change in relation to the process of modernization (understood as industrialization and urbanization) has engaged the attention of generations of social scientists and historians outside of China. The efforts of Chinese scholars above, to put the Chinese experience into a universal scheme of historical development are, then, part of a larger, ongoing historical debate. In order to put the Chinese experience of crime and modernization in historical perspective, we must first consider the ways in which western scholars have understood this question.

In the nineteenth and early twentieth centuries, scholars who looked at the relation between crime and modernization took the position that there was a simple correlation—modernization was accompanied by increased crime. Frederick Engels, Robert E. Parks, L. Reiman, Emile Durkheim, George Simmel and Louis Wirth all, from their different perspectives, argued that the transition from traditional, rural society to modern urban industrial society may have liberated individuals from the material and moral restrictions under which they and their ancestors had lived for generations, but that it had also brought a shocking breakdown of identity, a loss of moral principles, and an isolation or anonymity that either failed to discourage, or actually encouraged violent criminal behavior. At the same time, these factors, along with increased opportunities and feelings of relative deprivation brought on higher rates of property offenses, particularly of theft.[11] In short, urbanization and industrialization led to a breakdown in the traditional stability and civility that had characterized the more closely-knit pre-

---

9. *Ibid.*, 14.
10. Hao Hongkui, "Xiandaihua dui fanzuilu shengjiang de yingxiang," 9.
11. See the discussion in Zehr, *Crime and the Development of Modern Society*, 19-21 and in Shelley, *Crime and Modernization*, 4-5.

modern society; this breakdown of tradition was manifest in increased rates of both violence and theft.

The idea that modernization (and particularly urban living) is historically associated with higher crime rates is attractively simple and conforms to the prejudices of the late twentieth century. For this reason, it survives as a sort of common knowledge. Quantitative historical research has, however, fundamentally challenged the received wisdom. In place of the simple positive correlation between rising crime rates and modernization, research carried out over the past few decades has suggested three possible models for our understanding of the relationship between crime rates and modernization. These three models will be discussed below. Then we shall turn to the question of how these models might help in our understanding of the experience of crime and modernization in China.

The first model to be considered is that known as *"de la violence au vol."* This was first proposed by French historians who understood modernization in terms of the transition from feudal to bourgeois society. As they saw it, French court records indicated a long-term shift in the ratio of cases of violence to cases of theft. Modernization, it seemed, was accompanied by an evolution of criminality from a pre-modern (feudal) pattern dominated by crimes of violence to a modern (bourgeois) pattern dominated by theft. The reasons for this transition were to be found in the emergence of private property as the fundamental organizational principle of bourgeois society.[12]

The *violence-au-vol* model was refined by Howard Zehr. In his study of crime in nineteenth-century France and Germany, Zehr concluded that the relationship between crime rates and modernization could be understood in terms of two different stages. In the first stage, the initial transition from rural agricultural to urban industrial society was marked by rapid increases in both violent crimes and property offenses. But these were overshadowed in the second stage by a more significant long-term trend in which decreasing levels of violent crime were accompanied by increasing levels of theft. In the long term, then, Zehr argues that there is a shift from pre-modern patterns of criminality, characterized by rural violence, to a modern pattern in which rising theft rates, indicative of the spread of modern economic values and the increased opportunities for theft become the "characteristic of modern urban society."[13]

While Zehr's research was limited to nineteenth-century France and Germany, his conclusions inspired a much more ambitious study by Louise I. Shelley, published in 1981 as *Crime and Modernization: the Impact of Industrialization and Urbanization on Crime.* Shelley took Zehr's idea that modernization resulted in a short-term universal increase in crime rates, followed by a long-term shift

---

12. Reinhardt, "Crime and Royal Justice in Ancien Regime France," 437.
13. Zehr, *Crime and the Development of Modern Society,* 138-39, 142.

from violence to theft and applied it to a study that took in not only Western Europe, but also the United States, the former Soviet Union and Eastern European socialist states, and selected countries of the developing world.[14] Synthesizing statistical analyses from a mass of secondary sources, Shelley concluded that "The changes in crime patterns observed first in England, Germany, and France as a result of the industrial revolution have accompanied modernization elsewhere."[15]

As Shelley saw it, in the short term, modernization was accompanied by increases in violent crime and theft. Violent crime increased as rural folk brought their violent ways to the cities, while theft was exacerbated by the displacement and deprivation experienced by first-generation migrants. Modernization was also linked to increases in prostitution and in juvenile offenses.[16] But once this initial, traumatic transitional stage had been completed, the mature modern society experienced a slowing of the rate at which crime increased.[17] The rates of violent crime declined relative to the more rapidly increasing rates of property offenses, led by theft.

This pattern seemed to be universal. It could be observed in the contemporary experience of the developing countries as well as in the history of the developed world. Through their more effective control of society, socialist countries were able to suppress the overall crime rates in comparison to those of the more free-wheeling capitalist world, but they were unable to prevent either overall increases in crime or the shift from crimes of violence to property offenses. Indeed, Shelley doubted the capacity of any government to control the changes in crime that accompanied the development of urban industrial society: "As the primary causes of criminality appear to be rooted both on the societal and the personal level in the social structure and the disruptions of social transformation, there is little that can be done by governments or individuals to control the problem of crime . . . changes in criminal behavior occur only with changes in social structure and the transfor-mations in crime patterns reflect fundamental societal change."[18]

In the work of Shelley and of Howard Zehr we thus have a second model for the understanding of the relation between crime and modernization. In this model, a short-term, traumatic transition to urban industrial society is marked by increasing rates of violence, particularly in cities that are recipients of large numbers of migrant populations. In the long term, however, the *violence-au-vol* proposition holds good—modern societies are relatively less violent, and more larcenous, than traditional societies.

---

14. The PRC was not one of those countries considered in Shelley's study.
15. Shelley, *Crime and Modernization*, 138.
16. *Ibid.*, 46, 52.
17. *Ibid.*, 69.
18. *Ibid.*, 64-65.

A third model is proposed by a group of scholars including Eric Johnson and Eric Monkkonen. In a number of quantitative historical studies of the history of crime in Europe, Johnson, Monkkonen and their colleagues found that while "violence certainly did decrease over the centuries," there was "no solid evidence that property crimes actually increased."[19] As they rejected the *violence-au-vol* thesis, these scholars drew on the theoretical contributions of Norbert Elias to suggest a different scenario. In work originally published in 1939, Elias argued that from the late Middle Ages through the early modern period, Western societies had undergone a "civilizing process" that went hand in hand with the development of the modern state.[20] Part of this civilizing process involved the state's assertion of a monopoly over violence and a consequent imposition of self-control over violent behavior by the aristocrats of the princely courts of Europe as they made the transition from knight to courtier.[21]

Following Elias, Johnson, Monkkonen and their colleagues suggest that in reference to crime, the process of modernization can best be understood as a process of civilization in which the rate of violence, which had been quite high in the traditional rural world dropped significantly in most Western European and Scandinavian countries in the seventeenth and eighteenth centuries.[22] The apparently high crime rates observed in some urban areas might be ascribed either to the initial shock of the transition to modernity[23] or, as Johnson forcefully argued, they might be due to the hardship and economic deprivation experienced by specific migrant groups (distinguishable by their race or ethnicity) in specific cities and by patterns of enforcement that might also be linked to the issue of race or ethnicity. Thus Johnson points out that Poles and Lithuanians migrating to German cities in the late nineteenth and early twentieth centuries were met with discrimination from employers and from the police and the courts, thus explaining the apparently high crime rates of the cities that received these migrants.[24] Similarly, John Stack has shown that in the cities of mid-Victorian England, Irish children were more likely to be imprisoned than English children—a difference attributable partly to the greater poverty of the Irish immigrant population and partly to an anti-Irish prejudice that inclined the public, the police, and the courts to view Irish as incorrigible criminals and thus to "prosecute, convict, and imprison them more readily than the English."[25]

---

19. Eric A. Johnson and Eric H. Monkkonen, "Introduction," 7.
20. Elias, *The Civilizing Process*, xii-xiv.
21. Johnson and Monkkonen, "Introduction," 4-5.
22. *Ibid.*, 13.
23. Sharpe, " Crime in England," 24.
24. Johnson, "Cities Don't Cause Crime," 138.
25. Stack, "Children, Urbanization, and the Chances of Imprisonment in Mid-Victorian England," 133.

Which, if any, of these proposed models for the understanding of the relationship between crime and modernization can help us in the interpretation of China's experience? As we consider this question, we must be aware of the limitations involved. The simple *violence-au-vol* model, the refined, two-stage version proposed by Zehr and Shelley, and the civilizing process model are all based on analyses of a century or several centuries of historical development in the West. It might be more appropriate to analyze Chinese criminal trends for the twentieth century, rather than to look simply at the decade or so of China's modernization under Deng Xiaoping. Unfortunately, the turmoil that wracked China during the first half of the twentieth century makes it virtually impossible to gather complete and reliable statistical information for that period.[26] Similar problems face the researcher who looks for crime statistics for the first thirty years of the People's Republic. The best we can do at this point is to work with the information at hand, and to ask whether or not any preliminary patterns appear and, if so, to what extent they may be reasonably interpreted in terms of one of the available models of the relationship of crime to modernization.

The statistical information that we do have for the 1980s and early 1990s are suggestive of certain trends that are comparable to developments elsewhere. First the much more rapid increases in the rate of theft and other property offenses relative to violent offenses such as homicide and rape do seem to lend some credence to the *de la violence au vol* thesis. These figures cannot, however, overcome the various weaknesses of that theory. Although it seems to make some sense in the very long term, *violence-au-vol* cannot adequately take into account variations in the experience of different countries. Why, for example, should Sweden have experienced its greatest increase in theft rates, not during the industrialization of the late nineteenth century, but under the post-war welfare state?[27] Why should crime increase in some urban areas under modernization, but not in others? Furthermore, the apparent shift of criminality from violence to theft may be, to a greater or lesser extent, attributable, not to actual changes in the incidence of crime in the context of urbanization, but, rather, to changes in enforcement patterns.[28] The Chinese record certainly gives ample reason to believe that enforcement patterns should be taken seriously when trying to understand crime rates on the basis of the figures of arrests and trials.

---

26. Yan Jingyao states that while the Beijing and Nanjing governments of the Republican period both published criminal statistics, these were manufactured in order to convince Western observers that the Chinese criminal justice system was developing along Western lines and that for research purposes, they have no value. Yan Jingyao, *Zhongguo de fanzui wenti*, 16.

27. Osterberg, "Criminality, Social Control, and the Early Modern State," 83-84.

28. Weinberger, "Urban and Rural Crime Rates and Their Genesis in Late Nineteenth- and Early Twentieth-Century Britain," 200.

Second, the Chinese record gives no evidence for a civilizing process. The rising crime rates of the 1980s, the increases in juvenile offenses, the rebirth of old crimes (trafficking n women and prostitution) and the development of new offenses (economic crimes, smuggling, drug trafficking and drug use) seem to indicate that, at least in some respects, China is experiencing a decline in civilization. Of course, it is always possible that the 1980s were part of a transitional phase that will, in the long run, be overshadowed by a reassertion of state power, and in particular a strengthening of the state's monopoly on violence and thus the eventual repetition of the pattern that Johnson and Monkkonen argue is the Western European experience—declining levels of violence in a modernizing society.

Here again, however, the limitations of the model for the understanding of developments in the West should also inspire us to be cautious about its application to China's historical development. As it is based upon the same statistical records as is *violence-au-vol*, the civilizational process theory may also be undermined by the doubt that can be cast upon the reliability and interpretation of those records. Changes in the definition of violence and the willingness to prosecute various acts (fights, slaps, and vehicular homicide, for example) might have an effect on the apparent shifts in the level of violence. The scale of the decline in homicide might even be affected by changes in medical science—as J. S. Cockburn points out, most of those who died in the early modern age from wounds and broken bones would not do so today. Thus violence that resulted in homicide, and thus contributed to the higher homicide rates of early modern England would, in modern times, be attempted homicide at best. The lower homicide rate of modern England thus cannot be taken to indicate an exactly corresponding lower incidence of violence.[29]

The model that seems to bear the most relevance to China's experience in the 1980s is that put forth by Louise Shelley. Indeed, Shelley's book directly influenced those Chinese criminologists who, in the late 1980s, took the position that modernization is inevitably accompanied by increased crime rates. The universality of Shelley's conclusions proved attractive to scholars who had been trained in the Marxist tradition and then sought laws of historical development that could explain a phenomenon that seemed to contradict the older Party dogma about the ability of socialist China to avoid the rising crime rates that had accompanied modernization in the West.[30] China's increased crime rates, increased juvenile offenses, prostitution, and violence, all associated with a wave of industrialization and urbanization coincide nicely with Shelley's thesis of an initial, traumatic transitional period in which modernizing countries experience

29. Cockburn, "Patterns of Violence," 103.
30. Wang Zhemin and Huang Jingping, *Jingji fazhan yu fanzui bianhua*, 15-16.

rapidly rising crime rates—indeed, rates of increase more rapid than those observed in the developed world.

At the same time, it seems clear that in order to reach an adequate understanding of the relationship between crime and modernization in China (and elsewhere as well), Shelley's model needs to be refined in order to take into account differences in the rates of criminality in different urban settings and also to take into account differences in the level of enforcement. As was demonstrated in the preceding chapters, the statistical record in China reflects varying levels of enforcement, not simply varying levels of crime. The higher levels of hooliganism, rape, and theft observed in local jurisdictions and on the national scale in the context of the Strike Hard Campaign of 1983-84 are only the most striking example. Increases in rates of theft, particularly rates of "serious theft" do not simply reflect variations in the level of enforcement and in the greater availability of things to be stolen; they are also linked to inflationary trends that tended to increase the value of items taken from others, and thus to effectively lower the threshold of criminal responsibility.

Finally, increased crime rates in China in the 1980s may be partially attributable to China's relatively young population in the 1980s and to world-wide trends such as the growth of the international drug trade. Increased incidence of crime in certain rural and urban areas and the linkage in the Chinese literature of crime with transience and unemployment gives support to the argument that it is not simply urbanization and an alleged break-down of traditional social structures and morals, but rather material deprivation and discrimination that are the causes of crime. Thus despite the incidence of certain types of crime (trafficking in women and female infanticide, for example) that have roots in Chinese culture, China's experience of crime in the context of rapid modernization bears a strong resemblance to the development of crime under modernization elsewhere. Theoretical models such as that proposed by Louise Shelley for the understanding of the relationship between crime and modernization, although derived from the Western experience, are relevant to our understanding of developments in China. By the same token, such models must, if they are to attain the level of universality which they aim for must be tested against the historical experience of China as well as of the West.

MODERNIZATION AND THE CRIMINAL JUSTICE SYSTEM

If the development of crime rates and patterns of crime in China has been comparable to that experienced in the West and in other developing countries, can the same be said for the development of the criminal justice system? Have the police, the legal system, and the punitive regime of the People's Republic developed (or are they developing) in ways similar to those observed in the modern West? Or is the Chinese criminal justice system fundamentally different than the criminal justice systems of the West? If it is, then can the difference be attributed to China's Marxist-Leninist system, or is it best explained in terms of the continued strength of traditional institutions or ideas inherited from the Chinese past? Can problems such as the evident inattention to legal procedure, insufficient protection of defendants' and prisoners' rights, the use if confession, torture, and over-use of the death penalty best be explained as remnants from the Chinese past, or are they better understood by reference to the ideology, the structure, and the material conditions of the institutions of criminal justice as they existed in the late 1980s? In order to answer these questions, we shall first consider what the characteristics of a modern criminal justice system should be. Then we may ask whether the proposed model of legal modernity is relevant to an analysis of China's criminal justice system and whether or not Chinese criminal justice has developed along the lines of the proposed model.

Our definition of legal modernity is derived from the work of Max Weber. For Weber, the modernization of law was a process by which "a multitude of actually prevailing systems of law locally or personally limited in application" were replaced by "a body of rational law claiming universal validity."[31] According to the Weberian model, the rules of law must be "uniform and unvarying," equally applicable to all people within the territory under which they are governed. The law must also be transactional: "rights and obligations are apportioned as they result from transactions (contractual, tortuous and so on) between parties rather than aggregated into clusters that attach to persons because of determinants outside the particular transactions." Finally, laws must be universalist, rather than particular and intuitive, so that "the application of law is reproducible and predictable."[32]

According to the same model, modern law must be administered through institutions and techniques which themselves have the characteristics of modernity. The legal system must be hierarchical, with a network of lower and higher courts of appeal and review, all conforming to the same rational standards, so that the system will be predictable. Second, the system must be organized bureaucratically and operate impersonally according to standardized procedures and deciding cases on the basis of written rules. Third, the system must be staffed by full-time professionals whose qualifications come from their mastery of the legal system itself. Fourth, there must be a body of professionally trained lawyers to mediate between the legal system and the people who have to deal with it. Fifth, the system must be amendable through its own regular methods for revision of rules and

---

31. Weber. *The Interpretation of Social Reality*, 241.
32. This and the following paragraph summarize the Weberian model of legal modernity presented in Galanter, "The Modernization of Law," 1046-1049.

procedures as required by changing needs or preferences. Seventh, although functioning as an arm of the state, the modern legal system must be distinctly separate from the legislative and the executive functions. Finally, one would expect the use of only as much violent force, coercion, and punishment as are necessary to accomplish the tasks of restraining and reforming the offender.

Certainly this model cannot be taken as a literal description of the legal system of any particular country. Nevertheless, it is fair to say that the criminal justice systems of Western Europe and North America developed toward this ideal in the nineteenth and twentieth centuries. Concurrently, we note the development of the modern professional police force and, in punishment, a shift from the techniques of public shaming, torture, and execution toward systems of incarceration whose initial aim was not merely to punish the offender, but to isolate and then reform him/her. Interpretations of the significance of this modern transformation of criminal justice vary. Many have regarded the development of the modern Western systems of policing, law, and punishment as the outcome of a humanitarian effort that has protected the individual from the coercive power of the state. Others, most notably Michel Foucault, see instead the growth of ever-more rational, scientific, efficient, but repressive systems of control in which the state and a corps of professional "experts" who are empowered to isolate and manipulate not only the body, but the very soul of the individual in the effort to produce social conformity. The resulting modern society is, for Foucault, not the realm of freedom; instead, it is the "carceral city" in which each individual is entrapped in a series of interlocking systems of observation, control, and reform.[33]

If we can agree that the criminal justice systems of the modern West developed roughly along the lines sketched out above, then what of the development of modern criminal justice in China? Some would argue that the essential characteristics of Chinese criminal justice in the 1980s were derived from or are attributable to the influence of the ideas, the techniques, and the institutions of the Chinese past. For example, the People's Republic uses a household registration system. So to did the dynastic governments of China as far back as the Qin (221-206 BCE). The People's Republic sends prisoners to remote border areas (particularly to Xinjiang) in order to combine the punishment and reform of criminals with the tasks of opening up new agricultural land and increasing the Han Chinese population of these non-Han areas. So to did the Qing Dynasty send criminals into exile in Xinjiang, for similar reasons.[34] The People's Republic strongly encourages (and in practice, sometimes forces) criminals to confess and works (or claims to work) to reform them; dynastic Chinese laws such as the Qing Code required confession and looked also to the possible reform of the offender.

---

33. Foucault, *Discipline and Punish*, 307-308.
34. For a description, see Waley-Cohen, *Exile in Mid-Qing China*.

The pre-modern legal system prescribed the use of torture in order to elicit both confessions and testimony; torture was an endemic problem in the practice of criminal justice in the 1980s. Under the Qing and other dynasties, law was viewed as an instrument; the coercive power of the state was ultimately derived from the power of the emperor and employed by his agents in an attempt to accomplish the task of the moral transformation of the people that was understood to be essential to the maintenance of the stability of the Chinese universe. The Communist Party uses the criminal justice system as an instrument of social engineering. The legal philosophy of China was highly concerned with the prevention of deviant behavior through the inculcation of morality, and this value placed on prevention was reflected in the laws and in the techniques of rulership adopted by dynastic governments. The People's Republic, too, places great theoretical emphasis on the innate goodness of the individual, the possibility of reform, and the importance of preventing crime rather than simply detecting and punishing it after the fact.

On another level, one might argue, as has Lung-kee Sun, that many contemporary Chinese institutions and many aspects of contemporary Chinese behavior are understandable as manifestations of the "deep structure" of Chinese culture. The core of this "deep structure" is, according to Sun, the definition of the individual in the context of his/her exchange of feelings and care with other individuals in the context of a hierarchical collective whose fundamental model is the patriarchal family.[35] In the field of traditional Chinese criminal justice, this preference for hierarchy and collectivism was evident, for example, in the provision that the punishment of an offender would be decided, in part, on the basis of the family relationship of the offender to the victim as well as in such institutions of policing as the household registration system. In the modern era, the same assumptions or core values may be seen to pervade the new institutions of policing and of criminal justice.

These apparent continuities with the Chinese past have been interpreted in a variety of ways. In the 1970s and 1980s some Western scholars, seeking enlightenment and possible solutions to the problems of crime, recidivism, and an unresponsive legal system in the West, thought that they had found answers to the problems of the modern West in a Chinese present in which the Chinese past lived on. Discussing China's criminal justice system as it appeared on the eve of reform in the late 1970s, Victor Li suggested that the European-style formal legal system of police, courts, and procuratorates, trials, and prisons was misleading; that in fact, the Chinese approach to crime was inspired, not by the adversarial European approach, but by traditional Chinese Confucian values.[36]

---

35. Sun Longji, *Zhongguo wenhua de shenceng jiegou*, 14-15; Sun, "Contemporary Chinese Culture: Structure and Emotionality," 2-3.
36. Li, *Law Without Lawyers*.

Following Li, a number of American academics found in the legal system of the People's Republic a repository of humanitarian Confucian values which, at their best, express a confidence in human nature and a faith in the capacity of the state, the Party, and society to prevent crime and to reform deviants. The Chinese approach to social control, they suggested, holds lessons that from which the West might profit.[37] These lessons included the use of legal education programs for the general public, the importance of citizen involvement in the process of dispute resolution, and the involvement of citizens in crime control initiatives.[38] Beyond these practical suggestions lay another potential lesson for Americans. As Ronald Troyer put it:

> In the United States, the dominant approach begins with presuppositions about the innate depravity of human beings. We devise criminal justice systems and laws on this basis and are then surprised when people turn out to be brutes. This in turn becomes a rationale for even harsher laws and more punitive approaches. But the problem never changes.[39]

What Americans could really learn from Chinese criminal justice, Troyer argued, was to take a more optimistic view of human nature and construct a criminal justice system that would look toward the possibilities for good that are innate in each and every individual. The Chinese approach seemed, in short, to be more humane and more caring than that of the American criminal justice system.

Western and Chinese critics of the Chinese system, on the other hand, located the problems of Chinese criminal justice in the Chinese past. China's criminal justice system was regarded as "backward," its problems described (in Chinese Marxist terms) as "the dregs of feudalism."[40] In this analysis, the solution to torture and other violations of human rights is to be sought in a process of modernization in which the Chinese criminal justice system joins those of the liberal democracies.

It is neither desirable nor necessary that we entirely rule out the influence of ideas and practices inherited from the Chinese past in our effort to understand the development of criminal justice in the 1980s. But it would be misleading if we were to simply regard the Chinese criminal justice system as an area passed by in China's drive toward modernity, to relegate it to the status of a backward, feudal relic that has yet to be modernized or to regard it as the repository of some ancient Oriental wisdom that has been long-forgotten (or was never even learned) in the West. It would be equally misleading if we were to assume that the Chinese

---

37. See the essays in Troyer, Clark and Rojek, ed. *Social Control in the People's Republic of China*.
38. Troyer, *Social Control*, 195.
39. *Ibid*.
40. For examples, see the discussion in Dutton, *Policing and Punishment*, 6-12.

criminal justice system is so unique that it cannot fairly be discussed in terms of the western model of modernity.

As Stanley Lubman has observed, evaluation of the Chinese criminal justice system in terms of the Weberian model is justified to the degree that Chinese legal scholars and legal workers accept many of the characteristics of that model as their own goals in the ongoing task of constructing a Chinese socialist legal system.[41] In fact, under pressure from the Western nations, the modernization of China's systems of police, criminal law, and punishment along Western lines began during the last years of the Qing and proceeded throughout the Republican period. Western-style laws and legal institutions were introduced, police advisers brought over, and modern prisons constructed.[42] Thus in the 1980s Chinese legal scholars saw the Chinese legal system and its development as a part of international trends.[43]

With this background of westernization and modernization in the first half of the twentieth century, along with the adaptation of Soviet law to the purposes of the People's Republic in the 1950s, it is hardly surprising that the legal system of the 1980s did, in many respects, conform to the Weberian model of modernity. China's laws, its legal institutions, and its legal theory were all derived from European models. The Criminal Law and the Criminal Procedure Law of 1979 were constructed as universal laws to be uniformly applied to all people under Chinese jurisdiction. Liability for punishment was incurred through a criminal transaction between offender and victim. The institutions of the legal system were hierarchical bureaucracies in which the handling of cases was guided by a body of written rules and procedures. The legal system was based on neither theological nor superstitious beliefs. Although professional staff were in insufficient supply, there was a clear commitment to the professionalization of the police, the courts, and the procuratorates, as well as to the training of a corps of professional lawyers. The legal system was amendable through institutional procedures including the passage of new legislation and the publication of legal interpretations.

The essentially modern nature of China's legal system should lead us to consider the possibility that those aspects of Chinese criminal justice that we find most disturbing—inattention to procedure, violation of the rights of defendants, confession, torture, and the use of the death penalty—might best be explained, not in terms of the Chinese past, but in terms of the structure and conditions of the Chinese legal system as they stood in the 1980s. For example, the importance attached to confession and the frequent resort to torture in order to obtain it may

---

41. Lubman, "Emerging Functions of Formal Legal Institutions in China's Modernization," 260.

42. On legal reform, see Meijer, *The Introduction of Modern Criminal Law in China*. Dutton, *Policing and Punishment* includes descriptions of prison reform. The development of modern police is discussed in Wakeman, *Policing Shanghai*.

43. Gan Yupei, "Dangdai xingfa kexue yanjiu zhong de shijiexing quxiang," 688-89.

be best be understood, not as an unfortunate inheritance from the past, but, rather, in terms of the difficulties of police work in China, lack of police training and resources, and pressure to produce results. Lack of attention to procedure and violation of defendants' rights in the courts may be understood by reference to the hierarchical structure of China's Soviet-style legal system and by the leadership function of the Communist Party, rather than in terms of an alleged historical tendency of the Chinese not to be concerned with legal procedure.

If there is any continuity with the past at all, it may be at the "deep structural" level—long-held cultural assumptions may inform the Chinese people's choice and adaptation of modern Western institutions and techniques. The Chinese acceptance of Marxism itself may arguably be related to the "fit" between already established Chinese preferences for collectivism and socialist economic and social organization. But wherever we see apparent continuity with the past in specific institutions, practices, or elements of political discourse (references, for example, to "Chinese tradition" or "Chinese morality") we should be aware that there is not a single, ongoing tradition—there are, instead, many practices, ideas, institutions, and techniques, created in the present and legitimized by reference to the past. Therefore, although the Chinese past remains relevant to our understanding of Chinese criminal justice system of the 1980s, the essential characteristics of that system are best located in that system itself, rather than in the past. There are, I would argue, two basic characteristics that defined the Chinese criminal justice system in the 1980s—characteristics that have a good deal to do with the problems of that system: poverty and the legal instrumentalism.

China's lack of human and material resources appear to have been a major problem for the construction and the operation of the Chinese criminal justice system in the 1980s. As a result of years of Party disdain for law, China in the late 1970s was a place with virtually no lawyers, a decrepit court system, a decimated procuratorate, and a police force that had served as a tool of factional political struggle. Such judges and procurators as existed were often ill-trained, or untrained. For ten years during the Cultural Revolution, the state had even lost its monopoly on coercive force as the masses dispensed "justice" on their own account. The lack of human resources was exacerbated by a lack of material resources—buildings, office supplies, living quarters for court and procuratorial staff, and low wages for everyone concerned would be an obstacle to the construction of any modern legal system, no matter how progressive, liberal, or forward-looking it might be in theory. Many of the problems of the Chinese legal system of the 1980s—including, I would argue, inattention to procedure, the use of torture, and the mistreatment of prisoners—were related to the poverty that afflicted the criminal justice system.

The second characteristic of the Chinese criminal justice system in the 1980s was instrumentalism. Legal instrumentalism is, of course, not unique to China. As Kalman Kulcsar points out, it has been the case in socialist states generally, and in many developing nations as well, that law becomes an instrument for the modernization of society.[44] But such instrumentalism is not limited to the socialist and to the developing nations. Lawrence M. Friedman argues that " In modern times, law is an instrument; the people in power use it to push or pull toward some definite goal. The idea of law as a rational tool underlies all modern systems, whether capitalist, socialist, fascist, democratic or authoritarian."[45] Instrumentalism is based on the fundamentally modern assumption that the rational human being, as he/she applies the scientific method to the problem of material and cultural development, can employ various instruments—the law among them—in order to guide that development in the right direction.

What was distinctive and problematic about legal instrumentalism in China (and the same can be said for other socialist and many developing countries as well) was its linkage to a political system in which a single ruling political party sought to use law as an instrument for the management and for the improvement of society. The Chinese police, procuratorates, courts, and labor camps were understood to be weapons or tools in the hands of the Communist Party. Instrumentalism in this sense represents a significant diversion from the Weberian model of legal modernity, for it places the courts, along with the police, the procuratorate, and the labor reform system under the unified leadership of the Communist Party and puts them in the service of its ultimate goal—the modernization of Chinese society. The legal instrumentalism of the 1980s, along with the leading role of the Chinese Communist party, gave the criminal justice system under Deng a certain degree of continuity with the criminal justice system of the Maoist era. The two were certainly not identical—the existence of formal codes of law and the emphasis, in the Deng era, on common criminals rather than on political offenders distinguish the post-Mao criminal justice system from the system as it operated under Mao. What remained the same were the idea of harnessing criminal justice to long-term utopian goals of social transformation (as well as transformation of individual offenders) and certain concrete practices through which the Party exercised leadership over the concrete practice of criminal justice—procuratorial and adjudication committees, the use of Party policy to direct the application of law, and the practice of a high degree of cooperation between police, procuratorates, and courts (sometimes to the point of virtually collapsing the separate stages of the criminal procedure), and the use of campaign tactics.

Instrumentalism in combination with the one-party system was clearly one of the major causes of many of the abuses that characterized criminal justice during the 1980s—the loosely-drawn laws that allowed judicial personnel to bend

---

44. Kulcsar, *Modernization and the Law*, 106.
45. Friedman, *A History of American Law*, 29.

procedural rules, the sacrifice of defendants' rights in the name of efficiency, the reluctance of the authorities to pursue and punish cases of torture, and even the tendency to over-rely on the death penalty are all linked to the assumption that the law is simply one of many means to a morally unchallengeable end—an instrument that may be used, altered, or set aside at will. These problems were exacerbated by modernization and social change so fast and by pressure to keep up with and to control the direction of change so intense that, as in many modernizing states, there was a tendency in China for those in power to "set over-ambitious goals" for the law and for the legal system and to "hope for far too spectacular results."[46] This inevitably led to a perception of failure as the criminal justice system proved incapable of fulfilling its assigned task and the Party's plans for the construction of a morally and aesthetically attractive modern spiritual civilization were overtaken by popular culture, changing mores, and crime.

Such was the fate of criminal justice in the 1980s. Thus the problems of the Chinese criminal justice system of that decade—problems pointed out not only by Western observers but also by Chinese scholars—had their roots not simply in the Chinese past, but in the context of the single-minded pursuit of modernity by a Chinese central leadership plagued by regionalism, weakness, inadequate infrastructure, lack of trained legal professionals, and poorly paid personnel. And so, China's experience of crime and criminal justice in the context of the modernization drive of the 1980s was traumatic and full of inequities, abuses, torture, and abuses of power. Many of these problems were exacerbated during the anti-crime campaigns of the early to mid-1980s. To some extent, the arbitrary powers of the state were increased and the rights of defendants weakened as the criminal justice system was refined and amended during the anti-crime campaigns of the early and mid-1980s.

But while the story of crime, criminal justice, and modernization in China during the 1980s is in many ways a sad and frustrating one, it is not neither unique nor uniquely bad. In many respects, the relationship between crime, criminal justice, and modernization in China bears resemblance to that seen elsewhere in human history. To say so, and to point out that the weaknesses and problems of China's criminal justice system were weaknesses and problems closely linked to China's poverty as well as to its pursuit of modernity under the conditions of single-party leadership is not to deny the seriousness of the torture, the arbitrary detentions, the shocking conditions of labor camps, the numerous executions or other human rights abuses that pervaded the practice of criminal justice in China in the 1980s and continued into the next decade. Nor should it be read as an apologetic for the use of the criminal justice system against non-violent political dissidents. It should, however, make us aware that problems such as the emphasis

---

46. Kulcsar, *Modernization and the Law*, 112.

on confession, the violation of defendants' rights and the use of torture are not as alien as we imagine, and that neither the structure of crime nor the fundamental characteristics of the Chinese criminal justice system will really change until China undergoes further significant economic as well as political development.

AFTERWARD

In 1996 and 1997 the National People's Congress of the PRC passed legislation that extensively revised the Criminal Procedure and Criminal Laws that were originally promulgated in 1979.[47] In all likelihood, these are the laws that will take Chinese criminal justice into the next century. We might ask, then, whether or not the changes made in 1996 and 1997 will bring about any fundamental changes in the system of criminal justice that developed during the anti-crime campaigns of the early to mid-1980s. The answer would seem to be a qualified "yes."

The amendments made to the criminal and criminal procedure laws fall into two categories: rhetorical and substantive. On the rhetorical side, the language of class struggle has been toned down considerably in the amended laws. The revised Criminal Procedure Law states that it is formulated on the basis of the constitution and that its tasks include the punishment of criminals in order to safeguard "the progress of socialist construction." References to Marxism-Leninism, Mao Zedong Thought, the dictatorship of the proletariat and the safeguarding of the socialist revolution in Articles One and Two of the 1979 Criminal Procedure Law have been eliminated from the corresponding articles of the new law. The removal of Marxist-Leninist revolutionary rhetoric brings the law up to date with the real status of the Chinese Communist Party, which is no longer a revolutionary organization seeking to bring about Marxian socio-economic change but has become a ruling party that seeks national economic development and preservation of social and economic stability.

The transformation of the Communist regime is also indicated in some of the substantive changes of the law. In the criminal code, counter-revolution has been

---

47. The text the Criminal Procedure Law as amended in 1996 may be found in *Zhonghua renmin gongheguo xingshi susongfa*, 40-100. The text of the revised Criminal Law may be found in Guowuyuan fazhiju, ed., *Zhonghua renmin gongheguo xin fagui huibian 1997 diyiji*, 16-124.

eliminated, replaced by the new offense of endangering state security.[48] The vaguely defined, morally charged offense of hooliganism has been eliminated. In its place, the various types of behavior that fell under the rubric of hooliganism have been explicitly defined and included under a variety of other offenses. According to the provisions of the new Criminal Procedure Law, the public security organs will no longer be able to detain criminal suspects indefinitely for "shelter and investigation." In contrast to the previous system of "verdict first, trial second," judges will now be required to hear the evidence in court and make their decision afterward. Defense lawyers, previously allowed to participate in the criminal process only in the trial stage, may now be retained by a criminal suspect from the first day on which he/she has been questioned or subject to a coercive measure. Procurators and defense lawyers are to be allowed to debate the evidence and to cross-examine witnesses in court.[49]

Much of the revision carries with it the hope that the criminal procedure in China will ultimately become more open and achieve a greater degree of conformity to procedure. The increased attention given to defendants' rights and specifically to the greater regulation and oversight of police administrative detention and to the role of the defense lawyer before and during trial could reduce the incidence of arbitrary detention and torture while at the same time lending the Chinese criminal justice system a greater aura of legality and fairness both within China and in the eyes of Western observers. The increased numbers of professionally trained lawyers, procurators, and judges turned out by Chinese law schools since the 1980s seems to increase the likelihood of the laws being implemented in practice. Also encouraging is the possibility that leaders at the Party center believe that a greater degree of openness in the criminal justice system can help to reduce corruption and incompetence on the part of judiciary personnel. NPC Chairman Li Peng's suggestion that all trials other than those involving state secrets, personal privacy, or juvenile cases be open to the public and that jury systems be established in the base level people's courts indicate that at least some in the Chinese leadership are thinking along these lines.[50]

But while we acknowledge the significance of the progress that has been made, there is reason to be skeptical about the possibility that changes in the law will bring about rapid and thorough changes in the practice of criminal justice or that they will appreciably increase the ability of the criminal justice system to address the problem of crime.

The factors mitigating against a quick resolution of the problems of Chinese criminal justice are both logistical and philosophical. On the logistical side,

---

48. "Zhonghua renmin gongheguo xingfa" (Criminal law of the PRC),
49. See the discussion in Lawyers Committee for Human Rights. *Opening to Reform?* 9-18.
50. Kwan, "Li Peng Pushes for Trials," 1.

changes in the law will not resolve problems associated with poorly trained staff, lack of material resources, low pay, the pressure to achieve fast results, and the need for the labor reform system to generate revenue in order to defray the costs of imprisonment. Inasmuch as these problems are among the reasons for China's police, procuratorates and courts to have resorted to arbitrary detention, interrogation under torture, the denial of defendants rights and the abusive exploitation of prisoner labor in the 1980s, we can expect to see the same abuses continue into the next century, regardless of what the law may say about them. The gradual influx of younger and better-trained personnel may mitigate these problems in the long run, but it will not lead to rapid short-term improvement. Nor can we expect crime rates to respond to changes in the criminal and criminal procedure laws. As economic reform and opening to international trade place continued pressure on the moribund state-run industries, bankruptcies and restructuring may bring about increased unemployment, increased disparities in the distribution of wealth, and thus further increases in crime. This is not to say that changes in the law are meaningless, but simply to point out that it would it would be unreasonable to expect changes in the law to achieve a quick fix for problems rooted more in the concrete social and economic circumstances under which the organs of criminal justice operate than in the letter of the law itself.

While logistical considerations limit the capacity of any laws to bring about change in the behavior of either the law enforcers or of deviants in society, philosophical principles limit the ability of the criminal justice to achieve fundamental change. Nothing in the revised laws indicates a change in the theoretical basis of Chinese criminal justice or in the guiding principles, policies, and techniques for addressing crime that developed in the context of the anti-crime campaigns of the 1980s. The Chinese regime continues to subscribe to the belief that a combination of preventive/reformative strategies in order to deal with crime in combination with resort to harsh punishment in the face of increasing social instability and rising crime rates. Indeed, many of the harsher penalties that had been added to the original Criminal Law during the anti-crime campaigns of the 1980s were written into the code as it was amended in 1997. In the practice of criminal justice, continuity with the approach developed in the mid-1980s was demonstrated when the promulgation of the revised Criminal Procedure Law in March 1996 was followed by yet another Strike Hard campaign, by renewed emphasis on comprehensive management,[51] and by a strong crackdown on China's small political dissident movement.

Finally, it is clear that the revisions of the criminal and criminal procedure laws have had no affect on the theoretical assumption of legal instrumentalism and upon the continued role of the criminal justice system as a tool or weapon in the

---

51. Hu Kangsheng. "Xiugai xingshi susongfa shi Zhongguo yifa zhiguo de biaozhi," 9.

hands of the Chinese Communist Party. As long as legal instrumentalism is not challenged and the leadership of the Communist Party over the legal organs remains in place, then it remains possible for central or local Party leaders to determine the direction, targets, and severity of criminal justice and to set the law aside in particular cases or at particular times when, in their estimation, the situation demands it.

The revision of the criminal and criminal procedure laws is to be welcomed as a step in the right direction. In the drafting and promulgation of codes of criminal law and criminal procedure in 1979, the development of the criminal justice system in the context of the anti-crime campaigns of the 1980s, and the revisions of the laws in the 1990s may appear as parts or stages in a longer process of legal development that also includes increased emphasis on legal education, the construction of the civil code and other areas of law, and educational legal exchange with Western countries including the United States of America and Britain. But the fundamental characteristics of the administration of criminal justice as they developed in the early 1980s run deeper than the letter of the law. As long as the Party remains above the law and the law remains an instrument of attempted social management and social engineering in the hands of the Party, and as long as the underlying factors of poverty, growing differences in the distribution of wealth, and the heavy workload imposed upon an untrained and insufficient cadre of police, procurators, lawyers and judges are not addressed, there is a real danger that in the short term, the practical significance of changes in the law will remain limited. Indeed, progressive changes in the written laws may at times seem to lead not to substantial improvements in the administration of criminal justice, but to an even greater gap between legal theory and legal practice.

REFERENCES

INTERVIEWS:

Interviews with persons in the field of legal studies and with persons involved in the practice of criminal justice were carried out in Beijing in 1992. The names of those interviewed have not been included unless the interview was arranged and carried out under official auspices.

1. Beijing. February 3, 1992.
2. Li Shukun, procurator. Supreme People's Procuratorate, Beijing. May 22, 1992.
3. Beijing. March 13, 1992.
4. Beijing. March 3, 1992.
5. New York. November 30, 1992.
6-a. Beijing. January 14, 1992.
6-b. Beijing. March 25, 1992.
7. Beijing. January 5, 1992.
8. Beijing. December 21, 1991.
9. Beijing. February 19, 1992.
10. Beijing. May 15, 1992.
11. Beijing. December 28, 1991.
12. Zhou Daoluan, Director of the Policy Research Office, Supreme People's Court. Beijing. May 16, 1992.
13. Beijing. May 28, 1993.

BOOKS, DISSERTATIONS, AND ARTICLES:

Amnesty International. *China Punishment Without Crime: Administrative Detention.* AI Index: ASA 17/27/91 London: Amnesty International Publications, 1991.

Amnesty International. *China Violations of Human Rights: Prisoners of Conscience and the Death Penalty in the People's Republic of China.* London: Amnesty International Publications, 1984.

Amnesty International. *China: Torture and Ill-Treatment of Prisoners.* AI Index: ASA 17/07/87. New York: Amnesty International Publications, 1987.

An Chunlian. *Lun xingshi susong guanxia* [On jurisdiction in the criminal process]. Beijing: M.A. thesis, People's University, 5 July 1989.

Anhui sheng gonganting. "Zhibiao zhiben yiqizhua" [Cure the symptoms and the roots of the disease simultaneously]. In Gonganbu bangongting, ed. *Zonghe zhili shehui zhian jingyan xuanbian, dier ji* [Selected experiences in the comprehensive management of public security]. Beijing: Qunzhong chubanshe, 1986: 25-26.

Anhui sheng gaoji renmin fayuan yanjiushi. "Cong panchu sixing anjian zhong kan jin jinian lai nongcun fasheng zhongda xianxing fanzui de xin qingkuang" [The new situation of current serious crimes in the rural areas in recent years as seen in capital cases]. *Renmin sifa* [People's adjudication] 12:3-6 (1983).

Ankang xianzhi [Gazetteer of Ankang county]. Xi'an: Shaanxi renmin chubanshe, 1989.

Asia Watch. *Prison Labor in China.* New York, 1991.

Bakken, Borge. "Crime, Juvenile Delinquency, and Deterrence Policy in China." *The Australian Journal of Chinese Affairs* 30:29-58 (1993).

_____. *The Exemplary Society: Human Improvement, Social Control and the Dangers of Modernity in China.* Oslo: Department of Sociology, University of Oslo, 1994.

Bao Suixian. "Dui Zhongguo sixing wenti de shenceng sikao" [Thinking seriously about the issue of the death penalty in China]. In Yang Dunxian and Cao Zidan, ed., *Gaige kaifang yu xingfa fazhan—1992 nian xingfa xueshu yantaohui lunwen jingxuan* [Reform, opening, and the development of criminal law—selected papers from the 1992 research conference on criminal law studies]. Beijing: Zhongguo jiancha chubanshe, 1993: 167-176.

Bao Shengqing. "Xingshi jiejiao renyuan chongxin fanzui de tedian yuanyin ji duice" [The characteristics, causes of, and countermeasures to new offenses committed by personnel released from labor reform and labor re-education]. *Fanzui yu gaizao yanjiu* [Studies in Crime and Reform], 1:49-50 (1991).

Bao Gang. "Tantan qianghua laodong gaizo shouduan" [On Strengthening the methods of labor reform]. *Fanzui yu gaizao yanjiu* [Studies in Crime and Reform], 2:4-6 (1991).

Bao, Ruowang (Jean Pasqualini) and Rudolph Chelminski. *Prisoner of Mao*. New York: Coward, McCann and Geoghegan, Inc. 1973.

Baum, Richard. "Modernization and Legal Reform in Post-Mao China: The Rebirth of Socialist Legality." *Studies in Comparative Communism* 19.2:69-103 (1986).

Beijingshi zhongxiaoxuesheng liushi yu weifa fanzui lianhe diaochazu. "Buke hushi de yige yanzhong shehui wenti" [A serious social problem that cannot be ignored]. *Beijing sifa* [Beijing jurisprudence] 4:27-28, 30 (August, 1985).

Berman, Harold J. *Soviet Criminal Law and Procedure: The RSFSR Codes*. Cambridge, Mass.: Harvard University Press, 1966.

_____. *Justice in the USSR*. Cambridge, Mass.:Harvard University Press, 1966.

Bi Xiaonan. "Queyou mingxian haozhuan, mianlin xin de wenti" [Truly a clear turn for the better, but facing new problems]. *Renmin sifa* 1:10-11 (1987).

Black, George and Robin Munro. *Black Hands of Beijing: Lives in Defiance in China's Democracy Movement*. New York: John Wiley and Sons, Inc., 1993.

Bo Juyi. "Xing, li, dao" [Penal law, rites, and the way] In *Bo Juyi ji* [Works of Bo Juyi] (four volumes). Beijing: Zhonghua shuju, 1979, vol. 4:1352-1353.

Bodde, Derk and Clarence Morris. *Law in Imperial China*. Taibei: Xinyue tushu gufen youxian gongsi, 1971.

"By Laws or by Cadres." *The Economist*, 6 February 1988: 34.

"Caizhengbu, sifabu guanyu xinzeng fanren he laojiao renyuan jingfei wenti de buchong tongzhi" [Supplementary circular of the ministry of finance and the ministry of justice regarding the question of expenses of newly added prisoners and labor re-education personnel]. Document dated 21 March 1984, in *Zhonghua renmin gongheguo falu guifanxing jieshi jicheng*: 1595.

Cao Manzhi, ed. *Zhongguo qingshaonian fanzuixue* [Youth criminology in China]. Beijing: Qunzhong chubanshe, 1987.

Cao Yi. "Guangzhou shi maiyin funu qingkuang poxi" [Analysis of women prostitutes in Guangzhou]. *Shehuixue yu shehui diaocha* [Sociology and social research] 6:44-46 (1989).

Chalidze, Valery. *Criminal Russia: Essays on Crime in the Soviet Union* Translated from the Russian by P.S. Falla. New York: Random House, 1977.

Changshan xianzhi [Gazetteer of Changshan county]. Hangzhou: Zhejiang renmin chubanshe, 1990.

Chen Guangzhong. "Zhongguo xingshi susongfaxu sishi nian, shang" [Forty years of Chinese criminal process law studies, part 1]. *Zhengfa luntan* [Politics and law tribunal] 4:5-14 (August 1989).

Chen Guyuan. *Zhongguo fazhishi* [History of Chinese law]. Beijing: Zhongguo shudian, 1988. Reprint of the 1934 edition.

Chen Xingliang, ed. *Jingji fanzui yian tanjiu* [Analysis of difficult economic cases]. Beijing: Zhongguo shehui kexue chubanshe, 1990.

_____, ed. *Jingji xingfaxue (zonglun)*. [Economic crime (general part)]. Beijing: Zhongguo shehui kexueyuan, 1990.

Chen Yu, Tang Guofang, Xu Shiying and Chen Xiuping. "Yanda hou xinshou nufan de qingkuang he tedian" [The situation and characteristics of women offenders newly received after the strike hard campaign]. In Jiangsusheng faxuehui qingshaonian fanzui yanjiuhui and Jiangsu sheng shehui kexueyuan zhengfa yanjiusuo, ed., *Qingshaonian fanzui yanjiu* [Studies in youth crime]: 197-210.

Chen Zhongshun. "Daxue jingshen weisheng" [Psychological health in the university]. *Zhongguo shenjing jingshen jibing zazhi* [Chinese journal of neurological and psychological disease] 11.2:92-94 (1985).

Chen Zixian. "Yanjin xingxun bigong weizhe yifa chengchu" [Coercion of confessions under torture is strictly forbidden; violators will be punished according to law]. *Beijing Sifa* [Beijing Adjudication] 4:6 (June 1984).

"Chinese Leaders Call for Stability." Beijing: U.P.I., 24 December 1993.

Chiu, Hung-dah. "China's Legal Reform." *Current History* 84.503:268-271 (September 1985).

Chiu, Hung-dah. "China's Changing Criminal Justice System." *Current History* 87.530:265-268, 271-272 (September 1988)

Chong Fa. "Bo fanzui youli lun" [Refutation of the theory that crime is justified]. *Beijing ribao* [Beijing daily] 7 November 1983:3.

Cockburn, J.S. "Patterns of Violence in English Society: Homicide in Kent, 1560-1985." *Past and Present* 130:70-106 (February 1991).

Cohen, Jerome Alan. *The Criminal Process in the People's Republic of China, 1949-1963: An Introduction.* Cambridge, Mass.: Harvard University Press, 1968.

"Concepts of Law in the Chinese Anti-Crime Campaign." *Harvard Law Review* 98.1870:1890-1908 (1985).

Confucius. *The Analects.* Translated and with an introduction by D.C. Lau. Harmondsworth: Penguin Books, 1979.

"Congkuai reng ying jianchi yifa banshi." [In rapid punishment, handling of work in accordance with law should still be upheld]. *Renmin sifa* [People's Adjudication] 9:15-16 (1981).

The Criminal Law and the Criminal Procedure Law of China. Beijing: Foreign Languages Press, 1984.

Da Dan. "Dui 203 ming maiyin renyuan bijiao fenxi" [Comparative analysis of 203 prostitutes]. *Qingshaonian yanjiu* [Studies in youth crime] 6:43-47 (1990).

Dai Zihong. "Wunianlai nuxing weifa fanzui de jiben qingkuang" [The basic situation of female criminal offenses in the past five years]. *Zhejiang faxue* [Zhejiang Jurisprudence] 4:25-26 (1989).

Dangdai Zhongguo de gongan gongzuo [Public security work in contemporary China]. Beijing: Dangdai Zhongguo chubanshe, 1992.

Dangdai Zhongguo de shenpan gongzuo (shang) [Judicial work in contemporary China (vol. 1)]. Beijing: Dangdai Zhongguo chubanshe, 1993.

Davis, Stephen P. "The Death Penalty and Legal Reform in China." *Journal of Chinese Law* 1.2:303-334 (fall 1987).

"Dazhong chengshi ying jinkuai jianli jingshenbing guanzhi yiyuan" [Large and medium cities should establish mental hospitals as rapidly as possible]. *Renmin gonganbao* [People's Police], 24 May, 1988: 1.

Dazu xian jianchazhi. [Dazu County Procuratorial Gazetteer]. Dazu County, Sichuan: Dazu County Procuratorate, 1988.

Deng Xiaoping. "Combat Economic Crime." In *Selected Works of Deng Xiaoping (1975-1982)*: 380-382.

Deng Xiaoping. *Build Socialism With Chinese Characteristics.* Beijing: Foreign Languages Press, 1985.

Deng Xiaoping. *Fundamental Issues in Present-Day China*, New York: Pergamon Press, 1987.

Deng Xiaoping. "The Present Situation and the Tasks Before Us." In *Selected Works of Deng Xiaoping (1975-1982)*: 224-258.

Deng Xiaoping. "Talk at a Meeting of the Standing Committee of the Political Bureau of the Central Committee (17 January 1986], in Deng, *Fundamental Issues in Present-Day China*: 136-140.

Deng Xiaoping. "Speech at the Third Plenary Session of the Central Advisory Commission of the Communist Party of China." In Deng, *Build Socialism With Chinese Characteristics*: 54-64.

Deng Qun. "Shilun jingji fazhan yu fanzui zengzhang de guanxi" [On the relation between economic development and increases in crime]. *Qingshaonian fanzui yanjiu* [Studies in youth crime] 3/4:1-6 (1989).

Deng Youtian and Deng Xiuming. "Dangqian zhongxiaoxue shisheng weifa fanzui de zhuangkuang yu tedian" [The current situation and characteristics of primary and middle school drop-out lawbreaking and crime]. *Qingshaonian fanzui yanjiu* [Studies in youth crime] 11:12-16 (1989).

Ding Yichou. "Zhuanzheng xia de 'fazhi'" ["Rule of law" under dictatorship]. *Jiushi niandai* [The nineties] 192:17 (January 1986).

"Diwujie quanguo renmin daibiao dahui changwu weiyuanhui di shisan ci huiyi guanyu xingshi susongfa shishi wenti de jueding" [Decision of the thirteenth meeting of the standing committee of the fifth national people's congress regarding the question of implementation of the criminal procedure law]. Document dated 12 February 1980, in *Zhonghua renmin gongheguo falu guifanxing jieshi jicheng*: 676.

Domenach, Jean-luc. *Chine: l'archipel oublié*. Paris: Fayard 1992.

Dongning xianzhi [Gazetteer of Dongning county]. Harbin: Heilongjiang renmin chubanshe, 1989.

Dutton, Michael R. *Policing and Punishment in China: From Patriarchy to "the People."* Cambridge: Cambridge University Press, 1992.

Elias, Norbert. *The Civilizing Process: The History of Manners*. Translated by Edmund Jephcott. New York: Urizen Books, 1978.

Fang Qiang. *Fazhi xinlixue gailun* [Introduction to legal psychology]. Beijing: Qunzhong chubanshe, 1986.

Feldbrugger, F.J.M. and William B. Simonas, ed. *Perspectives on Soviet Law for the 1980s*. The Hague: Martinus Nijhoff, 1982.

Forster, Robert and Orest Ranum, ed. *Deviants and the Abandoned in French Society: Selections from the Annales Economies, Societes, Civilisations, Volume 4.* Baltimore and London: The Johns Hopkins University Press, 1978.

Foucault, Michel. *Discipline and Punish: The Birth of the Prison.* Translated from the French by Alan Sheridan. New York: Vintage Books, 1979.

Friedman, Lawrence. *A History of American Law (Second Edition).* New York: Simon and Schuster, 1985.

Galanter, Marc. "The Modernization of Law." In Lawrence Friedman and Stewart Macaulay, ed. *Law and the Behavioral Sciences, Second Edition.* Indianapolis: The Bobbs Merrill Co., 1977: 1046-1055.

"Ganyu 'xia dayu'" [Dare to 'rain hard']. *Renmin sifa* [People's adjudication] 9: 2 (1989).

Gan Yupei. "Dangdai xingfa kexue yanjiu zhong de shijiexing quxiang" [Global tendencies in contemporary research in the science of criminal law]. In Gan Yupei and Zhang Wen, ed. *Fanzui yu xingfa xinlun*: 688-89.

Gan Yupei and Zhang Wen, ed. *Fanzui yu xingfa xinlun* [New essays on crime and punishment], Beijing: Beijing daxue chubanshe, 1991.

Gao Mingxuan. *Zhonghua renmin gongheguo xingfa de yunyu he dansheng* [The gestation and birth of the criminal law of the People's Republic of China]. Shijiazhuang: Falu chubanshe, 1981.

_____. *Xin Zhongguo xingfaxue yanjiu zongshu (yijiu sijiu-yijiu bawu)* [The summary of penal law studies in China (1949-1985)]. Henan renmin chubanshe, 1986.

Gao Shuqiao and Li Congzhu. *Fanzui diaocha jiqi tongji fangfa.* [Crime surveys and their statistical methodology]. Beijing: Qunzhong Chubanshe, 1986.

Gao Xun. "Jianchi zai dang de lingdao xia yifa duli xingshi jianchaquan" [Uphold the independent exercise of procuratorial power under the leadership of the party]. *Zhongguo fazhibao* [China legal system news] 119:3 (5 November 1982).

Ge Tingfeng. "Zhuanzhe shiqi de nongcun fanzui wenti" [The rural crime problem in a period of change]. *Shehuixue yu shehui diaocha* [Sociology and social investigation] 5:45-50 (1989).

"Geji difang renmin jianchashu zuzhi tongze" [General regulations governing the organization of people's procurators at various levels]. *Renmin ribao* [People's Daily] 5 September 1951:2.

"Geji renmin fayuan xingshi anjian shenpan chengxu zongjie" (Summary of adjudication procedure of criminal cases in the people's courts of all levels). Document issued 17 October 1956 by the SPC, in *Zhonghua renmin gongheguo falu guifanxing jieshi jicheng*: 627-637

Ginsburgs, George and Arthur Stahnke. "The Genesis of the People's Procuratorate in Communist China, 1949-1951." *China Quarterly* 24:1-37 (1964).

_____. "The People's Procuratorate in Communist China: The Period of Maturation, 1951-54." *China Quarterly* 25:53-91 (1965).

Giovannetti, Dana. "The Principle of Analogy in Sino-Soviet Criminal Laws." *Dalhousie Law Journal* 8: 382-401 (1984).

Gong Xiaobing and Liu Shuguang. "Jianli sifa xingzheng jiguan tiqing shenyi zhidu quyi" [Humble opinions on establishment of the justice administrative organs' system of requesting review]. *Faxue dongtai* [Developments in legal studies] 15:1-7 (30 August 1983).

Gonganbu bangongting, ed. *Zonghe zhili shehui zhian jingyan xuanbian, dier ji* [Selected experiences in the comprehensive management of public security]. Beijing: Qunzhong chubanshe, 1986.

"Gonganbu buzhang Liu Fuzhi da benkan bianjibu wen" [Minister of public security Liu Fuzhi answers questions from the editors]. *Minzhu yu fazhi* [Democracy and the legal system] 2:2-4 (February 1984).

Gonganbu faguiju, ed. *Zhifa shouce—gongan jiguan banli xingshi anjian chengxu zhuanji* [Law enforcement manual—special volume on the procedure for public security organs' handling of criminal cases]. Beijing: Qunzhong chubanshe, 1991.

"Gonganbu faguiju fujuzhang Liu Enqi 'guanyu gongan jiguan banli xingshi anjian chengxu guiding de shuoming.'" [Assistant head of the law and regulations office of the ministry of public security Liu Enqi's "explanation regarding procedural regulations for the public security organs' disposition of criminal cases"]. Talk dated 7 April 1984, in Gongan faguiju, ed. *Zhifa shouce—gongan jiguan banli xingshi anjian chengxu zhuanji*: 37-42.

Gonganbu fazhisi, ed. *Zhifa shouce* [Law enforcement handbook].Beijing: Qunzhong chubanshe, 1991.

_____, ed. *Zhifa shouce dishierji* [Law enforcement manual, vol. 12]. Beijing: Qunzhong chubanshe, 1990.

"Gonganbu guanyu chuli waiguo luoti renxiang youpiao wenti de pifu" [Reply of the ministry of public security regarding the question of the disposition of foreign postage stamps bearing nude human likenesses]. Document dated 6 June 1982, in Liang Guoqing, ed. *Xin Zhongguo sifa jieshi daquan*: 1178.

"Gonganbu guanyu jianjue daji xiang guomindang tewu jiguan xie xin guagou de fanzui fenzi de tongzhi" [Ministry of public security notice regarding striking firm blows against criminals writing letters of contact to nationalist intelligence organs]. Document dated 15 August 1981, approved and transmitted by the state council), in *Zhonghua renmin gongheguo falu guifanxing jieshi jicheng*: 294-95.

"Gonganbu guanyu laojiao, laogai gongzuo ganbu gangwei butie he zhuozhang de buchong tongzhi" [Supplementary circular of the ministry of public security regarding post subsidies and uniforms of labor re-education and labor reform cadres]. Document dated 16 December 1981, in *Zhonghua renmin gongheguo falu guifanxing jieshi jicheng*: 1582-83.

"Gonganbu guanyu shourong shencha xuanchuan wenti de qingshi' de pifu" [Ministry of public security's reply to request for instructions regarding the question of propaganda on shelter and investigation]. Document dated 14 October 1988, in Zuigao renmin fayuan yanjiushi, ed. *Sifa shouce, diwuji*: 75.

"Gonganbu guanyu yange yifa banshi, zhixing zhengce, shenru kaizhan chu 'liuhai' douzheng de tongzhi" [Ministry of public security circular regarding doing things strictly according to law, carrying out policy, and deeply unfolding the struggle to eliminate the 'six evils']. In Gonganbu fazhisi, ed. *Zhifa shouce (dishierji)*: 231-238.

"Gonganbu guanyu zhengdun he jiaqiang dui liucuan fanzuifenzi shourong shencha gongzuo de tongzhi" [Circular of the ministry of public security regarding rectification and strengthening of shelter and investigation of roving criminal elements]. Document dated 1 November 1978, in Gonganbu zhengce falu yanjiushi, ed. *Zhifa shouce, diyi ji*: 248-250.

"Gonganbu guanyu zhuanfa Beijingshi gonganju 'guanyu changkuang qiye danwei luoshi shehui zhian zonghe zhili qingkuang de diaocha baogao' de tongzhi" (Ministry of public security circular transmitting the Beijing city public security bureau's investigative report on the implementation of comprehensive management of public security in factory and mining units). Document dated 9 August 1982 in Xie Anshan and Yan Li, ed. *Zonghe zhili shehui zhian gongzuo shouce*: 44.

"Gonganbu, laodong renshibu, nongmuyuyebu, jiaoyubu, shangyebu guanyu fanren xingman shifanghou luohu he anzhi de lianhe tongzhi" [Joint circular of the ministry of public security, the ministry of labor, the ministry of agriculture, herding, and fisheries, the ministry of education, and the ministry of commerce regarding settlement and employment of criminals released on completion of sentence]. Document dated 5 May 1983, in Shanxisheng zhengfa guanli ganbu xueyuan, xingfa jiaoyanshi, ed. *Yanli daji yanzhong jingji fanzui he yanzhong xingshi fanzui yilaide wenjian xuanbian, shang*: 120-26.

"Gonganbu, sifabu guanyu jianjue yifa chengchu yi zican shouduan taobi chengchu de fanzui fenzi de tongzhi" [Circular of the ministry of public security and ministry of justice regarding resolute punishment according to law for criminal elements who use self-mutilation as a means of escaping punishment]. Document dated 25 August 1988, in *Zhonghua renmin gongheguo falu guifanxing jieshi daquan (zengbuben)*: 742-3.

Gonganbu yushenju, ed. *Yushen anli xuanbian (yi)* [Selected preliminary hearing cases (one)]. Beijing: Qunzhong chubanshe, 1985.

_____, ed. *Yushen anli xuanbian (er)* [Selected preliminary hearing cases (two)]. Beijing: Qunzhong chubanshe, 1984.

Gonganbu zhengce falu yanjiushi, ed. *Zhifa shouce, dierji* [Law enforcement manual, vol. 2]. Beijing: Qunzhong chubanshe, 1980.

_____ ed. *Zhifa shouce, diyi ji* [Law enforcement handbook, vol. 1]. Beijing: Qunzhong chubanshe, 1982.

"Gonganbu, zuigao renmin fayuan, zuigao renmin jianchayuan guanyu yange kongzhi zai sixing zhixing xianchang jinxing paishe he caifang de tongzhi" [Ministry of public security, SPC, SPP circular regarding strictly controlling photography and reporting at execution grounds]. Document dated 16 July 1990, in *Zhonghua renmin gongheguo falu guifanxing jieshi jicheng (zengbuben)*: 68.

Gu Yingchun. *Qingshaonian fanzui zonghe zhili gailun*. Beijing: Qunzhong chubanshe, 1986.

Gu Xiaoyan. *Zhongguode jianyu*. [China's prisons]. Changchun: Jilin renmin chubanshe, 1987.

"Guanyu tiqing quandang zhongshi jiejue qingshaonian weifa fanzui wenti de baogao." [Report reminding the entire Party to emphasize the resolution of the youth crime problem]. Attachment to "Zhonggong zhongyang zhuanfa zhongyang xuanchuanbu deng bage danwei 'Guanyu tiqing quandang zhongshi jiejue qingshaonian weifa fanzui wenti de baogao' de tongzhi (jielu)" [Central committee of the communist party notice transmitting the central propaganda ministry and seven other units' "report suggesting the entire party emphasize the resolution of the problem of youth lawbreaking and crime (excerpts)]. Document dated 17 August 1979, in Xie Anshan and Yan Li, ed. *Zonghe zhili shehui zhian gongzuo shouce*: 7-8.

"Guanyu yange kongzhi shiyong shourong shencha shouduan de tongzhi" [Notice regarding strict control of the use of shelter and investigation]. Document dated 31 July 1985, in Shanxisheng zhengfa guanli ganbu xueyuan, xingfa jiaoyanshi, ed. *Yanli daji yanzhong jingji fanzui he yanzhong xingshi fanzui yilai de wenjian xuanbian, shang*: 73-75.

Guangdong sheng gaoji renmin fayuan yanjiushi. "Jingji fanzui changjue, fayuan shouan xiajiang de qingkuang, yuanyin ji duice" [Reasons and counter-measures for the decrease in cases received by the courts while economic crime rages]. *Renmin sifa* [People's adjudication] 9:3-4 (1989).

Guangdong sheng laogaiju. "Xin shiqi dui zuifan de zai renshi ji gaizao duice" [Criminals in the new era: recognition and strategies for reform] *Fanzui yu gaizao yanjiu* [Studies in crime and reform] 5:28-9 (1989).

Guo Xiang. "Zhongguo dangqian de baoli fanzui he yufang duice" [Violent crime in today's China and its preventive counter-measures]. *Qingshaonian fanzui yanjiu* [Studies in youth crime] 11:1-7 (1988).

"Guowuyuan bangongshi guanyu zuohao fanren xingman shifang hou luohu he anzhi gongzuo de tongzhi" [Office of the state council notice regarding doing a good job of arranging residence and employment for prisoners released on completion of sentence]. Document dated 16 July 1984, in Shanxisheng zhengfa guanli xueyuan, xingfa jiaoyanshi, ed. *Yanli daji yanzhong jingji fanzui he yanzhong xingshi fanzui yilai de wenjian xuanbian, shang*: 307-8.

Guowuyuan fazhiju, ed. *Zhonghua renmin gongheguo xin fagui huibian 1997 diyiji* [Collection of new laws and regulations of the PRC 1997, volume 1]. Beijing: Zhongguo fazhi chubanshe, 1997.

"Guowuyuan guanyu jiang qiangzhi laodong he shourong shencha liangxiang cuoshi tongyiyu laodong jiaoyang de tongzhi" [Notice of the state council on the unification of the two measures of forced labor and shelter and investigation together with re-education through labor]. Document dated 29 February 1980 in Gonganbu zhengce falu yanjiushi, ed. *Zhifa shouce, dierji*: 238-239.

"Guowuyuan guanyu jianjue quti maiyin huodong he zhizhi xingbing manyan de tongzhi" [State council circular regarding firmly eliminating prostitution and stopping the spread of sexually transmitted diseases]. Document dated 1 September, 1986 in Liang Guoqing, ed. *Xin Zhongguo sifa jieshi daquan*: 1194-1195.

Han ying cidian [Chinese-English dictionary]. Beijing: Shangwu yinshuguan, 1978.

Hao Hongkui. "Xiandaihua dui fanzuilu shengjiang de yingxiang" [The influence of modernization on fluctuations in crime rates]. *Qingshaonian fanzui yanjiu* [Studies in youth crime] 6:6-9 (1988).

Hao Qingshan. "Zuohao pibu gongzuo de beian shencha gongzuo" [Do a good job of the registration and review of cases for approval of arrest]. *Renmin jiancha* (People's Procuratorate) 3 (1980), reprinted in *Renmin jiancha xuanbian*: 215-218.

He Bingsong. "Woguo de fanzui qushi, yuanyin yu xingshi zhengce, shang" [Our country's crime trends, causes and criminal policy, part one]. *Zhengfa luntan* [Politics and law tribunal] 5:37-45 (1989).

_____. "Woguo jinnian lai fanzui gaikuang" [An overview of crime in our country in recent years]. *Qingshaonian fanzui yanjiu* [Studies in youth crime] 9:19-21 (1989).

He Fangbo, ed. *Kangsu anjian baili pingxuan* [One-hundred protested cases with commentary]. Beijing: Zhongguo renmin daxue chubanshe, 1992.

Heilongjiang sheng renmin jianchayuan Nenjiang fenyuan. "Guanyu qingshaonian fanzui wenti de diaocha baogao" [Investigative report on the problem of youth crime]. *Faxue yu Shijian* [Law and practice] 1:26-29 (January 1985).

Heilongjiang Haerbin shi zhongji renmin fayuan. "Dui qingshaonian fanzui de qingkuang, tedian, he yuanyin de chubu fenxi" [Preliminary analysis of the situation, characteristics, and causes of youth crime]. *Renmin sifa* [People's Jurisprudence] 9:2-3 (1981).

Hengtai xianzhi [Hengtai county gazetteer]. Jinan: Jilu shushe, 1992.

Hewitt, John D., Eric W. Hickey and Robert M. Regoli. "Dealing With Juvenile Delinquency: The Re-Education of the Delinquent in the People's Republic of China," in Jim Hackler, ed. *Official Responses to Problem Juveniles: Some International Reflections*. Onati, Spain: The Onati Institute for the Sociology of Law, 1991: 67-81.

Hood, Roger. *The Death Penalty: A World-wide Perspective (Second Revised and Updated Edition)*. Oxford: Clarendon Press, 1996.

Hooper, Beverly. *Youth in China*. Harmondsworth: Penguin Books, 1985.

Hougang shizhi [Hougang city gazetteer]. Harbin: Heilongjiang renmin chubanshe, 1990.

Hu Congshun. "1,269 ming zaiya nufan fanzui tedian de fenxi" [Analysis of the characteristics of the offenses of 1,269 women criminal prisoners]. *Qingshaonian fanzui yanjiu* [Studies in youth crime] 9:31-34 (1989).

Hu Kangsheng. "Xiugai xingshi susongfa shi Zhongguo yifa zhiguo de biaozhi" [Amendment of the criminal procedure law is a sign of china's rule by law]. *Zhongguo Falu* [China Law] 2:9 (1996).

Hu Shiyou. "Gaohao shehui zhian de zonghe zhili" [Do a good job of comprehensive management of public security]. *Faxue zazhi* [Legal science magazine] 4:17 (1981).

"Huang Huoqing jianchazhang dao Hubei jiancha gongzuo yaoqiu jinkuai ba gexiang jiancha gongzuo quanmian kaizhan qilai" [Chief procurator Huang

Huoqing inspects work in Hubei, demands that all aspects of procuratorial work be fully developed as quickly as possible]. *Renmin jiancha* (People's Procuratorate) 1 (1980), reprinted in *Renmin jiancha xuanbian*: 56-60.

"Huang Huoqing tongzhi zai quanguo jiancha gongzuo zuotanhui shang de zongjie" [Comrade Huang Huoqing's summary comments at the national procuratorial work conference]. Talk dated 31 July 1979, in *Renmin Jiancha* (People's Procuratorate) 3 (1979), reprinted in *Renmin jiancha xuanbian*: 23-34.

Huang Tiemao. "Zhixing sixing sheji zuijia buwei de shangque" [Discussion on shooting the optimal place in carrying out capital punishment]. *Renmin sifa* [People's Adjudication] 7:22 (1987).

Huang Siyuan. "Jue buke hushi nu qingshaonian weifa fanzui" [Lawbreaking by young women cannot be ignored]. *Sifa* [Jurisprudence] 70:21, 26 (May 1987).

Huang Jingxiang. "Shenzhenshi qingshaonian fanzui zhuangkuang ji tedian" [The situation and characteristics of youth crime in Shenzhen]. *Qingshaonian fanzui yanjiu* [Studies in youth crime] 3-4:19-21 (1990).

Huma xianzhi [Huma county gazetteer]. Nanjing: Zhongguo wenshi chubanshe, n.d.

Human Rights Watch/Asia. "New Evidence of Chinese Forced-Labor Imports to the U.S." New York: Human Rights Watch/Asia, 24 March, 1994.

Hunan sheng gaoji renmin fayuan yanjiushi. "Dui jingji fanzui huodong daji buli de xianxiang bixu yinqi zhongshi" [The weakness of blows against economic crime demands attention]. *Renmin sifa* [People's adjudication] 12:12 (1985).

Jia Chunfeng, *Lun shehui zhuyi jingshen wenming* [On socialist spiritual civilization]. Beijing: Hongqi chubanshe,1984.

Jia Lufeng and Feng Shou. *Zhongguo xibu dajianyu* [Major prisons in west China]. Nanjing: Jiangsu renmin chubanshe 1986.

Jiang Hua. "Guanyu renmin fayuan zai ren, cai, wu fangmian de yanzhong kunnan qingkuang de baogao" [Report concerning the people's courts' severe difficulties in respect to personnel, finances, and infrastructure]. Report dated 30 June 1983, in *Jiang Hua sifa wenji*: 305-312.

_____. "Sifa renyuan zhifa yao xuefa" [Judicial personnel must learn law to implement law]. Originally published in *Hongqi* (Red Flag) 8 (1979), reprinted in *Zhonghua renmin gongheguo xingshi susong faxue cankao ziliao, diyiji, zonglei*: 211-219.

Jiang Hua sifa wenji [Jiang Hua on jurisprudence: selected articles]. Beijing: Renmin fayuan chubanshe, 1989.

"Jiang Hua tongzhi zai bufen gao, zhongji renmin fayuan he junshi fayuan fuze tongzhi zuotanhui jieshu de jianghua" [Comrade Jiang Hua's talk at the conclusion of a discussion meeting with the responsible cadres of some intermediate people's and military courts]. Talk dated 10, 11 April 1979. *Renmin sifa* [People's Adjudication] 4 (1979), reprinted in *Zhonghua renmin gongheguo xingshi susongfa xuexi cankao ziliao, diyiji, zonglei*: 186-202.

"Jiang Hua tongzhi zai Henan sheng gaoji renmin fayuan ganbu hui shang de jianghua" [Comrade Jiang Hua's talk at the Henan provincial higher people's courts cadres conference]. *Renmin Sifa* [People's Adjudication] 7:6-14 (1980).

"Jiang Hua tongzhi zai liang ci bufen gao, zhongji renmin fayuan he junshi fayuan fuze tongzhi zuotanhui shang de jianghua" [Comrade Jiang Hua's talks at two symposiums of the responsible comrades of some higher and middle peoples and military courts]. Talks dated 8 March and 2 April 1979, in *Zhonghua renmin gongheguo xingshi susongfa xuexi cankao ziliao, diyiji, zonglei*: 168-186.

"Jiang Hua tongzhi zai quanguo gaoji renmin fayuan yuanzhang huiyi shang de jianghua" [Comrade Jiang Hua's talk at the national conference of presidents of higher people's courts].Talk dated 8 March 1980, in *Zhonghua renmin gongheguo xingshi susongfa xuexi cankao ziliao, diyiji, zonglei*: 219-226.

Jiang Rentian. "Dui qiangjianzui zhong 'weibei funu yizhi' wenti de zai renshi" [Rethinking the question of 'violation of the woman's will' in rape cases]. *Faxue Yanjiu* [Studies in Law] 5:39-45 (1984).

Jiangsu sheng faxuehui qingshaonian fanzui xuehui and Jiangsu sheng shehui kexueyuan zhengfa yanjiu suo ed. *Qingshaonian fanzui yanjiu* [Studies in youth crime]. Nanjing: n.p., 1987.

"Jiaoyubu, gongqingtuan zhongyang, gonganbu, guanyu zhuanfa 'Jinxi xian qiming zhongxiao xuesheng jiehuo daoqiang yumou sharen anjian de qingkuang diaocha' de tongzhi" [Ministry of education, central committee of the communist youth league, ministry of public security, notice transmitting the 'investigation of the case of seven Jinxi county middle-school students' group theft of guns and plotting of murder']. Document dated 23 July 1979, in Xie Anshan and Yan Li, ed., *Zonghe zhili shehui zhian gongzuo shouce*: 60-65.

"Jiaqiang dui jingshen bingren de jianhu gongzuo" [Strengthen guardianship of the mentally ill]. *Shanghai fazhibao* [Shanghai Legal System News] 14 March 1988: 1.

"Jiaqiang he gaige gongan gongzuo baozhang guojia changzhi jiuan" [Strengthen and reform public security work, guarantee long-term peaceful order for the country]. *Zhongguo fazhibao* [China legal system news] 6:1 (May 1983).

Jin Guangzheng, Zhu Zhongbao and Yue Maohua. "Lun shehui zhian de zonghe kongzhi" [On the comprehensive control of public security]. *Zhengfa luntan* [Tribune of political science and law] 4: 63-64 (1986).

Jin Jixiang and Liu Zhengxiang. "Dui dangqian baowai jiuyi zhong jige wenti de fenxi he jianyi" [Analysis and suggestions on several current problems in release for medical care]. *Sifa* [Jurisprudence] 2:19 (1986).

Jin Liangnian. *Kuxing yu Zhongguo shehui.* [Torture and Chinese society]. Hangzhou: Zhejiang renmin chubanshe, 1991.

Jin Mosheng. "Jiancha jiguan ying huifu chuizhi lingdao tizhi" [The procuratorial organs should restore the system of vertical leadership]. *Minzhu yu fazhi* [Democracy and legal system] 6:3 (June 1982).

_____. "Yifa congzhong congkuai zhengzhi yanzhong xingshi fanzui" [Punish serious criminal offenders severely and rapidly according to law]. *Guangming ribao* [Enlightenment daily] 15 May 1981:3

Jin Zhong. "Suzhu yundong: Zhonggong daju zhenya fanzui" [Resorting to a movement: the Chinese Communists make a big crackdown on crime]. *Qishiniandai* [The seventies] 165:50-51 (October 1983).

Jin Zitong, Gu Xiaorong and Zheng Daqun. *Zui yu fa* [Crime and Punishment]. Shanghai: Shanghai shehuikexueyuan chubanshe, 1989.

Jinan shi gonganju. "Luoshi jiceng zhian baowei gongzuo de hao banfa" [A good method for implementing base-level public security protection work]. In Gonganbu bangongting, ed., *Zonghe zhili shehui zhian jingyan xuanbian, dier ji*: 19.

"Jingshen bingren fanzui de yiban tedian" [The general characteristics of offenses committed by the mentally ill]. *Renmin gonganbao*, 20 May 1988: 3.

"Jingshen bingren weihai zhian riyi tuchu" [Mental patients' endangerment of public order increases daily]. *Renmin gonganbao*, 6 November 1990: 1.

"Jixu guanche 'yanda' fangzhen—benkan jizhe zoufang zuigao renmin fayuan fu yuanzhang Lin Zhun" [Continue to implement the guiding principle of 'strike hard'—our reporter interviews vice-president of the supreme people's court, Lin Zhun]. *Renmin sifa* [People's Adjudication] 1:9 (1987).

Johnson, Eric A. "Cities Don't Cause Crime: Urban-Rural Differences in Late Nineteenth- and early Twentieth-Century German Criminality." *Social Science History* 16:129-176 (spring 1992).

_____ and Eric H. Monkkonen. "Introduction," in Johnson and Monkkonen, ed., *The Civilization of Crime: Violence in Town and Country Since the Middle Ages*: 1-13

_____, ed., *The Civilization of Crime: Violence in Town and Country since the Middle Ages*. Urbana: University of Illinois Press, 1996.

Jones, William C. "The Criminal Law of the People's Republic of China." *Review of Socialist Law*, 6.4:405-423 (December 1980).

_____, (translator). *The Great Qing Code*. Oxford: Clarendon Press, 1994.

Juviler, Peter H. *Revolutionary Law and Order: Politics and Social Change in the USSR*. New York: The Free Press, 1976.

Kang Shuhua ed. *Fanzuixue tonglun* [General Criminology]. Beijing: Beijing daxue chubanshe, 1992.

Ke Gezhuang and Gu Xiaorong. "Guanyu 'jueding' de sujili wenti" [On the retroactive force of the "decision"]. *Faxue* [Legal science] 12:19-20 (1983).

Kong, Xiaohong "Legal Interpretation in China" *Connecticut Journal of International Law* 1.2:491-506 (spring 1991).

Kulcsar, Kalman. *Modernization and the Law*. Budapest: Akademiai Kiaodo, 1992.

Kwan, Daniel. "Li Peng Pushes for Juries and Open Trials." *South China Morning Post*, Thursday September 17, 1998: 1.

Ladany, Laszlo. *Law and Legality in China: The Testament of a China-watcher*. Honolulu: University of Hawaii Press, 1992.

Lawyers Committee for Human Rights. *Opening to Reform? An Analysis of China's Revised Criminal Procedure Law*. New York: Lawyers Committee for Human Rights, 1996.

Leng, Shao-chuan and Hungdah Chiu. *Criminal Justice in Post-Mao China: Analysis and Documents*. Albany: State University of New York Press, 1985.

Li Baoguo. "Qiantan shangpin jingji yu shehui fanzui" [On commodity economy and crime]. *Qingshaonian fanzui yanjiu* [Studies in youth crime] 3/4:7-12 (1989)

Li Cheng and Tang Huayong. "Qiantan yifa congzhong congkuai yanzheng yanzhong fanzui de wenti" [Discussion of the question of severe and rapid punishment of serious crime according to law]. *Beijing sifa* [Beijing jurisprudence] 6:27-29 (20 December 1983).

Li Guangxian, Ning Hanlin, and Ma Kechang, ed. *Zhonghua renmin gongheguo xingfalun* [On the criminal law of the People's Republic of China]. Changchun: Jilin renmin chubanshe, 1984.

Li Hong and Huang Chi. "Lun qiangjianzui de waiyan" [On the scope of the offense of rape]. *Faxue Zazhi* [Legal Studies Magazine] 2:25 (1987).

Li Long. "Mao Zedong tongzhi guanyu laodong gaizao zuifan de lilun he shijian" [Comrade Mao Zedong's theory and practice concerning the reform of criminals through labor]. *Zhengzhi yu falu* [Politics and Law] 7:3-10 (1983).

Li Meijin. "Shixi Zhongguo muqian de jingji fazhan dui shehui fanzui wenti de yingxiang" [On the influence of China's current economic development on the crime problem in society]. *Qingshaonian fanzui yanjiu* [Studies in youth crime] 8-9:33-35 (1990).

Li Qi and Dai Yanling. "Jiushi niandai de Zhongguo laogai gongzuo" [China's Labor Reform Work in the 1990s]. *Fanzui yu gaizao yanjiu* [Studies in Crime and Reform] 1:46-48 [1991).

Li Tianfu, Yang Shiqi and Huang Jingping. *Fanzui tongjixue* [Criminal statistics]. Beijing: Qunzhong chubanshe, 1988.

Li, Victor. *Law Without Lawyers: A Comparative View of Law in China and the United States*. Boulder: Westview Press, 1978.

Li Xiaoying. "Shaonu xing zuicuo de chengyin" [Contributing factors in juvenile women's sex offenses]. *Qingshaonian fanzui yanjiu* [Studies in youth crime] 2:30-34 (1989).

Li Yuqian. "Dangqian yunei fanzui huodong xin dongxiang ji qi duice" [Current developments and countermeasures to prison crime]. In Sifabu, falu zhengce yanjiushi, laogaiju, ed. *Laogai laojiao de lilun yu shijian*: 138-148.

Li Zenghui. "Dangqian minzhe diqu xingshi fanzui de tedian qushi he duice" [Current characteristics, trends and counter-measures to crime in the Fujian-Zhejiang area]. *Fanzui yu gaizao yanjiu* [Research in crime and reform] 3:18-22, 13 (1989).

Li Zhongfang. *Xing yu fa* [Sex and law]. Jilin: Beifang funu ertong chubanshe, 1989.

Li Zhunren, ed. *Zhongguo chongxin fanzui yanjiu* [Research on recidivism in China]. Beijing: Falu chubanshe, 1992.

Liang Guoqing, ed. *Jiancha yewu gailun* [An introduction to the procuratorial profession]. Beijing: Zhongguo jiancha chubanshe, 1991.

_____, ed. *Xin Zhongguo sifa jieshi daquan* [Complete judicial interpreta tions of new China]. Beijing: Zhongguo jiancha chubanshe, 1990.

Lifton, Robert J. *Thought Reform and the Psychology of Totalism: A Study of "Brainwashing" in China*. New York: W.W. Norton and Co. 1961.

Lin Li. "Woguo de fanzui yu kongzhi" [Our country's crime and its control], *Fanzui yu gaizao yanjiu* [Studies in Crime and Reform] 3:24-27 (1993).

Linhai xianzhi [Gazetteer of Linhai County]. Hangzhou: Zhejiang renmin chu-banshe, 1989.

Liu Cuixiao. "Faxuejie dui qingshaonian fanzui de yuanyin he tedian taolun de zongshu" [Summary of legal circles' discussion of the characteristics and causes of youth crime]. *Faxue Dongtai* [Developments in Legal Studies] 12:1-6 (1 June 1983).

Liu Cuiying. "Nuxing weifa fanzui de shehui xinli tedian ji yufang cuoshi" [The social psychological characteristics of women's offenses and their preventive measures]. *Qingshaonian fanzui yanjiu* [Studies in youth crime] 2:11-13, 21 (1990).

Liu Dalin, ed. *Zhongguo dangdai xing wenhua: Zhongguo liangwanli "xing wenhua" diaocha baogao* [Sexual behavior in modern China: A report of the nation-wide "sex civilization" survey on 20,000 subjects in China]. Shanghai: Sanlian shudian, Shanghai fendian, 1992.

Liu Guangren. "Dangqian Beijingshi weichengnianren weifa fanzui ji yufang" [Juvenile delinquency and its prevention in Beijing in recent years]. *Qingshaonian fanzui yanjiu* [Studies in youth crime] 5:33-35 (1989).

Liu Hua. "Hooliganism." *Chinese Sociology and Anthropology* 27.3:57-63 (spring 1995).

Liu Jun. "Guangzhou Municipality's Public Security Shows Clear Improvement" Guangzhou: *Nanfang ribao* [Southern daily] 26 November 1983:1, translated in FBIS *China Report* 10 April 1984: 51-52.

Liu Shengrong and Zhi Jun. "Yantai shi maiyin anjian de diaocha" [Investigation of prostitution cases in Yantai]. *Qingshaonian fanzui yanjiu* [Studies in youth crime] 1:9-13 (1990).

Liu Siqi. "Xingxun bigong lujin buzhi de yuanyin" [Causes for the persistence of forcing confessions under torture in spite of repeated bans]. *Renmin gongan* [People's Police] 2 August, 1991: 3.

Liu Yunxiang. "Daoqie leiguanfan de sixiang xingge tedian he gaizao duice" [Characteristics of the thought and personality of recidivist and habitual thieves and counter-measures for their reform]. *Fanzui yu gaizao yanjiu* [Studies in crime and reform] 5:38-44 (1991).

Liu Zhengqing, ed. *Xingshi fanzui anli congshu (zousi, zhizao, fanmai dupinzui)* [Criminal cases series (smuggling, producing, and trafficking in drugs)]. Beijing: Zhongguo jiancha chubanshe, 1991.

Lu Dong. "Jixu gaohao 'yanda,' di sanzhanyi, zhengqu shehui zhian wending haozhuan" [Continue to do a good job of the third battle of 'strike hard,' fight for a stable improvement in public security]. *Renmin sifa* [People's Adjudication] 6:3-4 (1986).

Lu Xiaoying. "Shaonu xing zuicuo de chengyin" [Contributing factors in juvenile women's sex offenses]. *Qingshaonian fanzui yanjiu* [Studies in youth crime] 2:30-34 (1989).

Lu xing [The Punishments of Lu]. In *Sishu wujing* [The four books and five classics]. Beijing: Beijingshi Zhongguo shudian, 1984, *shang*: 132-136.

Lubman, Stanley. "Emerging Functions of Formal Legal Institutions in China's Modernization." *China Law Reporter* 2.4:196-266 (fall 1983).

Luo Bing. "Deng Xiaoping yujie yu da daibu" [Deng Xiaoping's encounter with bandits and the mass arrests]. *Zhengming* [Contention] 72:6-10 (1 October 1983).

Luo Bingzhong. "Dangqian xingshi da an shangsheng de yuanyin ji duice" [Reasons and counter-measures for the current increase in serious criminal cases]. *Fanzui yu gaizao yanjiu* [Studies in crime and reform] 3:26-29 (1989).

Luo Feng. "Fanzui xianxiang gaishu" [An overview of crime]. In Wang Zhong fang, ed. *Zhongguo shehui zhian zonghe zhili de lilun yu shijian:* 135-151.

Ma Jie. "Lun shehui zhian zonghe zhili de lilun jianshe" [On the construction of a theory of comprehensive management of public security]. In Ma Jie, ed. *Zhongguo shehui zhian zonghe zhili yanjiu*: 92-93.

_____. "Lun gaige yu shehui zhian zonghe zhili" [On reform and the comprehensive management of public security]. *Fanzui yu gaizao yanjiu* [Studies in crime and reform] 3:10-15 (1988).

_____, ed. *Zhongguo shehui zhian zonghe zhili yanjiu* [Research on China's comprehensive management of public security]. Beijing: falu chubanshe, 1990.

Ma Qibin, ed. *Zhongguo gongchandang zhizheng sishinian (1949-1989)* [Forty years of rule by the Chinese Communist Party: 1949-1989]. Beijing: Zhonggong dangshi ziliao chubanshe, 1989.

Ma Shucai and Yan Xiujun. "Qianxi guanjiao ganbu sixiang zhuangkuang" [Preliminary analysis of the ideological state of labor reform cadres]. *Fanzui yu gaizao yanjiu* [Studies in crime and reform] 3:66-68 (1991).

Ma Weiguo. "Guanmao zong xieding jiang dui laogai jingji chansheng de yingxiang tanxi" [Analysis of the impending influence GATT on the labor reform economy]. *Fanzui yu gaizao yanjiu* [Studies in crime and reform] 3:27-28 (1993).

Ma Xiwu. "Zai sifa zuotanhui shang dui liangge shenli chengxu chubu zongjie de jidian shuoming" [Explanation of several points of the preliminary summation of the two adjudication procedures at the adjudication conference]. Talk dated June 1955 in *Zhonghua renmin gongheguo falu guifanxing jieshi jicheng*: 615-620.

Ma Zhongzhi, ed. *Zhian chufa anli xiangjie* [Analysis of SAPA cases]. Beijing: Qunzhong chubanshe, 1989.

Mao Tse-tung. "On Practice." In *Selected Readings from the Works of Mao Tse-tung*: 65-84.

Mao Zedong. "Qingniantuan de gongzuo yao zhaogu qingnian de tedian" (Youth League work must take the characteristics of youth into consideration) in *Mao Zedong xuanji, di wu juan*: 83-87.

Mao Zedong xuanji, di wu juan [Selected works of Mao Zedong, volume 5]. Beijing: Renmin chubanshe, 1987.

Mathews' Chinese-English Dictionary. Cambridge: Harvard University Press, 1966.

Meijer, Marinus J. *The Introduction of Modern Criminal Law in China.* Arlington, Va.: University Publications of America, 1976.

_____. "The New Criminal Law of the People's Republic of China." *Review of Socialist Law* 6. 2:125-139 (June 1980).

Meisner, Maurice. *Mao's China and After: A History of the People's Republic.* New York: The Free Press, 1986.

Min Cheng. "Xinshou zuifan burenzui xinli fenxi" [Analysis of the psychology of new prisoners who refuse to admit guilt]. *Fanzui yu gaizao yanjiu* [Studies in crime and reform] 3:41-43 (1991).

Minzhengbu xingzheng quhuachu, ed. *Zhonghua renmin gongheguo xingzheng quhua shouce* [Handbook of the administrative divisions of the PRC]. Beijing: Guangming ribao chubanshe, 1986.

Mulan xianzhi [Gazetteer of Mulan County]. Harbin: Heilongjiang renmin chubanshe, 1989.

Nan Shan. "Xinkeji geming tiaojian xia de fanzui wenti" [On the problem of crime in the new scientific and technological revolution]. *Qingshaonian fanzui yanjiu* [Studies in youth crime] 6:14-16 (1986).

Nanjing shi sifaju zhengce yanjiushi laogai laojiaochu Yangmeitang laojiaosuo. "Dangqian nu qingshaonian fan zuicuo de tedian" [The characteristics of current female youth offenders]. In Jiangsu sheng faxuehui qingshaonian fanzui yanjiuhui and Jiangsu sheng shehui kexueyuan zhengfa yanjiusuo, ed., *Qingshaonian fanzui yanjiu*: 189-196.

"Nanjing panchu sharenfan Luo Wenxuan sixing" [Nanjing sentences murderer Luo Wenxing to death]. *Renmin ribao* [People's daily] 25 June 1981: 4.

Nee, Victor and David Mozingo, ed. *State and Society in Contemporary China.* Ithaca: Cornell University Press, 1983.

Ng, Vivien W. "Ideology and Sexuality: Rape Laws in Qing China." *Journal of Asian Studies*, 46.1:57-70 (February 1987).

"Nongcun qingnian fanzui weihe zengduo" [Why youth crime in the villages is increasing]. *Nongmin ribao* [Peasants Daily], 21 December 1990: 3.

Osterberg, Eva. "Criminality, Social Control, and the Early Modern State: Evidence and Interpretations in Scandinavian Historiography." *Social Science History* 16.1:67-98 (spring 1992).

Ouyang Tao. "Dangqian woguo jingji lingyu jizhong fanzui de tedian" [Characteristics of several types of economic crime in our country]. *Faxue dongtai* [Developments in legal studies] 15:1-5 (2 July 1982).

——————, ed. *Daoqiezui, guanqiezui* [Theft and habitual theft]. Beijing: Zhongguo jiancha chubanshe, 1991.

Pan Zhenhua. "Lun laogai danwei yao zuohao jingji wenzhang" [On the need for labor reform units to do a good job on their economies]. *Fanzui yu gaizao yanjiu* [Studies in crime and reform] 7:34-36 (1993).

Pang Xinghua. "Qita leixing de fanzui" [Other types of crime]. In Kang Shuhua, ed. *Fanzui xue tonglun* [General criminology]: 340-353.

——————. "Shaonu xing zuicuo yanbian guocheng yu xinli tedian" [The development and psychological characteristics of juvenile female sex offenses]. *Qingshaonian fanzui yanjiu* [Studies in youth crime] 9:28-30 (1989).

"Peng Zhen tongzhi zai quanguo gongan juzhang huiyi shangde jianghua" [Comrade Peng Zhen's speech at the national meeting of public security bureau chiefs]. Talk dated 16 September 1979, in *Zhonghua renmin gongheguo xingshi susongfa xuexi cankao ziliao, diyiji, zonglei*: 114-129.

"Peng Zhen tongzhi zai quanguo jiancha gongzuo zuotanhui, quanguo gaoji renmin fayuan he junshi fayuanzhang de huiyi, di san ci quanguo yushen gongzuo huiyi shang de jianghua" [Comrade Peng Zhen's talk at the national procuratorial work forum, national meeting of presidents of higher people's courts and military courts and third national preliminary examination work conference]. Talk dated 27 July 1979, in *Zhonghua renmin gongheguo xingshi susongfa xuexi cankao ziliao, diyiji, zonglei*: 94-104.

Peng Zhen wenxuan (1941-1990) [Selected works of Peng Zhen, 1941-1990]. Beijing: Renmin chubanshe, 1991.

Perrot, Michelle. "Delinquency and the Penitentiary System in Nineteenth-Century France." In Robert Forster and Orest Ranum, ed. *Deviants and the Abandoned in French Society: Selections from the Annales Economies, Societes, Civilisations, volume 4*: 213-245.

Perry, Mary Elizabeth. *Crime and Society in Early Modern Seville.* Hanover, New Hampshire: The University Press of New England, 1980.

Pi Yijun. "Maiyin xianxiang de chengyin tantao" [Exploration of the contributing factors in the phenomenon of prostitution]. *Qingshaonian fanzui yanjiu* [Studies in youth crime] 6:27-33 (1990).

Pu Yi. *From Emperor to Citizen: The Autobiography of Aisin-Gioro Pu Yi.* New York: Oxford University Press, 1987.

"Qieshi zhuahao jindong mingchun shehui zhian gongzuo" [Resolutely do a good job of public security work this winter and next spring]. *Dazhong bao* [The masses] 26 November 1982: 1.

Qin Kun. "Shanghai shi renmin jianchayuan gongzuo baogao (zhaiyao)" [Work report of the Shanghai people's procuratorate (excerpts)]. *Jiefang ribao* [Liberation daily] 3 May 1983: 8.

"Quandang dongshou, fadong qunzhong, zhengqu zhian qingkuang genben haozhuan" [Mobilize the entire party, mobilize the masses, strive for a basic turn for the better in public security]. *Renmin ribao* [People's daily] 25 July 1981: 1.

"Quanguo fayuan yuanzhang zuotanhui zai jing zhaokai" [National conference of presidents of people's courts held in Beijing]. *Renmin sifa* [People's adjudication] 9:2-5 (September 1984).

Quanguo renda changweihui fazhi gongzuo weiyuanhui xingfashi. *Lun "Zhong hua renmin gongheguo xingfa" de buchong xiugai* [On the supplementation and amendment of the criminal law of the PRC]. Beijing: Falu chubanshe, 1992.

"Quanguo renda falu weiyuanhui dui 'guanyu yanjin maiyin piaochang de jueding (caoan' shenyi jieguo de baogao" [Report of the NPC committee on law concerning the results of deliberations on the draft "Decision regarding strict prohibition of prostitution and whoring"] in *Renda changweihui gongbao* (Bulletin of the SC of the NPC) 5 October, 1991: 51.

"Quanguo renmin daibiao dahui changwu weiyuanhui guanyu shishi xingshi susongfa guihua wenti de jueyi" [Resolution of the standing committee of the NPC regarding the question of plans for implementation of the criminal procedure law]. In *Zhonghua renmin gongheguo falu guifanxing jieshi jicheng*: 678-79.

"Quanguo zhengdun shehui zhian shoudao mingxian chengxiao" [Nationwide rectification of public security shows clear results]. *Renmin ribao* [People's daily] 2 September 1982: 5.

"Quota Means Death Penalty for Petty Offenders." *South China Morning Post* 20 September 1983: 1.

Reinhardt, Steven G. "Crime and Royal Justice in Ancien Regime France: Modes of Analysis." *Journal of Interdisciplinary History* 13.3:437-460 (winter 1983).

Ren Yiqiu. "Zhiding xingshi sifa jieshi de jige yuanze" [Several principles of the formulation of criminal justice judicial interpretations]. *Faxue yu shijian* [Law and practice] 1:31-32 (January 1992).

Renda changweihui gongbao [Bulletin of the Standing Committee of the NPC]. Beijing: Standing Committee of the NPC, 5 October 1991.

"Renmin jianchayuan xingshi jiancha gongzuo shixing xize" [Provisional regulations for criminal procuratorial work of the people's procuratorates]. In *Zhonghua renmin gongheguo falu guifanxing jieshi jicheng*: 679-684.

Renmin jiancha xuanbian [Selections from *People's Procuratorate*]. Beijing: Renmin jianchayuan chubanshe, 1981.

Renshou xianzhi [Gazetteer of Renshou county]. Chengdu: Sichuan renmin chubanshe, 1990.

"Ruhe jielu xiaoji yin'an de dongxi" [How to reveal dark, negative things]. *Duiwai xuanchuan cankao* [Reference for external propaganda] 13:12 (1 July 1983).

Scherer, John L., ed. *China Facts and Figures Annual 1984*. Gulf Breeze, Florida: Academic Press, 1984.

Schram, Stuart R., ed. *The Scope of State Power in China*. London and Hong Kong: School of Oriental and African Studies, University of London and The Chinese University Press, The Chinese University of Hong Kong, 1985.

Scobell, Andrew. "The Death Penalty in Post-Mao China," *The China Quarterly* 123:503-520 (September 1990).

Scobell, Andrew. "The Death Penalty under Socialism, 1917-1990: China, the Soviet Union, Cuba, and the German Democratic Republic." *Criminal Justice History: An International Annual* 12:160-234 (1991).

The Second Session of the Sixth National People's Congress (Main Documents). Beijing: Foreign Languages Press, 1984.

Selected Readings From the Works of Mao Tse-tung. Peking: Foreign Languages Press, 1971.

Selected Works of Deng Xiaoping (1975-1982). Beijing: Foreign Languages Press, 1984.

Seymour, James D. and Richard Anderson. *New Ghosts Old Ghosts: Prisons and Labor Reform Camps in China*. Armonk, N.Y.: M.E. Sharpe, 1998.

Sha Zhengxin. "Xiangzhen qiye qingshaonian fanzui chutan" [Preliminary investigation of youth crime in local rural enterprises]. In Jiangsu sheng faxuehui qingshaonian fanzui xuehui and Jiangsu sheng shehui kexueyuan zhengfa yanjiusuo ed., *Qingshaonian fanzui yanjiu*: 164-165.

Shaan xianzhi [Gazetteer of Shaan county]. Zhengzhou: Henan renmin chubanshe, 1988.

Shan Zhanzong, Ouyang Tao, Zhang Sihan and Zhou Daoluan. "Tantan jingji lingyu zhong yanzhong fanzui anjian de dingzui he liangxing wenti" [On problems concerning the conviction and penal discretion against serious crimes in the economic sphere]. *Faxue yanjiu* [Studies in law] 3:11-17 (1983).

Shanghai gongan nianjian bianjibu, ed. *Shanghai gongan nianjian (1988)* [Shanghai Public Security Yearbook, 1988]. Shanghai: Shanghai shehui kexue chubanshe, 1988.

Shangshui xianzhi [Gazetteer of Shangshui county]. Zhengzhou: Henan renmin chubanshe, 1990.

Shanxisheng gaoji renmin fayuan, Shanxisheng renmin jianchayuan,. "Guanyu yanli daji xingshi fanzui huodong yilai panchu de xingshi anjian tichu shensu de jidian yijian" [Some opinions regarding petitions for review of criminal cases sentenced since striking severe blows against serious criminal activities]. Document dated 3 May 1985, in Shanxi sheng zhengfa guanli ganbu xueyuan, xingfa jiaoyanshi, ed. *Yanli daji yanzhong jingji fanzui he yanzhong xingshi fanzui yilai de wenjian xuanbian, xia ce*: 22-24.

Shanxisheng zhengfa guanli ganbu xueyuan, xingfa jiaoyanshi, ed. *Yanli daji yanzhong jingji fanzui he yanzhong xingshi fanzui yilai de wenjian xuanbian, shang, xia liang ce* [Selected documents since striking severe blows against serious economic crime and serious crime, volumes 1 and 2]. Taiyuan: Shanxisheng zhengfa guanli ganbu xueyuan, xingfa jiaoyanshi, 1986.

"Shanyu yunyong falu wuqi yu fanzui fenzi zuo jianjue douzheng" [Excel in using the weapon of law in determined struggle against criminals]. *Renmin sifa* [People's Adjudication] 8:4-5 (1981).

Shao Daosheng. "Qiwu qijian de fanzui fazhan qushi ji duice" [Trends and counter-measures of crime for period of the seventh five-year plan]. *Weidinggao* [Rough manuscripts] 9:16-21 (1986).

Sharpe, James A. "Crime in England: Long-Term Trends and the Problem of Modernization." In Eric A. Johnson and Eric H. Monkkonen, ed., *The Civilization of Crime: Violence in Town and Country Since the Middle Ages*: 17-34.

Shelley, Louise I. *Crime and Modernization: The Impact of Industrialization and Urbanization on Crime*. Carbondale: Souther Illinois University Press, 1981.

Shen Qingyun. "Sheng zhengfa weiyuanhui zhaokai dianhua huiyi yaoqiu gedi: yifa congzhong congkuai daji xianxing fanzui huodong zhengqu wosheng shehui zhian de jin yibu haozhuan" [Provincial politico-legal affairs commission holds telephone conference demanding of all localities: strike blows against current criminal activities severely and rapidly according to law, strive for a further improvement in the public security of our province]. *Shaanxi ribao* [Shaanxi daily] 8 July 1983: 1.

Shi gaoji renmin fayuan jingji shenpanting. "Dui dangqian touji daoba anjian de fenxi" [Analysis of current speculation and profiteering cases]. *Beijing sifa* [Beijing adjudication] 17:10-12 (20 January 1982).

Shi Po. "Qingshaonian fanzui yu jiating jiaoyu" [Youth crime and family education]. *Beijing fazhibao* [Beijing legal system news] 6 October 1990:2.

Shierda yilai zhongyao wenxian xuanbian, shang [Selected important documents since the twelfth congress, vol. 1]. Beijing: Renmin chubanshe, 1988.

"Shiwei zhengfa weiyuanhui zhaokai zonghe zhili zhengdun zhian jingyan jiaoliuhui" [Municipal committee politico-legal commission holds meeting to exchange experiences in the rectification of public security through comprehensive management]. *Beijing sifa* [Beijing jurisprudence] 17:9 (1982).

"Shourong shencha guanli gongzuo zanxing guiding" [Provisional regulation for the management of shelter and investigation]. Document dated 15 February 1984, in Zuigao renmin fayuan yanjiushi, ed., *Sifa shouce, diwuji*: 250-252.

"Shouyao fenzi bei panchu sixing" [Leading elements sentenced to death]. *Minzhu yu fazhi* [Democracy and the legal system] 1:39 (1984).

Si Song. "Yifa congzhong congkuai daji xingshi fanzui fenzi" [Strike severe and rapid blows against criminal offenders according to law]. *Tianjin ribao* [Tianjin daily] 8 June 1981: 2.

Sifabu falu zhengce yanjiushi, laogaiju, ed. *Laogai laojiao gongzuo de lilun yu shijian* [Theory and practice of reform through labor and re-education through labor]. Shijiazhuang: Falu chubanshe, 1988.

"Sifabu fu kaifang chengshi nengfou zhangtie xingshi panjue bugao de qingshi" [Ministry of justice reply to the request for instructions concerning whether or not open cities are permitted to post notices of criminal sentences]. Document dated 9 October 1980, in Liang Guoqing, ed., *Xin Zhongguo sifa jieshi daquan*: 471-72.

"Sifabu, gonganbu, zuigao renmin jianchayuan, zuigao renmin fayuan guanyu dui fanren xingman he laojiao qiman renyuan zanting fanghui shehui de jinji tongzhi" [Ministry of justice, Ministry of Public Security, SPP, and SPC urgent notice regarding temporary halting the return to society of criminals having complete their sentences and labor re-education personnel having completed their terms]. Document dated 19 August 1983, in Shanxisheng zhengfa guanli xueyuan, xingfa jiaoyanshi, ed. *Yanli daji yanzhong jingji fanzui he yanzhong xingshi fanzui yilai de wenjian xuanbian, shang*: 155-156.

"Sifabu, gonganbu, zuigao renmin jianchayuan, zuigao renmin fayuan guanyu jiang yibufen xingman he jiechu laojiao de zanliu renyuan fanghui shehui de tongzhi" [Circular of the ministry of justice, the ministryof public security, the SPP and the SPC regarding return of a portion of sentence-completed criminals and personnel released from labor re-education who were temporarily retained]. Document dated 9 December 1983, in Shanxisheng zhengfa guanli xueyuan, xingfa jiaoyanshi, ed., *Yanli daji yanzhong jingji fanzui he yanzhong xingshi fanzui yilaide wenjian xuanbian, shang*: 217-19.

"Sifabu guanche zhongxuanbu 'guanyu daji xingshi fanzui de xuanchuan wenti de jidian yijian' de tongzhi" [Ministry of justice circular on carrying out the Central ministry of propaganda's "opinions on the question of propaganda on striking blows against criminal offenders"]. Document dated 14 October 1983, in Liang Guoqing, *Xin zhongguo sifa jieshi daquan*: 292-93.

"Sifabu guanyu di, shi chouban laogai, laojiaochang de baogao" [Report of the ministry of justice regarding localities and cities establishing labor reform and labor re-education facilities]. Document dated 20 February 1984, in Shanxi sheng zhengfa guanli ganbu xueyuan, xingfa jiaoyanshi, ed. *Yanli daji yanzhong jingji fanzui he yanzhong xingshi fanzui yilai de wenjian xuanbian, shang ce*: 253-54.

"Sifabu guanyu jin yibu jiaqiang anquan fangfan gongzuo de jinji tongzhi" (Ministry of justice urgent circular regarding further steps in strengthening safety and prevention work). Document dated 17 January 1987, in *Zhonghua renmin gongheguo falu guifanxing jieshi jicheng*: 1603-1605.

"Sifabu guanyu kaizhan gaizao zhiliang kaocha gongzuo de tongzhi" [Circular of the ministry of justice regarding carrying out investigation of the quality of reform]. Document dated 24 February 1984, in *Zhonghua renmin gonghe-guo falu guifanxing jieshi jicheng (zengbuben)*: 750-52.

"Sifabu guanyu panchu sixing fanren de shiti liyong wenti de fuhan" [Ministry of justice reply concerning the use of corpses of criminals sentenced to death].

Document dated 13 June 1981, in *Zhonghua renmin gongheguo falu guifanxing jieshi jicheng*: 986.

"Sifabu guanyu yanjin lanyong fanren he laojiao renyuan waichu gao shengchan jingying de tongbao" [Notice of the ministry of justice regarding strict prohibition of indiscriminate use of prisoners and labor re-education personnel to be sent out to do production or run businesses]. Document dated 30 April 1985, in *Zhonghua renmin gongheguo falu guifanxing jieshi jicheng*: 1600-1601.

"Sifabu guanyu yanli daji xingshi fanzui huodong zhong chongfen fahui lushi zuoyong de tongzhi" [Ministry of justice notice on giving full play to the function of lawyers during the campaign to strike hard blows against criminal offenders]. Document dated 14 October 1983, in Shanxi sheng zhengfa guanli ganbu xueyuan, xingfa jiaoyanshi, ed. *Yanli daji yanzhong jingji fanzui he yanzhong xingshi fanzui yilai de wenjian xuanbian, shang*: 200-201.

"Sifabu, laogaiju, laojiaoju guanyu xinzeng fanren, laojiao renyuan jingfei wenti de tongzhi" [Circular of the labor reform and labor reeducation departments of the ministryof justice regarding the question of expenses of newly added prisoners and labor re-education personnel]. Document dated 7 December 1984, in *Zhonghua renmin gongheguo falu guifanxing jieshi jicheng*: 1597.

Sifabu laojiaoju. "1984 nian jiejiao renyuan genzong diaocha qingkuang de zonghe baogao" [Comprehensive report on follow-up study of labor re-education personnel released in 1984]. *Fanzui yu gaizao yanjiu* [Studies in crime and reform] 2:28-29 (1990).

Sifabu yanjiusuo 'laogai jingji tizhi yanjiu' ketizu. "Zailun laogai jingji tizhi de gaige" [Revisiting the restructuring of the economics of labor reform]. *Fanzui yu Gaizao Yanjiu* [Studies in Crime and Reform] 6:2 (1990).

Sifabu yanjiusuo yunei anjian ketizu. "Jin shinian lai quanguo yunei anjian de tedian ji jinhou duice yanjiu" [Research on the characteristics of cases inside the prisons nation-wide over the past decade and future counter-measures]. *Fanzui yu gaizao yanjiu* [Studies in crime and reform] 5:12-18 (1990).

Sifabu yanjiusuo 'zuifan xin qingkuang yanjiu' ketizu. "Xin de lishi shiqi zaiya zuifan de xin qingkuang, xin tedian" [The new situation and characteristics of criminals in custody in the new historical era]. *Fanzui yu gaizao yanjiu* [Studies in crime and reform] 4:1-7 (1990).

Sishu Wujing [The Four Books and Five Classics]. Beijing: Beijingshi zhongguo shudian, 1984.

Song Lei. "Sheji xinyongka de zhapian fanzui yingdang yinqi zhongshi" [Crimes of credit card fraud should attract our attention]. *Faxue dongtai* [Developments in legal studies] 24:1-8 (25 October 1985).

Stack, John A. "Children, Urbanization, and the Chances of Imprisonment in Mid-Victorian England." *Criminal Justice History: An International Review* 13:113-139 (1992).

Su Zhongheng. "Jixu guanche yifa congzhong congkuai fangzhen, shenwa yincang yanzhong xingshi fanzui fenzi" [Continue to implement the guiding principle of severe and rapid punishment, dig deep for hidden serious criminal elements]. *Nanfang ribao* [Southern daily] 25 August 1984: 4.

Sun Fei. *Woguo xingshi susongfa di er chengxu lun* [On the secondary procedure in our country's criminal procedure law]. Beijing: People's University M.A. thesis, 30 November 1984.

Sun Longji (Lung-kee Sun). *Zhongguo wenhua de shenceng jiegou* [The deep structure of Chinese culture]. Taibei: Tangshan chubanshe, 1990.

Sun, Lung-kee. "Contemporary Chinese Culture: Structure and Emotionality." *The Australian Journal of Chinese Affairs* 26:1-41 (July 1991).

Sun Peisheng and Liu Xiuhua, ed. *Kangsu anli xuanbian* [Selected protested cases]. Beijing: Qunzhong chubanshe, 1988.

Tao Liqiang and Luo Xiaopeng. "Dangqian nongmin fanzui de tedian ji fazhan qushi" [The current characteristics, causes, and developmental trends of peasant crime]. *Fanzui yu gaizao yanjiu* [Studies in crime and reform] 4:15-18 (1989).

Tianjinshi gaoji renmin fayuan bangongshi. "Dakai jumian, yanzheng jingji fanzui" [Make the breakthrough, severely punish economic crime]. *Renmin sifa* [People's adjudication] 1:3-4 (1986).

Tianjinshi laogaiju. "Tianjinshi dui xingman shifang qiman jiejiao renyuan qingkuang de diaocha baogao [Report on Tianjin municipality's investigation of the situation of persons released upon completion of terms in prison or from re-education through labor). In Sifabu falu zhengce yanjiushi, ed., *Laogai laojiao gongzuo de lilun yu shijian*: 379-392.

Tianjinshi fanzui wenti diaocha wenji. [Selected Research on the Crime Problem in Tianjin]. Tianjin: Tianjin renmin chubanshe, 1985.

"Tianjin shi renmin jianchayuan gongzuo baogao" [Work report of the Tianjin people's procuratorate]. In *Tianjin ribao* [Tianjin daily] 25 April 1983: 3.

Troyer, Ronald J., John P. Clark and Dean G. Rojek, ed. *Social Control in the People's Republic of China*. New York: Praeger, 1989.

Tu Fazhong. "Tantan dui zuifan jinxing zhengzhi sixiang gongzuo de yuanze" [On the principles for carrying out political and ideological education of prisoners]. In Sifabu falu zhengce yanjiushi, ed. *Laogai laojiao gongzuo de lilun yu shijian*: 42-48.

van der Sprenkel, S. *Legal Institutions on Manchu China: A Sociological Analysis*. London: The Athlone Press, 1962.

Von Senger, Harro. "Recent Developments in the Relations Between State and Party Norms in the People's Republic of China." In Stuart R. Schram, ed. *The Scope of State Power in China*: 171-207.

Wakeman, Frederic Jr. *Policing Shanghai 1927-1937*. Berkeley: University of California Press, 1995.

Waley-Cohen, Joanna. *Exile in Mid-Qing China: Banishment to Xinjiang*. New Haven: Yale University Press, 1991.

Wang Chun. "Sifa shijian zhong jige you zhengyi wenti de tantao qingkuang zongshu" [Summary of the state of debate on several controversial issues in the practice of jurisprudence]. *Faxue dongtai* [Developments in legal studies] 15:1-5 (1 June 1985).

Wang Duoyou. "Dui fan maiyin zuicuo nu laojiao renyuan de diaocha poxi" [Investigation and analysis of women prostitution offenders in re-education through labor]. *Fanzui yu gaizao yanjiu* [Studies in crime and reform] 4:20-23 (1988).

Wang Fusen. "Jingshen bingren ganrao tielu yunshu riyi yanzhong"[Mental patients' obstruction of railway traffic worsens daily]. *Renmin gonganbao* [People's Police] 31 May 1988: 3.

Wang Ge. "Dangqian nongcun shehui wenti yu shehui guanli wenti jianxi" [Analysis of current social problems and questions of social management in rural areas]. *Shehuixue yu shehui diaocha* [Sociology and social investigation] 5:27-31 (1988).

Wang Guiwu. "Jianding zhengque di zhixing yifa congzhong congkuai fangzhen" [Resolutely and correctly implement the guiding principle of severe and rapid punishment]. *Hongqi* [Red flag] 24:31-33 (1981).

Wang Hanbin. "Daji xingshi fanzui, weihu shehui zhian" [Strike blows against crime, protect public security]. *Renmin ribao* [People's daily] 11 June 1981: 1.

Wang Hongxing and Lang Qingrong. "150 ming nuxing zuifan diaocha" [Research on 150 female criminals]. *Qingshaonian fanzui yanjiu* [Studies in youth crime] 9:35 (1989).

Wang Huaian, ed. *Zhonghua renmin gongheguo falu quanshu*. Changchun: Jilin renmin chubanshe, 1989.

Wang Minyuan. "Xingshi beigao ren quanli yanjiu" [The rights of criminal defendants in China]. In Xia Yong, ed. *Zouxiang quanli de shidai: Zhongguo gongmin quanli fazhan yanjiu*: 499-550.

Wang Shaolan. "Maiyin funu weifa xinli qianxi" [Preliminary analysis of the lawbreaking psychology of prostitutes]. *Fanzui yu gaizao yanjiu* [Studies in crime and reform] 5:22-25 (1987).

Wang Tai. "Shilun laodong gaizao de jiben lilun yiju" [Tentative Discussion of the Basis of the Fundamental Theory of Labor Reform]. In Zhou Mingdong, Xu Zhangrun, and Zhu Ye, ed. *Laodong gaizao faxue gailun cankao ziliao*: 247-248.

Wang Xiansheng. "Shenli qiangjian anjian ruhe fangcuo de tihui" [Reflection on how to avoid errors in the adjudication of rape cases]. *Faxue* [Legal Science] 7:24-25 (1985).

Wang Xinru. "Shenpan weiyuanhui dingan ying yu gaibian" [The adjudication committees' deciding of cases should be changed]. *Zhengzhi yu falu* [Politics and Law] 2:24-25 (February 1989).

Wang Yanxin and Zhen Jianping. "Gaige yu wanshan xingshi renyuan anzhi jiuye zhidu de zonghe sikao" [Comprehensive consideration for the reform and improvement of the system for the settlement and employment of released prisoners]. *Fanzui yu gaizao yanjiu* [Studies in crime and reform] 1:46-49 (1993).

Wang Yongqi, ed. *Faxue jichu lilun cankao ziliao* [Reference material on basic legal theory]. Beijing: Beijing daxue chubanshe, 1981.

Wang Yunsheng, ed. *Xingshi fanzui anli congshu (fanghai shehui fengshang fanzui]* [Criminal case series (crimes in violation of public morality)]. Beijing: Zhongguo jiancha chubanshe, 1991.

_____, ed. *Xingshi fanzui anli congshu (liumangzui)* [Criminal case series (hooliganism)]. Beijing: Zhongguo jiancha chubanshe, 1990.

Wang Zengfeng. "Jiefang sixiang, zhuazhu jiyu, jiakuai fazhan disan chanye" [Liberate thought, grasp the opportunity, hasten development of the third industrial sector]. *Fanzui yu gaizao yanjiu* [Studies in Crime and Reform] 3:9-12 (1993).

Wang Zhemin and Huang Jingping, ed. *Jingji fazhan yu fanzui bianhua* [Economic development and changes in crime], Beijing: Zhongguo renmin daxue chubanshe, 1992.

Wang Zhongfang, ed. *Zhongguo shehui zhian zonghe zhili de lilun yu shijian* [The theory and practice of China's comprehensive management of public security]. Beijing: Qunzhong chubanshe, 1989.

Weber, Max. *The Interpretation of Social Reality*. Edited and with an introductory essay by J.E.T. Eldridge. New York: Schocken Books, 1980.

Wei De. "Zhezhong fanzui huodong ying zai yanli daji zhi li" [This sort of criminal activity is the type that should be subject to severe punishment]. *Minzhu yu fazhi* [Democracy and the legal system] 1:39 (1984).

Wei Bomin and Ren Licheng. "Xuanchuan woguo laogai zhengce de chuchuang: Beijingshi jianyu jiedai laifang waiguo youren qingkuang zongshu" [A display window for the propagandization of our country's labor reform policy: a summary of the situation of Beijing city prison's reception of visiting foreign friends]. *Duiwai Baodao Cankao* [Reference for external propaganda] 14:9-12 (15 July 1987).

Weinberger, Barbara. "Urban and Rural Crime Rates and Their Genesis in Late Nineteenth- and Early Twentieth-Century Britain." In Eric A. Johnson and Eric H. Monkkonen, ed. *The Civilization of Crime: Violence in Town and Country Since the Middle Ages*: 198-216.

"Woguo jingshenbing huanzhe yida 1000 wan" [Our country's mental patients already amount to ten million]. *Fazhi ribao* [Legal system daily] 14 May, 1993: 1.

"Wosheng laogai laojiao qiye jianchi gaige kaifang, gan dao guoji shichang shang qu zhanju yixi zhi di" [Our province's labor reform and labor re-education enterprises uphold reform and openness, dare to stake their place in the international market]. *Liaoning fazhibao* [Liaoning legal system news] 19 April 1988: 1.

"Woshi jingshenbing guanzhi gongzuo xiaoguo hao" [Our city's management and treatment of mental disease gains good results]. *Hangzhou ribao* [Hangzhou Daily] 24 October 1990: 3.

Wu, Harry Hongda. *Laogai—the Chinese Gulag*. Boulder: Westview Press, 1992.

Wu, Harry, and Carolyn Wakeman. *Bitter Winds: A Memoir of My Years in China's Gulag*. New York: John Wiley and Sons, Inc., 1994.

Wu Kaiyu. "Liushisheng fanzui chengyin qianxi" [Causational factors of school-drop-out crime]. *Qingshaonian fanzui yanjiu* [Studies in youth crime] 2:25-29 (1989).

Wu Lei ed. *Zhongguo sifa zhidu* [China's judicial system]. Beijing: Zhongguo renmin daxue chubanshe, 1988.

Wushun xianzhi [Wushun County gazetteer]. Hohhot: Neimenggu renmin chubanshe, 1988.

Xia Yong, ed. *Zouxiang quanli de shidai: Zhongguo gongmin quanli fazhan yanjiu* [Toward the era of rights: perspectives on the development of civil rights in china]. Beijing: Zhongguo zhengfa daxue chubanshe, 1995.

Xiang Xuezhi. "Zhengque renshi shehui zhuyi chuji jieduan fanzui wenti" [Correctly recognize the crime problem during the primary stage of socialism]. *Qingshaonian fanzui yanjiu* [Studies in youth crime] 6:11-15 (1988).

Xiao Jianming. "Lun jingji fazhan yu fanzui wenti" [On economic development and the crime problem]. *Qingshaonian fanzui yanjiu* [Studies in youth crime] 5:12-17 (1988).

Xie Anshan and Yan Li, ed. *Zonghe zhili shehui zhian gongzuo shouce* [Work manual for the comprehensive management of public security]. Changchun: Jilin renmin chubanshe, 1986.

Xie Bing and Liu Zhenghui. "Tan gaige zhong de laogai gongzuo" [On labor reform work under reform]. *Sifa* [Jurisprudence] 10:15 (1986).

Xie Baogui. "Jingji fanzui de gainian" [The concept of economic crime]. In Yang Dunxian and Xie Baogui, ed. *Jingji fanzui xue*: 25-40.

Xin Ru and Lu Chen, ed. *Zhonghua renmin gongheguo falu lifa sifa jieshi anli daquan* [Compendium of legislative and judicial interpretations of the law of the People's Republic of China, with cases]. Shijiazhuang: Hebei renmin chubanshe, 1991.

Xin Zhongguo sifa jieshi daquan [Compendium of legal interpretations of new China]. Beijing: Zhongguo jiancha chubanshe, 1990.

Xin'an xianzhi [Gazetteer of Xin'an county]. Zhengzhou: Henan renmin chubanshe, 1989.

Xing Guozheng. "Xinjiang jianguan gaizao zuifan gongzuo zhong "sanlu" piangao de yuanyin poxi" [Analysis of the reasons for the relatively high 'three rates' in the work of reform of criminals in Xinjiang]. *Sifa xingzheng* [Judiciary administration] 16:23-24 (1992).

Xing Jianting. "Guanyu jinyibu guanche zhongyang guanyu zhengdun shehui zhian de zhishi de jidian yijian" [Opinions regarding further implementation of the party center's directive on rectification of public security]. *Beijing sifa* [Beijing jurisprudence] 2:2-4 (20 February 1982).

Xing Kebo. "Lun baohu beigaoren de hefa quanyi" [On protection of the defendant's legal rights]. Beijing: M.A. thesis in criminal procedure law, Zhongguo renmin daxue, 5 June 1989.

Xing Yi. "Qi sheng shi fayuan shenli jingji fanzui anjian zuotanhui zai jing zhaokai" [Conference on the adjudication of economic criminal cases of seven provincial and municipal courts held in Beijing]. *Renmin sifa* [People's adjudication] 12:6 (1988).

Xingcheng xianzhi [Gazetteer of Xingcheng county]. Shenyang: Liaoning daxue chubanshe, 1990.

Xingshi susongfa cankao ziliao, diyiji (shangce) [Criminal procedure law reference materials, part one (volume one)]. Beijing: Beijing zhengfa xueyuan susongfa jiaoyanshi, 1980.

Xinxiang diqu zhongji renmin fayuan. "Guanyu qingshaonian fanzui qingkuang de diaocha fenxi" [Investigation and analysis of the youth crime situation]." *Sifa* [Jurisprudence] 7:16 (1985).

Xu Hanmin, ed. *Renmin zhian 40 nian* [40 years of people's public security], Beijing: Jingguan jiaoyu chubanshe, 1992.

Xue Guanghua. "Jianchi guanche zhixing yifa 'congzhong congkuai' fangzhen" [Continue to implement the guiding principle of "severe and rapid punishment" according to law]. *Renmin sifa* [People's adjudication] 7:6-8 (1985).

Yan Jingyao. *Zhongguo de fanzui wenti yu shehui bianqian de guanxi*. [Crime in relation to social change in China]. Translated from the original English text by Wu Zhen. Beijing: Beijing daxue chubanshe, 1986.

Yang Chunxi, Gao Mingxuan, Ma Kechang and Yu Shutong, ed. *Xingshi faxue da cishu* [Encyclopedia of criminal sciences]. Nanjing: Nanjing daxue chubanshe, 1990.

Yang Diansheng ed. *Laodong gaizao faxue* [Labor reform law]. Beijing: Beijing daxue chubanshe, 1991.

Yang Dunxian and Xie Baogui, ed. *Jingji fanzui xue* [The study of economic crime]. Beijing: Zhongguo jiancha chubanshe, 1991.

Yang Guoyue. "'Zonghe zhili' chengji xianzhu—lianheguo huiyi zhongshi wo dui qingshaonian de fazhi jiaoyu" [The results of "comprehensive control" are obvious—our legal education of teenagers and youth emphasized at the United Nations meeting]. *Duiwai Xuanchuan Cankao* [Reference for external propaganda] 15:12-14 (August 1984).

Yang Yintang. "Xianpan, houshen yinggai gechu" [First verdict, then trial should be eliminated]. *Minzhu yu fazhi* [Democracy and the legal system] 6:10-11 (1988).

"Yanli daji xingshi fanzui huodong" [Strike hard blows at criminal activities]. Beijing: *Renmin ribao* [People's daily] 14 August 1983:1.

"Yanli daji xingshi fanzui huodong, wei shixian shehui zhian de genben haozhuan er douzheng" [Strike hard blows at criminal activities, fight for a fundamental turn for the better in public security]. *Zhengzhi yu falu* [Politics and law] 2:1-3 (5 April 1984).

"Yibu juyou Zhongguo tese de chongxin fanzui yanjiu de lilun zhuanzhu—Zhong guo chongxin fanzui yanjiu zuotanhui fayan zhaiyao" [A distinctively Chinese theoretical work on research into recidivism—excerpts from speeches delivered at the conference on research on recidivism in China]. *Fanzui yu gaizao yanjiu* [Studies in crime and reform] 2:6-16 (1993).

"Yifa congzhong congkuai chengchu yanzhong xingshi zuifan" [Punish serious criminal offenders severely and rapidly according to law]. Beijing: *Renmin ribao* [People's daily] 26 August 1983: 1.

"Yifa congzhong congkuai daji xianxing fanzui huodong" [Severely and rapidly punish current criminal activities according to law]. *Shaanxi ribao* [Shaanxi daily] 8 July 1983: 1.

"Yifa yanzheng jingji fanzui fenzi quebao zhili, zhengdun jingji zhixu shunli jinxing" [Severely punish economic criminals according to law, guarantee the smooth implementation of control and rectification of economic order]. *Renmin sifa* [People's adjudication] 1:12-13 (1989).

"Yu Lei fubuzhang zai guanche shishi 'gongan jiguan banli xingshi anjian de chengxu guiding' dianhua huiyi shang de jianghua" (Vice-minister Yu Lei's talk during the telephone conference on the implementation of the 'procedural regulations for the public security organs' handling of criminal cases"). Document dated 7 April 1987, in Gongan faguiju, ed. *Zhifa shouce—gongan jiguan banli xingshi anjian chengxu zhuanji*: 42-47.

Yuanan xianzhi [Gazetteer of Yuanan county]. Beijing: Zhongguo zhengzhi jingji she chubanshe, 1990.

Yue Hua. "Qiangjian fa'an weishenmo jiangbuxialai?" [Why doesn't the incidence of rape decline?]. *Renmin Sifa* [People's Jurisprudence] 8:22-23 (1985).

"Yushen gongzuo guize" [Preliminary hearing regulations]. Document dated 20 August 1979, in Gonganbu faguiju, ed. *Zhifa shouce: gongan jiguan banli xingshi anjian chengxu zhuanji*: 234-242.

Zehr, Howard. *Crime and the Development of Modern Society: Patterns of Criminality in Nineteenth Century Germany and France*. London: Croom Helm Ltd., 1976.

Zeldes, Ilya. *The Problem of Crime in the USSR*. Springfield, Ill.: Charles C. Thomas, 1981.

Zeng Hanzhou. "Zai quanguo xingshi shenpan gongzuo huiyi shang de baogao (jielu)" [Report at the national criminal adjudication work meeting (excerpts)]. Report dated 21 October 1978, in *Renmin sifa* [People's Adjudication] 4 (1978), reprinted in *Zhonghua renmin gongheguo xingshi susongfa xuexi cankao ziliao, diyiji, zonglei*: 310-327.

"Zenyang zhengque lijie yifa congkuai ban'an" [How to correctly understand the rapid disposition of cases according to law]. *Renmin sifa* [People's Adjudication] 9:15 (1981).

Zhang Fanshi and Wang Ya'nan. "Fanzui shaonian renji guanxi diaocha yanjiu" [Research on the relational networks of juvenile criminals]. *Qingshaonian fanzui yanjiu* [Studies in youth crime] 11:13-23 (1985).

Zhang Guofu. *Zhonghua minguo fazhi jianshi* [A short history of the legal system of the Republic of China]. Beijing: Beijing daxue chubanshe, 1986.

Zhang Guohua. *Zhongguo falu sixiangshi xinbian* [A new history of Chinese legal thought]. Beijing: Beijing daxue chubanshe, 1991.

_____, ed. *Zhongguo falu sixiangshi* [The history of Chinese legal thought]. Shijiazhuang: Falu chubanshe, 1982.

Zhang Hua. "Nongcun hunyin zhong de lifa chongtu yanjiu"[Study on the conflict between ritual and law in rural marriage]. *Shehuixue yu shehui diaocha* [Sociology and social research] 4:47-50 (1991).

Zhang Jian. "Woguo zui da de laogai nongchang—Hubeisheng Shayang nong-chang gaikuang" [Our country's biggest labor reform farm—an overview of Hubei's Shayang farm]. *Fanzui yu gaizao yanjiu* [Studies in crime and reform] 5:64-66 (1991).

Zhang Jinfan. *Fashi jianlue* [Reflections on legal history]. Beijing: Qunzhong chubanshe, 1988.

_____, Lin Zhong and Wang Zhigang. *Zhongguo xingfa xinlun* [A new history of Chinese criminal law]. Beijing: Renmin fayuan chubanshe, 1992.

Zhang Kaisi. "Luetan congzhong congkuai yu zonghe zhili" [On severe and rapid punishment and comprehensive management]. *Zhongguo fazhibao* [China legal system news] 15 January 1982: 1.

Zhang Li. "Dangqian nu qingshaonian laojiao renyuan de zhuyao tedian" [Current major characteristics of women youth labor reeducation personnel]. In Jiangsu sheng faxuehui qingshaonian fanzui yanjiuhui and Jiangsu sheng shehui kexueyuan zhengfa yanjiusuo, ed. *Qingshaonian fanzui yanjiu*: 218-223.

Zhang Panfu and Deng Zengrong. "Jianchi dui xingshi jiejiao renyuan kaizhan diaocha yanjiu de jianyi" [Suggestion to continue to carry out research on prisoners released from labor re-education and labor reform]. *Fanzui yu gaizao yanjiu* [Studies in crime and reform] 4:42-43, 27 (1993).

Zhang Shaoquan and Deng Juncai. "Dangqian maiyin piaochang huodong de tedian ji qi duice" [The characteristics and of and countermeasures to current prostitution activities]. *Qingshaonian fanzui yanjiu* [Studies in youth crime] 6:6-9 (1990).

Zhang Shangzhou. *Zhonghua renmin gongheguo xingfa gailun* [Introduction to the criminal law of the PRC]. Beijing: Falu chubanshe, 1983.

Zhang Siqing, ed. *Zhonghua renmin gongheguo jiancha yewu quanshu* [Encyclo-pedia of the procuratorial profession of the PRC]. Changchun: Jilin renmin chubanshe, 1991.

Zhang Shu. "Shilun maiyin xinli jiegou de tezheng—dui 188 ming maiyin funu de diaocha" [A discussion of the characteristics of the psychological structure of prostitutes—investigation of 188 women prostitutes]. *Qingshaonian fanzui yanjiu* [Studies in youth crime] 1:14-19 (1989).

Zhang Xipo, ed. *Geming genjudi fazhishi* [Legal history of the revolutionary base areas]. Beijing: Falu chubanshe, 1994.

Zhang Xianqin. "Dui Sichuansheng tuotao fanzui anjian qingkuang de fenxi" [Analysis of prison escape cases in Sichuan province]. *Fanzui yu gaizao yanjiu* [Studies in crime and reform] 3:42-43, 37 (1991).

Zhang Zhong and Li Xiaobo. "Dui laogai laojiao ganjing tanwu, shouhui, weiji anjian de poxi ji duice" [Analysis of and counter-measures for cases of reform through labor and re-education through labor cadres and guards committing corruption, accepting bribes, and violating regulations]. *Sifa xingzheng* [Judiciary administration] 14:21-23 (1992).

Zhang Zhehui. *Woguo xingfa zhong de liumang fanzui* [The offense of hooligan ism in our country's criminal law]. Beijing: Qunzhong chubanshe, 1988.

Zhao Bingzhi, ed. *Zhongguo xingfade yunyong yu fazhan* [The application and development of China's criminal law]. Beijing: Fazhi chubanshe, 1989.

_____ and Zhao Guoqiang, ed. *Xingfa xiugai yanjiu zongshu* [Summary of research on the amendment of the criminal law]. Beijing: Zhongguo renmin gongan daxue chubanshe, 1990.

Zhao Rongguo. "Yanda tougai de nu shaonian zhong chuxian de xin qingkuang" [The new situation emerging among juvenile females entering labor reform during the strike hard campaign]. In Jiangsu sheng faxuehui qingshaonian fanzui yanjiuhui and jiangsu sheng shehui kexueyuan zhengfa yanjiusuo, ed. *Qingshaonian fanzui yanjiu*: 211-217.

Zhao, Ziyang. "Work Report of the Government." In *The Second Session of the Sixth National People's Congress [Main Documents)*. Beijing: Foreign Languages Press, 1984: 3-15.

Zhejiang sheng sifating laogaiju. "Guanyu xingman shifang renyuan gaizao zhiliang de diaocha baogao" [Report on investigation into the quality of reform of prisoners released on completion of sentence]. In Sifabu, falu zhengce yanjiushi, laogaiju, ed. *Laogai laojiao gongzuo de lilun yu shijian*: 368-378.

"Zhengque zhangwo jingji fanzui yu zhengdang jingji huodong de jiexian" [Correctly grasp the line between economic crime and normal economic activity]. *Renmin sifa* [People's adjudication] 12:21-22 (1984).

"Zhian juliusuo guanli banfa (shixing)" [Experimental method for management of public security detention centers]. Document dated 3 January 1990, in Gonganbu fazhisi, ed. *Zhifa shouce dishierji*: 244-49.

Zhonggong yanjiu zazhishe ed. *Zhonggong yuanshi cailiao xuanji zhonggong shiyi jie sanzhong quanhui yilai zhongyang shouyao jianghua ji wenjian xuanbian, xiace* [Selected Chinese Communist primary material: important talks and documents since the third plenum of the eleventh central committee of the Chinese Communist party, volume 2]. Taibei: Zhonggong yanjiu zazhishe, 1983.

"Zhonggong zhongyang bangongting zhuanfa gonganbu quanguo fulian liang dangzu guanyu jianjue quti maiyin huodong de baogao" [Office of the central committee of the Chinese Communist Party's transmission of the ministry of justice and the all-China women's federation party cell's report regarding determined elimination of prostitution]. Document dated 8 April 1983, in Liang Guoqing, ed. Xin Zhongguo sifa jieshi daquan: 1080.

"Zhonggong zhongyang guanyu 'dierjie quanguo jiancha gongzuo huiyi' ji Gao Kelin tongzhi 'guanyu guoqu jiancha gongzuo de zongjie he jinhou jiancha gongzuo fangzhen renwu de baogao' de pishi" [The Central Committee of the Chinese Communist Party's instructions regarding the 'resolution of the second national procuratorial work conference' and comrade Gao Kelin's 'summarization of past procuratorial work and report concerning the policies and tasks of procuratorial work now and in the future']. Document dated 12 June 1954, in Zuigao renmin jianchayuan yanjiushi, ed. *Jiancha zhidu cankao ziliao, diyi ji (xin zhongguo bufen)*: 35-57.

"Zhonggong zhongyang guanyu jianli jiancha jigou wenti de zhishi" [Directive of the central committee of the Chinese communist party regarding the question of establishing procuratorial organs]. In Zuigao renmin jianchayuan yanjiushi, ed. *Jiancha zhidu cankao ziliao, diyibian (xin Zhongguo bufen)*: 21-22.

Zhonggong zhongyang guanyu jiaqiang zhengfa gongzuo de zhishi [Chinese Communist Party Central Committee directive concerning the strengthening of politico-legal work]. Document dated 13 January 1982, in Zhonggong yanjiu zazhishe ed., *Zhonggong yuanshi cailiao xuanji*: 1096.

"Zhonggong zhongyang guanyu shenzhong chuli 'wenhua da geming' zhong da, za, qiang wenti de tongzhi (jielu)" [Excerpts from the Chinese Communist Party Center notice regarding prudent disposition of questions of beating, smashing and looting during the cultural revolution]. Document dated 13

August 1978, in *Zhonghua renmin gongheguo falu guifanxing jieshi jicheng*: 21.

"Zhonggong zhongyang guanyu yanli daji xingshi fanzui huodong de jueding (jielu)" (A) [Central Committee of the Chinese Communist Party decision regarding striking hard blows against criminal activities (excerpts)]. Document dated 25 August 1983, in Zhonggong zhongyang wenxian yanjiushi, ed. *Shier da yilai zhongyao wenxian xuanbian shang*: 385-389.

"Zhonggong zhongyang guanyu yanli daji xingshi fanzui huodong de jueding (jielu)" (B) [Central Committee of the Chinese Communist Party decision regarding striking hard blows against criminal activities (excerpts)]. Document dated 25 August 1983, in Dazu xian renmin jianchayuan, ed. *Dazu xian jianchazhi*: 132-133.

"Zhonggong zhongyang guanyu zhongyang renmin jianchashu sixiang guiding de tongzhi" [Circular of the Central Committee of the Chinese Communist Party regarding four regulations for the central people's procuratorial office]. Document dated 29 January 1950, in Zuigao renmin jianchayuan yanjiushi, ed. *Jiancha zhidu cankao ziliao, diyiji (xin zhongguo bufen)*: 20-21.

"Zhonggong zhongyang, guowuyuan guanyu daji jingji lingyu zhong yanzhong fanzui huodong de jueding" [Chinese Communist Party Central Committee, State Council decision on striking at serious economic crimes], in *Renmin ribao* [People's daily] 1 April 1982: 14

"Zhonggong zhongyang jinji tongzhi" [Urgent notice of the Central Committee of the Chinese Communist Party]. Document dated 11 January 1982, in Zhonggong yanjiu zazhishe ed., *Zhonggong yuanshi cailiao xuanji*: 1092.

"Zhonggong zhongyang pifa zuigao renmin jianchashu dangzu 'guanyu jiancha gongzuo fangzhen renwu de yijian de baogao' ji zhongyang zhengfa weiyuanhui dangzu de jianyi" [The central committee of the Chinese communist party's transmission of the Party group of the supreme people's procuratorate's "report regarding opinion on the situation of procuratorial work and the present guiding principles and tasks of procuratorial work" and the suggestions of the party group of the central committee's commission of politics and law]. In Zuigao renmin jianchayuan yanjiushi, ed. *Jiancha zhidu cankao ziliao, diyibian (xin Zhongguo bufen)*: 23-6.

"Zhonggong zhongyang pizhuan zuigao renmin jianchayuan dangzu guanyu jiancha yewu gongzuo huiyi qingkuang he jinhou gongzuo yijian xiang zhongyang de baogao" [The central committee of the Chinese Communist Party's approval and transmission of the SPP party cell's report to the center regarding the procuratorial work conference and opinions on future tasks] in Zuigao renmin jianchayuan yanjiushi, ed. *Jiancha zhidu cankao ziliao, diyi ji (xin zhongguo bufen)*: 58.

Zhonggong zhongyang wenxian yanjiushi, ed. *Shier da yilai zhongyao wenxian xuanbian, shang* [Selected important documents since the twelfth congress, volume 1]. Beijing: Renmin chubanshe 1988.

"Zhonggong zhongyang xuanchuanbu, xinwen chubanshu, guangbo dianying dianshibu, wenhuabu, gonganbu, haiguan zongshu guanyu tingzhi jinkou he bofang jiguang shipian (gushipian) de tongzhi" [Central Committee of the Chinese Communist Party, propaganda bureau, office of news and publishing, ministry of radio, film and television, ministry of culture, ministry of public security, and general customs office circular regarding stopping the import and broadcast of laser discs (feature films)]. Document identified as Central Committee Propaganda Bureau Document 17 of 1990, in Gonganbu fazhisi ed. *Zhifa shouce dishierji*, 1990: 218-220.

"Zhonggong zhongyang xuanchuanbu, zuigao renmin fayuan, zuigao renmin jianchayuan, gonganbu, sifabu guanyu yanfang fandong baokan liyong wo chujue fanren jinxing zaoyao wumie de tongzhi" [Propaganda bureau of the central committee of the Chinese Communist Party, SPC, SPP, ministry of public security, ministry of justice circular regarding strict prevention of reactionary publications' use of our execution of criminals to create slanderous rumors]. Document dated 21 November 1984, in *Zhonghua renmin gongheguo falu guifanxing jieshi jicheng*: 1503.

"Zhonggong zhongyang xuanchuanbu, zuigao renmin fayuan, zuigao renmin jianchayuan, gonganbu, sifabu, guanyu yanfang fandong baokan liyong wo chujue fanren jinxing zaoyao wumie de tongzhi" [Office of propaganda of the central committee of the Chinese Communist Party, supreme people's court, supreme people's procuratorate, ministry of public security, ministry of justice, circular regarding strictly preventing reactionary publications from using our execution of criminals to spread rumors and insults]. Document dated November 21 1984, in Shanxi sheng zhengfa guanli ganbu xueyuan, xingfa jiaoyanshi, ed. *Yanli daji yanzhong jingji fanzui he yanzhong xingshi fanzui yilai de wenjian xuanbian, shang ce*: 349-50

"Zhonggong zhongyang zhuanfa zhongyang xuanchuanbu deng bage danwei 'guanyu tiqing quandang zhongshi jiejue qingshaonian weifa fanzui wenti de baogao' de tongzhi (jielu)" [The Chinese Communist Party center's notice transmitting the central propaganda bureau and eight other units' 'report reminding the entire party to place emphasis on the resolution of the problem of youth lawbreaking and crime (excerpts)]. Document dated 17 August 1979, in Xie Anshan and Yan Li, ed. *Zonghe zhili shehui zhian gongzuo shouce*: 3-12.

Zhongguo falu sixiangshi bianxiezu. *Zhongguo falu sixiangshi ziliao xuanbian* [Selected reference materials on the history of Chinese legal thought]. Shijia-zhuang: Falu chubanshe, 1983.

Zhongguo falu nianjian (1987) [Law yearbook of China, 1987]. Beijing: Falu chubanshe, 1987.

Zhongguo falu nianjian (1988) [Law yearbook of China, 1988]. Beijing: Falu chubanshe, 1989.

Zhongguo falu nianjian [1989) [Law yearbook of China, 1989].Beijing: Falu chubanshe, 1990.

Zhongguo falu nianjian (1990) [Law yearbook of China, 1990]. Beijing: Falu chubanshe, 1990.

Zhongguo zhengfa daxue laogaifa jiaoyanshi, ed. *Fanzuixue cankao ziliao, di san zhuan* [Reference materials on criminology, volume 3]. Beijing: Zhongguo zhengfa daxue laogaifa jiaoyanshi, October, 1984.

Zhonghua renmin gongheguo falu guifanxing jieshi jicheng [Collected normative legal interpretations of the People's Republic of China]. Changchun: Jilin renmin chubanshe, 1990.

Zhonghua renmin gongheguo falu guifanxing jieshi jicheng (zengbuben). [Collected normative legal interpretations of the People's Republic of China (supplementary volume)]. Changchun: Jilin renmin chubanshe, 1991.

"Zhonghua renmin gongheguo renmin jianchayuan zuzhifa." [Organic law of the people's courts of the PRC]. Document promulgated in 1979, amended in 1983, in Wang Huaian, ed. *Zhonghua renmin gongheguo falu quanshu*: 51-53.

Zhonghua renmin gongheguo xingshi susongfa. [Criminal Procedure Law of the People's Republic of China]. Beijing: Falu chubanshe, 1996.

Zhonghua renmin gongheguo xingshi susongfa xuexi cankao ziliao, diyiji, zonglei [Reference study materials on the criminal procedure law of the PRC, volume one, general principles]. Beijing: Zhongguo renmin daxue faluxi, xingfa jiaoyanshi xingsu xiaozu, ziliaoshi, 1980.

Zhonghua Renmin Gongheguo falu quanshu [Collection of the laws of the People's Republic of China]. Changchun: Jilin renmin chubanshe, 1989.

Zhonghua Renmin Gongheguo falu quanshu, zengbuben [Collection of the laws of the People's Republic of China, supplementary volume]. Changchun: Jilin renmin chubanshe, 1990.

"Zhonghua renmin gongheguo xingshi susongfa caoan (chugao)" (Preliminary Draft of the Criminal Procedure Law of the People's Republic of China). Document dated 10 April 1963, in *Xingshi susongfa cankao ziliao, diyiji (shangce)*: 50-88.

"Zhongxiaoxuesheng liushi yanzhong yinqi guanzhu" [Serious primary and middle school dropout rate attracts attention]. *Liaoning fazhibao* [Liaoning legal system news] 25 November 1988: 1.

"Zhongyang jilu jiancha weiyuanhui, zhongyang zhengfa weiyuanhui guanyu panchu jingji fanzui anjian tongyi liangxing de tongzhi" [Central discipline inspection committee, central politico-legal committee notice concerning unified sentencing of economic criminal cases]. Document dated 15 May 1982, in Shanxisheng zhengfa guanli ganbu xueyuan, xingfa jiaoyanshi, ed. *Yanli daji yanzhong jingji fanzui he yanzhong xingshi fanzui yilai de wenjian xuanbian, shang ce*: 28.

Zhongyang zhengfa ganxiao, xingfa, xingshi susongfa jiaoyanshi, ed. *Zhonghua renmin gongheguo xingshi susongfa jiangyi* [Lectures on the criminal procedure law of the People's Republic of China]. Beijing: Qunzhong renmin chubanshe, 1981.

Zhou Daoluan, Sun Changli and Zhang Sahan. "Yifa congzhong congkuai daji yanzhong de xingshi fanzui" [Strike severe and rapid blows at serious criminal offenders according to law]. *Renmin ribao* [People's daily] 25 June 1981: 5.

Zhou Guanghan. "Sifa jieshi qianxi" [An analysis of judicial interpretation]. *Sifa* [Adjudication] 11:14 (1985).

Zhou Guojun. "Guanyu shourong shencha cunfei zhi yanjiu"[Research into the question of whether shelter and investigation should continue]. *Zhengfa luntan* [Politics and law tribunal] 1:36 (1989).

Zhou Huai. "Beijing zheng zai saodong" [Beijing in the midst of a crack-down]. *Zhengming* [Contention] 72:11-13 (1 October 1983).

Zhou Mi. *Zhongguo xingfashi* [History of Chinese criminal law]. Beijing: Qunzhong chubanshe, 1985.

Zhou Mingdong, Xu Zhangrun, and Zhu Ye, ed. *Laodong gaizao faxue gailun cankao ziliao* [Reference Materials on the General Theory of Labor Reform]. Beijing: Zhongyang guangbo dianshi daxue chubanshe, 1987.

Zhou Qingzheng, Fang Xueguang, and Guo Shengjun. "Yige zhide zhongshi de shehui wenti" [A social problem that deserves attention]. *Fanzui yu gaizao yanjiu* [Studies in crime and reform] 3:49-51 (1991).

Zhou Zhenxiang and Shao Jingchun, ed. *Xin Zhongguo fazhi jianshe sishinian yaolan* [Outline of forty years of construction of new China's legal system]. Beijing: Qunzhong chubanshe, 1990.

Zhu, Su-li. *A Critique of Social Control in Cross-Cultural Studies.* Ph.D. dissertation, Arizona State University, August 1992.

Zhu Yongling. "Laogai changsuo xing fanzui de biaoxian xingshi ji yufang" [Varieties of sex crime and their prevention in labor reform institutions]. *Fanzui yu gaizao yanjiu* [Studies in Crime and Reform] 3:24-26 (1991).

"Zhuahao jindong mingchun shehui zhian gongzuo" [Do a good job of public security work this winter and next spring]. *Fujian ribao* [Fujian daily] 24 November 1982: 1.

Zi Junyong. "Guanyu daoqie anjian shangsheng de yuanyin he duice" [Concerning the increase and counter-measures of theft cases]. *Qingshaonian fanzui yanjiu* [Studies in youth crime] 5:10-12 (1990).

"Zuigao renmin fayuan guanyu baosong sixing fuhe anjian de fanxiang guiding de tongzhi" [SPC circular regarding regulations on the itemized reporting of capital cases for review]. Document dated 12 December 1979, in *Zhonghua renmin gongheguo falu guifanxing jieshi jicheng*: 941-42.

"Zuigao renmin fayuan guanyu jianjue zhixing quanguo renda changwei 'guanyu yanzheng yanzhong pohuai jingji de fanzui de jueding' de tongzhi" [SPC notice concerning resolute implementation of the NPC SC "decision regarding the severe punishment of criminals who seriously undermine the economy"]. Document dated 15 March 1982 in Shanxisheng zhengfa guanli ganbu xueyuan, xingfa jiaoyanshi, ed. *Yanli daji yanzhong jingji fanzui he yanzhong xingshi fanzui yilai de wenjian xuanbian, shang*: 6-8.

"Zuigao renmin fayuan guanyu tongyi baosong sixing beian cailiao de tongzhi" [SPC circular regarding unification of official reporting of death sentences]. Document dated 9 April 1984, in *Zhonghua renmin gongheguo falu guifanxing jieshi jicheng*: 945.

"Zuigao renmin fayuan, gonganbu, minzhengbu, guojia laodong zongju guanyu anzhi pingfan shifang hou wujia kegui renyuan de tongzhi" [Supreme people's court, ministry of public security, ministry of civil administration, national central labor bureau notice regarding the settlement of homeless rehabilitated and released personnel]. Document issued 29 March 1980, in *Zhonghua renmin gongheguo falu guifanxing jieshi jicheng*: 205.

Zuigao renmin fayuan, xingshi shenpan di er ting, ed. *Xingshi shenpan jiandu shouce (diyiji)* [Manual for supervision of criminal adjudication (volume one)]. Beijing: Renmin fayuan chubanshe, 1986.

Zuigao renmin fayuan, xingshi shenpan di er ting, ed. *Xingshi shenpan jiandu shouce (dierji)* [Manual for supervision of criminal adjudication (volume two)]. Beijing: Renmin fayuan chubanshe, 1991.

Zuigao renmin fayuan yanjiushi, ed. *Sifa shouce, diwuji* [Adjudication manual, volume five]. Beijing: Renmin fayuan chubanshe, 1989.

"Zuigao renmin fayuan, zuigao renmin jianchayuan, gonganbu guanyu fan geming guagou anjian de zuiming, zuizheng wenti de tongzhi" [SPC, SPP, ministry of public security notice regarding the questions of the charge and the evidence in cases of counter-revolutionary contact]. Document dated 26 December 1979, in *Zhonghua renmin gongheguo falu guifanxing jieshi jicheng*: 293-94.

"Zuigao renmin fayuan, zuigao renmin jianchayuan, gonganbu guanyu maiyin piaosu anchang anjian ying ruhe chuli de yijian" [Opinion of the SPC, the SPP and the Ministry of Justice regarding the disposition of cases of prostitution and whoring] Document dated 7 August, 1984, in Liang Guoqing, ed. *Xin Zhongguo sifa jieshi daquan*: 1079-1082.

"Zuigao renmin fayuan, zuigao renmin jianchayuan, gonganbu yinfa 'guanyu dangqian banli qiangjian anjian zhong juti yingyong falu de ruogan wenti de jieda' de tongzhi" [Supreme People's Court, Supreme People's Procuratorate, Ministry of Public Security, circular issuing the "explanation of certain questions in the concrete application of law in the current disposition of rape cases"] in Xin Ru and Lu Chen, ed. *Zhonghua renmin gongheguo falu lifa sifa jieshi anli daquan*: 648.

"Zuigao renmin fayuan, zuigao renmin jianchayuan, gonganbu guanyu jianjue zhizhi jiang yijue fan, weijuefan youjie shizhong de tongzhi" [SPC, SPP, ministry of public security notice concerning resolutely putting a stop to public parading of convicted and not-yet-convicted criminals]. Document dated 1 June 1988 in *Zhonghua renmin gongheguo falu guifanxing jieshi jicheng*: 999.

"Zuigao renmin fayuan, zuigao renmin jianchayuan, gonganbu, sifabu, guanyu zhengque chuli sixing fanzui yishu yiwu deng wenti de tongzhi" [SPC, SPP, ministry of public security, ministry of justice circular regarding the correct handling of wills and bequests made by capital criminals and related questions]. Document dated 11 January 1984, in Liang Guoqing, ed., *Xin Zhongguo sifa jieshi daquan*: 450-51.

"Zuigao renmin fayuan, zuigao renmin jianchayuan, gonganbu, sifabu, wei shengbu, minzhengbu guanyu liyong sixing zuifan shiti huo shiti qiguan de zanxing guiding" [SPC, SPP, ministry of public security, ministry of justice, ministry of hygiene, ministry of civil administration, Provisional regulations regarding the use of the corpses or organs of capital offenders]. Document dated 9 October 1984, in Liang Guoqing, ed. *Xin Zhongguo sifa jieshi daquan*: 464-65.

"Zuigao renmin fayuan dangzu guanyu zhuajin fucha jiuzheng yuan jia cuo an renzhen luoshi dang de zhengce de qingshi baogao (jielu)" [Party cell of the SPC report requesting instructions regarding urgent rectification of unjust, false and erroneous cases and conscientious implementation of Party policy (excerpts)]. Document issued and approved by the Party center, 29 December 1978, in *Zhonghua renmin gongheguo falu guifanxing jieshi jicheng*: 191-193.

"Zuigao renmin fayuan, zuigao renmin jianchayuan guanyu dangqian banli daoqie anjian zhong juti yingyong falu de ruogan wenti de jieda" [Explanation concerning certain questions regarding the concrete application of law in the disposition of current theft cases]. Document dated 2 November 1984, in *Zhonghua renmin gongheguo falu guifan xing jieshi jicheng*: 345.

"Zuigao renmin fayuan, zuigao renmin jianchayuan, gonganbu, sifabu guanyu zhixing sixing yanjin youjie shizhong de tongzhi" [SPC, SPP ministry of public security, ministry of justice notice on strictly prohibiting public parading in the implementation of the death sentence]. Document dated 24 July 1986, in *Zhonghua renmin gongheguo falu guifanxing jieshi jicheng*: 995.

"Zuigao renmin fayuan, zuigao renmin jianchayuan, gonganbu, sifabu guanyu zhuajin shencha chuli kanshousuo ya renfan de tongzhi" [Notice of the SPC, SPP, ministry of public security, and ministry of justice regarding urgent investigation and disposition of offenders held in detention centers]. Document dated 6 April 1984, in Shanxi sheng zhengfa guanli ganbu xueyuan, xingfa jiaoyanshi, ed. *Yanli daji yanzhong jingji fanzui he yanzhong xingshi fanzui yilai de wenjian xuanbian, xia*: 13-15.

"Zuigao renmin jianchayuan guanyu gaipan 'sixing' anjian de jidian yijian (jielu))" [Some opinions on cases for the revision of sentence to "capital punishment" (excerpts)]. Document dated 14 September 1983, in Shanxi sheng zhengfa guanli ganbu xueyuan, xingfa jiaoyanshi, ed. *Yanli daji yanzhong jingji fanzui he yanzhong xingshi fanzui yilai de wenjian xuanbian, shang*: 185

"Zuigao renmin jianchayuan guanyu jixu zhuajin zhuahao daji yanzhong jingji fanzui huodong de tongzhi" [SPP notice on continuing to do a good, conscientious job of striking blows at serious economic crime]. Document dated 21 October 1983, in Shanxisheng zhengfa guanli ganbu xueyuan, xingfa jiaoyanshi, ed. *Yanli daji yanzhong jingji fanzui he yanzhong xingshi fanzui yilai de wenjian xuanbian, shang*: 202-206.

"Zuigao renmin jianchayuan guanyu zai yanli daji xingshi fanzui douzheng zhong juti yingyong falu de ruogan wenti de dafu" [SPP reply to certain questions concerning the concrete application of law in the struggle to severely punish criminal offenders]. Document dated 9 January 1984, in Liang Guoqing, ed. *Xin Zhongguo sifa jieshi daquan*: 36-39.

"Zuigao renmin jianchayuan, gonganbu, sifabu guanyu qiangzhi liuchang jiuye renyuan shanzi lichang zhuihui tuzhong kefou shiyong jieju he jiya de tongzhi" [Circular of the SPP, the ministry of public security, and the ministry of justice Regarding whether or not restraints and imprisonment may be used in returning prisoners forcibly retained for labor who left their units without permission]. Document dated 16 November 1984, in *Zhonghua renmin gongheguo falu guifanxing jieshi jicheng*: 1596-97.

Zuigao renmin jianchayuan xingshi anli congshu bianweihui, ed. *Liumangzui* [Hooliganism]. Beijing: Zhongguo jiancha chubanshe, 1990.

Zuigao renmin jianchayuan yanjiushi, ed. *Jiancha zhidu cankao ziliao, diyibian (xin Zhongguo bufen)* [Reference materials on the procuratorial system, volume one (new China)]. Beijing: Zuigao renmin jianchayuan yanjiushi, 1980.

INDEX

249

CORNELL EAST ASIA SERIES

FORTHCOMING

To order, please contact the Cornell East Asia Series, East Asia Program, Cornell University, 140 Uris Hall, Ithaca, NY 14853-7601, USA; phone (607) 255-6222, fax (607) 255-1388, internet: ceas@cornell.edu, http://www.einaudi.cornell.edu/eastasia/EastAsiaSeries.html.

3-99/.5 M pb/.2M hc

Milton Keynes UK
Ingram Content Group UK Ltd.
UKHW040629180124
436246UK00001B/24